Advance Praise for *I Surrender*

"Heart-stopping . . . *I Surrender* witnesses to the suffering and resilience of the Chilean people, the heroic lives of her companions, and most movingly, of her encounter with the divine in the midst of life-threatening perils."   **—Kathleen M. O'Connor,**
Columbia Theological Seminary

"In this gripping memoir, Kathy Osberger narrates her experience of being drawn into the courageous work of sisters, lay women, and clergy who stood up to the Pinochet dictatorship in defense of the lives of others. This story is an important chapter not only in Chile, but in the Catholic Church and the modern human rights movement."   **—Phillip Berryman, author,** *Latin America at 200;*
Memento of the Living and the Dead

"Two years into Pinochet's reign, a twenty-two-year-old enters his house of terrors. We meet nuns and teachers whose ingenuity outsmarts Pinochet's intelligence police and CIA accomplices. Riveting and inspiring, Osberger places the reader there, and you cannot look away."   **—Renny Golden, author,**
The Music of Her Rivers

"As one of many Chileans who were tortured and held in Pinochet's concentration camps, I embrace this memoir, told with truth and emotion. Chile's memory is awakened and preserved by these stories of risk and solidarity."   **—Mario Venegas, founder,**
Chicago Torture Justice Center and ChileAmigo Chicago

I Surrender

I SURRENDER

A Memoir of Chile's Dictatorship, 1975

Kathleen M. Osberger

ORBIS BOOKS

Maryknoll, New York 10545

Founded in 1970, Orbis Books endeavors to publish works that enlighten the mind, nourish the spirit, and challenge the conscience. The publishing arm of the Maryknoll Fathers and Brothers, Orbis seeks to explore the global dimensions of the Christian faith and mission, to invite dialogue with diverse cultures and religious traditions, and to serve the cause of reconciliation and peace. The books published reflect the views of their authors and do not represent the official position of the Maryknoll Society. To learn more about Maryknoll and Orbis Books, please visit our website at www.orbisbooks.com

Copyright © 2023 KMO Literary LLC
Published by Orbis Books, Box 302, Maryknoll, NY 10545-0302.

Cover Art: Marcha de Mujeres Familiares de Detenidos Desaparecidos (AFDD), Victoria Díaz Caro, Artesana, Colección de Isabel Morel de Letelier. Museo de la Memoria y Derechos Humanos. Special Permission granted by the Museo de la Memoria y Derechos Humanos, to include all images of the Chilean arpilleras displayed in this book.

Manufactured in the United States of America

Library of Congress Cataloging-in-Publication Data

Names: Osberger, Kathleen M., author.
Title: I surrender : a memoir of Chile's dictatorship, 1975 / Kathleen M. Osberger.
Other titles: Memoir of Chile's dictatorship, 1975
Description: Maryknoll, New York : Orbis Books, [2023] | Includes bibliographical references and index. | Summary: "While teaching grade school in Chile in 1975, Kathy Osberger was picked up and interrogated by Chile's secret police"—Provided by publisher.
Identifiers: LCCN 2023007250 (print) | LCCN 2023007251 (ebook) | ISBN 9781626985476 (trade paperback) | ISBN 9798888660058 (epub)
Subjects: LCSH: Osberger, Kathleen M. | Political prisoners—Chile—Biography. | Victims of state-sponsored terrorism—Chile—Biography. | Lay teachers—Chile—Biography. | School Sisters of Notre Dame. | Catholic Church—Chile—History—20th century. | Chile—Politics and government—1973-1988.
Classification: LCC F3101 .O83 A3 2023 (print) | LCC F3101 (ebook) | DDC 983.06/5092 [B]—dc23/eng/20230322
LC record available at https://lccn.loc.gov/2023007250
LC ebook record available at https://lccn.loc.gov/2023007251

*To the Chilean people
who have struggled so valiantly
for human rights and democracy*

Contents

*Part V. The Church Bears Witness:
October 15–31, 1975*

Part VI. The Day of the Dead: November 1–2, 1975

Part VII. Solidarity: November 3–8, 1975

Part VIII. Take Cover: November 9–19, 1975

Preface

September 11, 2023, marks the fiftieth anniversary of Chile's tragic coup d'état, orchestrated by the U.S. government, the CIA, corporate leaders, and the Chilean military to depose the democratically elected president of Chile, Salvador Allende. Even these many decades later, the loss of life, the inhumanity, and the traumatic memories remain vivid. The struggle waged over decades by the Chilean people to restore democratic rule and human rights continues to inspire.

I hope this memoir will plunge the reader into the reality of Chile in 1975, then in its second year under the Pinochet dictatorship. In intimate detail it describes the risks taken and the profound solidarity offered by Chilean citizens, faith communities, religious sisters, and clergy, who in their daily lives resisted the dehumanization of Pinochet's rule.

While this memoir is based on my own memories and experiences in 1975, it is anchored in the interviews undertaken in 2005 and 2007 that captured the shared experiences of the women I lived and worked with in Santiago. In reality, their lives are the story to which I was a privileged witness. To each of them I am eternally grateful. In the solitude of writing, my heart was warmed by the generosity of so many old and new friends who agreed to be interviewed, sharing their profound memories.

This memoir would not have come to fruition without the careful attention of those who critiqued the early drafts. They include Renny Golden, my sister Margaret (Peggy) Wilder and niece Elizabeth Wilder, Laurie Brands Gagné, Mary Hawley, Phillip Berryman, Isabel Donoso, Bernadette Ballasty, Helen Nelson, and the late Michael McConnell. Their keen insights propelled me forward. I am deeply grateful to Sandi Wisenberg, my developmental editor, for her clear eye and expert direction.

My now deceased parents, Alice and Daniel Osberger, held on to the letters I sent home, a tender reminder of their love. Though no longer with us, two persons I'd like to recognize are Don McNeill, CSC, and Claude Pomerleau, CSC, for the roles they played launching many experiential learning programs at the University of Notre Dame, which influenced me and generations of Notre Dame students and faculty.

I want to extend my gratitude to Maryknoll archivist Jennifer Halloran, New York Sisters of Charities archivist Mindy Gordon, and the Microfilm librarians at the University of Notre Dame Hesburgh Library. Valuable technical and editorial support was given to me by Carla Spann, Maribeth Nesbitt, Maria Ugarte, and my nephew, Read Wilder. Macarena Gana corrected my Spanish, and Dale Fast enhanced many photos to an unexpected crispness.

I am very grateful to all my family, dear neighbors, and lifelong friends, who have promised to be among the memoir's first readers. In particular, I'd like to recognize those friends who were shaped by years spent in Chile, Peru, or Central America, then devoted their lives to human rights and solidarity work. Special thanks go to Kathy Neidhardt and the late Martin Gárate, who in 2007 hosted me in Santiago.

Finally, I am indebted to Robert Ellsberg, publisher, Jon Sweeney, editor, and the entire staff at Orbis Books for their dedication to the publication.

Interviews

JOSÉ (PEPE) AHUMADA, Congregation of the Holy Cross (CSC): October 16 and November 12, 22, 23, 27, 2022, by email.

PAULA ARMSTRONG, School Sister of Notre Dame (SSND): April 4 and November 11, 2005, Sommerville, MA, in person, audio-taped and transcribed.

ROSITA ARROYO: March 13, 2007, Santiago, Chile, in person, audio-taped and transcribed.

BERNADETTE BALLASTY, School Sister of Notre Dame (SSND): March 9 and 10, 2007, in person, audio-taped and transcribed; multiple telephone calls, and email correspondence.

HELEN CARPENTER, Maryknoll Sister (MM): March 8, 2007, International Day of Women, Lo Prado, Santiago, Chile, at Casa Malen, in person, audio-taped, and transcribed.

MICHAEL CODY, Society of St. Columban (SSC): March 13, 2007, Santiago, Chile, Columban Center, in person, hand-written notes.

PATRICK ALOYSIUS CONNAUGHTON, Society St. Columban (SSC): October 17, 19, and November 8, 22, 2022, by email.

TOM CONNELLY, Society of St. Columban (SSC), from 1973 to 1989; later a legislative researcher at the *Biblioteca del Congreso Nacional de Chile*: October 14, 19, 29, 31, 2021, Santiago, Chile, Zoom call, email, and summary notes. He graciously provided archived materials about Fr. William Halliden and Enriqueta Reyes Valerio.

ISABEL DONOSO: March 14, 2007, Santiago, Chile, in person, audio-taped and transcribed; and February 15, 2022, by Zoom, summary notes, and email.

DAVID FARRELL, Congregation of the Holy Cross (CSC): August 31 and September 17, 2021, October 17 and December 3, 2022, Holy Cross House, Notre Dame, IN, by telephone, email, and summary notes.

LUCY GIACCHETTI, School Sister of Notre Dame (SSND): June 26, 2012, Chicago, IL, in person and a hand-written note.

KATHERINE GILFEATHER, Maryknoll Sister (MM): January 7, 12, 2022, Maryknoll Sisters Center, Ossining, NY, by phone, email, and summary notes.

ELIZABETH (LIZ) GILMORE, Society of the Holy Child Jesus (SHCJ): January 8, 10, 16, 27, 2022, Santa Barbara, CA, by telephone, email, and summary notes.

TOM HENEHAN, Maryknoll Father (MM): September 14, 2021, Chicago, IL, in person, email, and summary notes.

PEG LIPSIO, Maryknoll Sister (MM): October 12, 2022, Hendersonville, NC, by telephone, email, and summary notes.

ROBERT (BOB) MOSHER, Society of St. Columban (SSC): September 27, 2021, Wareham, MA, by telephone and summary notes.

BERNARD NAHLEN, MD: April 24 and 25, 2021, New Buffalo, MI, in person, with summary notes.

HELEN NELSON, School Sister of Notre Dame (SSND): March 9 and 10, 2007, Los Andes, Chile, in person, audio-taped and transcribed and emails.

DANIEL PANCHOT, Congregation of the Holy Cross (CSC): January 14, February 7, February 15, 2022, San Roque, Peñalolén, Santiago, Chile, by Zoom and emails.

BRIAN H. SMITH, Society of Jesus (SJ) (former member). In 1975, he lived in Santiago doing PhD research focused on the Catholic bishops in Chile; emeritus professor of religion, Ripon College, October 6, 2022, by email and phone.

MARY TRACY, Maryknoll Sister (MM): September 30, 2022, Argo, IL, by telephone and email.

PART I
JOURNEY
1953–1975

1

Descent

I remember leaving poinsettia hedges, lovely and large, behind me at the airstrip in Panama. Dew filtered the dawn heat that would evaporate, just as the brilliance of morning light would turn gray at my destination. Only a few hours after departing from the continent's midsection the plane descended, grazing for thousands of miles over the majestic Andes, the backbone of Chile, and its capital city, Santiago. Arriving in the aptly named shoestring-shaped country in the Americas' southern cone, it was as if I had skipped into a movie first rendered in dazzling tropical colors and emerged sprinkled in gray-green and black.

The new colors around me were not foliage but uniforms, the garb of the Third Reich imitated and fierce. Chile's police, *los Carabineros*, occupied every corner of the arrivals room of Pudahuel airport, swinging shiny machine guns as they surveyed the crowd. They stood menacingly proud in their crisscrossed leather vest belts. I began to tremble and did not know if it was caused by the Southern Hemisphere's bracing winter chill or by fear. I knew one fact clearly, Chile's violent *Golpe de Estado*, the September 11, 1973, military coup d'état against the democratically elected president, Salvador Allende, had ushered in General Augusto Pinochet's dictatorship, now nearly two years old.

I rescued my zippered suitcase from the confusion of the conveyor belt. I gripped my documents and the straps of my leather backpack, then waited to pass through the final check points before being released from the anonymous, querying eyes in the secluded customs area.

I felt alone and uncertain, missing my college friends Bernard Nahlen and Patrick Cimino. The three of us had traveled for the past month as itinerant students, hopping on and off the *Ticabus* as it traversed the Pan-American highway through southern Mexico, Guatemala, El Salvador, Nicaragua, Costa Rica, and Panama. We were part of the University of Notre Dame's inaugural Latin American Program in Experiential Learning (LAPEL), focused on one to two years of volunteer work and studies in Santiago, Chile, or Chimbote, Peru. While I flew ahead to Chile to begin a year of teaching in an elementary school, the others continued their overland trip for several more weeks.

I watched as the customs agent's hand slipped through my suitcase, where I had tucked a few reminders of my journey: startlingly beautiful hand-loomed weavings from San Antonio de las Aguas Calientes, a photo of the macaw who kept us awake nights in Guatemala, an intricately beaded necklace made and sold on the Panamanian roadside by Emberá indigenous women, and postcards of numerous places where I wondered if I would ever be lucky enough to return.

I didn't know then that I had been fortunate to traipse freely across Managua's streets, a mangle of heaved sidewalks and semi-intact buildings, the survivors of the devastating 1972 earthquake. Street signs were no more, so descriptive directions were given instead: "*¡Camina dos bloques y doblas donde el palo verde y sigues recto, pa'arriba hasta el mango!*" Walk two blocks and turn when you see the tree with the green trunk, continue straight ahead until you see a mango tree. This Managua would soon tremble and heave with the rise of the Sandinistas, the doom of the Somoza dynasty, and the deadly invasion of Contra forces. I didn't know then that I was seeing the Guatemalan Highlands before General Rios Montt, before the Civil Patrols and the genocide of the Mayan indigenous people. As I walked up the cathedral steps in San Salvador, I had no idea that five years later, in 1980, Archbishop Oscar Romero would be slain while saying Mass and that the kidnapped, raped, and dead bodies of four religious women from the United States would be unearthed. Nor that the same decade would end with the murdered bodies of six Jesuit priests, their housekeeper, and her daughter.

On July 28, 1975, hearing the repeated thud of rubber stamps on my passport at Santiago's Pudahuel airport, I didn't fully comprehend the frontier I was crossing. Instead, I felt relieved when the customs officer put down his rubber stamp, looked up at me, and nodded toward the exit door saying, "*Señorita, ya puedes pasar.*" You may pass.

Bernadette Ballasty, a School Sister of Notre Dame (SSND) from Connecticut, had agreed to meet me at the airport. We spotted each other quite easily. She was on the fringe of the crowd, a gentle face with high cheekbones, marine blue eyes, and a broad smile. Her short bangs and hair cut to her ear tips seemed to match the wheat color of the Irish-knit sweater she wore.

She called out my name, and we embraced in the awkward way that two strangers begin a friendship. All around us was the mayhem of families searching for their loved ones. The excitement and musicality of Chilean Spanish greeted my ears. Stepping off the sidewalk I gasped at my surroundings, seeing up close now the soaring horizon of mountain peaks draped in snow. The *cordillera,* as the vista is known, felt intimate even in its vastness.

In the next few days, I would be marveling at the same zigzagged horizon, drawn by the children at San Juan de Dios grade school, where I had come to teach. Their crayon drawings rendered Santiago's horizon, the Andes Mountains, as a row of upside-down waffle cones with snow dripping from the peaks like melting ice cream. Gazing at their work, I noticed that the serenity and constancy of the *cordillera* created an imme-diate calm in them as it did in me.

In April of my senior year at Notre Dame, the unexpected opportu-nity to live in Chile arose. I happened to bump into Fr. Don McNeill, CSC, as we were both walking across the main quad toward the Golden Dome. Fr. Don, or *"Don Alto"* as many called him for his basketball-player height, was young and well liked. He led courses in pastoral theology and was known for his persistent networking with students and faculty interested in radical structural change in the inner cities and the Third World, where the marginalized poor lived in vast slums. Don believed that genuine social change emerged out of deep personal relationships and immersion into the world of the poor. His courses and those of faculty members with a similar vision challenged students to think critically, examine their privileges and assumptions, and be willing to leave their comfortable lives, to cross over, serve, and be radically changed by the experience.

During our chance encounter Don told me about a pilot program in which Notre Dame graduates and students would be living and working in poor parish communities led by the Holy Cross priests in Chile and Peru. He asked if I would be interested in being part of it. I was enthralled by the chance to learn, make friends, and be immersed in the reality of Latin America for two years. My qualifications were sparse: a newly minted liberal arts degree, fluency in Spanish gained during high school, a semester in Spain, and a six-week social justice "plunge" the previous summer in the *barrios* of San Miguelito, Panama. I knew the Chilean people were living under a repressive military government, but that had also been true when I studied in Spain during the dictatorship of Francisco Franco and in Panama under Omar Torrijos.

Because I would be the only woman among the group going to Chile, the Holy Cross priests (CSC) in Santiago reached out to the School Sisters of Notre Dame (SSND) to see if I could live with them. The sisters had taught at Colegio St. George, a school led by the Holy Cross priests. The sisters offered to meet me upon arrival, provide hospitality, and arranged for me to teach and volunteer in the poorer neighborhoods, called *poblaciones*.

Bernadette led me to a car in the parking lot, a white Peugeot whose doors slammed with a tinny noise once I hoisted my bag into the back seat. Our conversation was halting, beginning in Spanish then in English, popping in and out of topics to orient me. I contributed to the frequent shifts, asking questions about the peculiar sights that claimed my attention as we drove into Santiago.

Soon we were on La Alameda, Santiago's central artery. We passed the Estación Central, where trains and buses converge and arriving passengers find themselves captive to a sidewalk mélange of vendors selling produce, trinkets, and crafts. I noticed that once we were away from the mountain vista and inside the hub of the city, the green-gray drabness returned. Gray permeated the air and clung to the ornate stone buildings reminiscent of colonial Spain. Brightly colored old school buses, heading to Lo Barnechea or La Bandera, spewed dense soot as they lurched away from the curb with passengers jammed in the entry well or clinging to the bus's back bumper. The noise was ferocious as buses cascaded around vehicles and pedestrians, with their brakes grinding and moaning.

On side streets I saw men in broken shoes leading horse-drawn carts to haul refuse. Nearby, women bundled in black shawls stood outside the *panaderías,* bakeries, carefully counting their coins. The winter drizzle seemed to cast a cloud of weariness, as their shoulders drooped under the weight of wet woolen ponchos.

Bernadette turned the car at Avenidas Matta and Portugal and drove a few blocks more until we reached Calle Padre Orellana, a tidy working-class street of single-story, attached dwellings with smoothed cement façades. She parked the car, glanced about, then quickly ushered me past the heavy wooden door into the house where she lived with Helen Nelson and Paula Armstrong, North American members of the SSND community. The SSNDs shared their convent home and community life with two lay women, Isabel Donoso, a Chilean, and Rosita Arroyo, from Peru.

Bernadette seemed apprehensive as she showed me around the house, an ample place with five bedrooms, four of which had large windows spanning the street. The other bedroom, living room, and kitchen had windows facing a walled-in garden patio, adding brightness to the dim interior. The furnishings were comfortable, yet modest. Chilean artifacts decorated the room: a painting of the red *copihue*, the national flower, hung in one corner; a hand-carved wooden statue stood in another; and a large embossed copper ashtray adorned the coffee table. Keepsakes from other parts of Latin America—carved gourds from Peru, woven wall hangings and basketry—were scattered about, as were shawls to fend off the chill. Bernadette quickly showed me how to light the portable paraffin heater in the living room.

Right away, I sensed that my favorite place in the house would be the kitchen, even though on this winter day it was the coldest room. It had yellow walls, white metal cupboards, and a view of the garden. From the kitchen we doubled back through the house, and Bernadette pointed out a small interior room, just off the front hallway, which was used as a chapel. I peeked in, saw a worn carpet, pillows propped against the walls, two chairs, an open Bible, and a crucifix on the wall. Consecrated hosts were held in reserve on a low table inside a copper box encrusted with blue lapis lazuli stones. Instead of the customarily lit vigil candle, a small red electric light glowed, a practical nod to spontaneous fires in this earthquake-prone region. Strangely, until one of my last days in the house, I never stepped back into this room.

I set my belongings in a front bedroom that had twin beds with thick covers, heavy drapes, an empty desk, and a half-filled closet. I hadn't given much thought to whether I'd have my own room or to my surroundings. Assuming they would be minimal, I was surprised by the comfort around me.

Bernadette and I went to the kitchen, where she poured powdered Nescafé into heavy white cups, followed by steaming milk. On the table sat yeasty bread rolls scored with a long crease down the middle. Bernadette stammered a bit as she told me she had been alone most of the past weekend, since Helen and Paula were visiting their families in the United States. She said Rosita would be home, after seeing off her first-grade class. Isabel planned to arrive later in the evening. I listened, breaking off a bit of my roll and putting a dab of jam on it, when Bernadette went on to say, "The others asked me not to talk about this right away, but I think you should know something."

The drop in her voice and halting speech made me a little panicked. "Well, sometimes we have visitors here, people who need help. They are people who need to be in a safe place if their lives are in danger."

The air between us was still. Gravity weighted each word as she spoke. "One of our visitors just left this morning."

I don't think I blinked. I just tried to take it in.

"We called him Juan," she said. "It has been very dangerous for several weeks, since his story came out in the international press. Some reports claimed he had been in an embassy and had left the country, but it wasn't true. He was here in our house. The DINA knew he hadn't left the country."

"The DINA?" I asked.

"The Directorate of National Intelligence, the secret police," she replied, and then continued, "The DINA held him in custody and tortured him with multiple burns. When they took him out to force him to finger a man they wanted to arrest, he escaped. Then he was taken to see Cardinal Silva's personal doctor. Afterwards he was brought here. It's been very dangerous. He left this morning, just before I went to pick you up at the airport."

Bernadette looked relieved, the weeks of tension falling off her shoulders as she described her last days spent with a brave but crumbling man who prowled the house like a cat, finding terror in every shadow.

"Are you talking about the man who was written up in *Time* magazine in June?" I asked, stunned, my thoughts cascading to unknown depths, while my speech slowed. "Bernadette, I know this story."

I was flooded with the memory of a perfect Midwest day about six weeks earlier, a hot sun rolling over newly sprouted grass and trees moving to a faint rustle of wind. I was preparing to leave from my home in South Bend, Indiana, anxious to meet my Notre Dame friends in Mexico, then travel through Central America and on to Chile. After a morning of errands with my mom, I plopped down on the couch. My mother came in with the mail. Sitting across from me, she paged through the latest issue of *Time* magazine, then paused, saying, "Let me read this to you."

The headline was, "Chile: Terror under the Junta."[1] The first two paragraphs were gripping, but when she reached the middle portion, I saw in front of my eyes an enormously powerful field of energy, like a compressed cloud of black static, which surrounded my head and slowly pressed through my skull. I had never had an experience like that before. When it was over, all I knew was that I was deeply connected to this story, but couldn't imagine how.

> Last month, with considerable fanfare, General Pinochet signed a new decree requiring police officials to notify a prisoner's family within 48 hours of his detention and, more important, prohibiting "illegal pressure on detainees," meaning torture. But in one two-week period since the decree, according to legal sources about 30 people were seized by the police; 19 of them have not been seen since. Among the recent victims is a socialist named Sergio Zamora Torres. Seized and tortured for six hours, Zamora eventually managed to get the protection of Raúl Cardinal Silva Henríquez, the head of Chile's increasingly oppositionist Roman

Catholic Church. Zamora was examined by Silva's doctor and found to show burns on his arms, legs, genitals and nose, plus evidence of a beating. With the help of the cardinal, he was able to get a safe-conduct pass out of the country, but at last word he was still in Santiago.

My mother's voice became more somber as she finished reading the piece. I roused myself from the intense sensation pinning me to the couch, trying to placate the worry in her voice. "It will be okay, Mom. I'm just going to teach in a grade school, and I'll be living with nuns. I'll be safe. You know the university wouldn't start the program if something dangerous could happen." I didn't say it, but I may have thought it: besides, we are Americans.

My mother never let on if she felt the same energy pass through the room. She just stared at me, past my blitheness. Studying her eyes, I felt her wondering if she could let me go. Go so far away to places she had been too busy raising kids to ponder, to worlds she never imagined.

I didn't have the heart to tell her what transpired in me as she read the magazine article. Instead, I swiftly mustered the pretense of youthful invincibility. I acted overconfident and changed the subject. Having just graduated, I couldn't permit parental worries to cancel my passport into the future. While I wasn't totally naïve about the potential for danger, it seemed unlikely that it would touch me. I had yet to discover that there are moments in history when neutrality is not only impossible but immoral.

Now on my first day in Chile, I was being handed not only a household secret, but a national security secret.

My eyes locked on Bernadette's face as she spoke about Zamora, the man they called "Juan." She described the terrible toll of his torture, then the clever way he eluded the DINA. The DINA had brazenly taken their wounded captive during the workday to the *Comité Pro Paz* (Pro-Peace Committee), an ecumenical organization that arose after the military coup to aid the hungry, the unemployed, those detained, and the families of those disappeared. Confident that Zamora would point out a comrade they had in their sights, the DINA never suspected that he might escape and expose their crimes. Alert staff members of the *Comité* recognized the operation under way, cried out, and scuffled. A chain of *Comité Pro Paz* employees pulled him into their offices and blocked the DINA from entering the church property. Led by unknown friends Zamora was moved through a warren of offices and ultimately brought to Cardinal Silva's personal doctor, who documented his wounds.[2]

Thus "Juan" arrived surreptitiously, through church channels, to the sisters' doorstep on Calle Padre Orellana. Bernadette told me that he suffered acute insomnia from the traumatic recall of his torture. He cringed at every knock on the door and knew that any slip of the tongue might mean captivity, more torture, and death.

After his arrival the sisters kept up their normal routines, leaving him in the quiet of their home while they left to teach school. Their behavior was equal parts disguise and relief—a disguise that nothing out of the ordinary was happening in their lives, should their house be under surveillance, and a relief for them to be away from the penetrating anxiety, pulsating fears, and terrors emanating from the cavernous psychic space "Juan" inhabited in their home. They too lived with the awareness that one misstep might bring the full force of the DINA upon them all.

Bernadette asked me not to mention to the others, expected home soon, that she had shared this story with me. She said she would tell them in due time. She reassured me that they had already agreed to take a respite from offering their home as a sanctuary. She looked spent. The final days and hours before "Juan's" transfer to an embassy had drained her.

I retreated to my room. I busied myself with the unpacking, a simple enough task, since I had packed light to ease hoisting my bag on and off the *Ticabus*. But this huge secret? I had no place to put it; it was beyond any realm of my experience. My thoughts buzzed, scrambled and unformed. Part of me felt awe for the courage of these women, who were risking their lives. The knowledge of Cardinal Silva's intervention to safeguard a hunted man's life seemed to sanction their heroics. I tamped down my fears by recalling Bernadette's comment that the sisters had decided not to provide sanctuary for a while. I suspected this was due in part to my arrival. More than anything I wanted to understand their motivation for such momentous risk taking. Then it occurred to me that, through their generous hospitality, I had become their latest gamble.

Could they trust me?

After I had rested a few hours, Bernadette called me to see if I would like to help prepare *la once*, an early evening Chilean custom to socialize and enjoy a snack, maybe some fresh bread with ham and cheese, or on special occasions piping hot *empanadas*. We walked to the neighborhood *panadería* to purchase bread. Bernadette handed me the *malla*, a mesh grocery bag. We queued behind numerous neighbor women, who had gathered just as the ovens released their aromas. While a few women chatted with those around them, others seemed somber, fiddling with coins. I noticed that several customers changed their minds, shrinking their orders, before loaves and palm-sized rolls were tossed into their *malla*. No one left the counter without doing some quick mental math and double-checking their change and receipt. The baker woman eyed each customer until both smiled with satisfaction, and *"¡Gracias!"* flew off the customer's lips as she left.

As we stepped closer to the counter my Spanish abilities diminished. The array of breads and their colloquial names whizzed by as the baker plucked loaves and buns from specific baskets. In vain I tried memorizing their sizes, shapes, and names. When our turn came the store quieted as all eyes fell on the *gringas*. I hoisted the *malla* to the counter, stinging with self-consciousness, like a chubby kid challenged to climb a rope. Blushing deeply, I imagined the slew of social rituals I needed to learn before I could hope to fit in.

The fresh bread and ham we enjoyed before dinner, tasted delicious, and the house seemed to warm as each member returned from work, settled in, and welcomed me. A pot of *porotos*, Chilean beans, bubbled on the stove behind us, blending its steamy flavors amid introductions and chatter.

Rosita was the first one home. She was twenty-six years old and seemed to bundle joy and enthusiasm into every moment. Life, spirit, and imagination filled her. A born storyteller, she had a captivating voice, gravelly and low. Her coarse, dark hair sprang freely about her head, falling to just above her shoulders. She stood slightly tipped to the side, a posture that no doubt brought her closer to her first-grade students. Woven Peruvian bags, stuffed full of papers and projects, dangled from her hands and shoulder. She dropped them to greet me with a hug and then launched into an urgent account of the day.

"*¿Sabes qué? No lo van a creer. . . .*" She spoke in wonderment about one of her student's achievements. I studied her face, spotting a sleepy left eye easily disguised by her effervescence, and hoped we would soon be friends.

Rosita's animated conversation sustained us for a while and then seemed to peter away. Apprehension hovered in the room whenever the conversation hit a lull.

"What plans did Isabel have tonight?" Rosita asked. "Did she say when she'd be home?"

I detected some collective worry about Isabel's safety. This was my first lesson in the undercurrent of a society coping with fearsome nights under curfew, enforced by the dictatorship.

"What kind of work does Isabel do?" I asked. An odd quiet met my question, followed by a round of glances.

After a moment, Bernadette brushed past the hesitancy in the room. "She works at the *Comité Pro Paz*, the ecumenical organization I mentioned to you earlier. It was started to help people after the *golpe*. She has to be very discreet and careful in her work, since the government is hostile toward the organization."

I pulled back and didn't ask any of the other questions forming in my mind. Just then, the lock in the front door clicked, followed by a vibrant voice saying, "*¡Hola, amigas! ¡Qué noche más fría!*"

Isabel was home and out of the cold. She rushed into the kitchen, savoring the warmth, then paused to welcome me. "*¡Qué gusto estar donde hay calor! Hola Kathy, soy Isabel. ¡Bienvenida a Chile!*"

She quickly switched into English. "Let me give you a warm Chilean welcome, because after all, I am Chilean!" She laughed heartily, as she gave me a hug.

She was of medium height, looked to be about thirty, with soft brown eyes and hair that curled around the contours of her face. I sensed that she had quite a spirit, intense, deep, and playful. Her nickname—*La Pulga*, the Flea—fit her. In a flicker she could bounce from laughter to a pensive attentiveness. Her energy appeared boundless.

Soon the night grew still as we retreated to our rooms. I heard fewer buses rumbling down Av. Matta and almost no footsteps on the sidewalk. I peeked out the window; most businesses on the block had already shuttered their doorways. Very few cars passed. The evening curfew at 1:00 a.m. was almost in effect as I drew the curtains. I picked one of the twin beds and tumbled in, trying to stay awake long enough to pry apart the day's experiences.

2

Invisible Passports

Had my heart been cultivated to live this moment in Latin America? I wish today, nearly five decades later, I could be sure. There is something comforting in the thought that this was all meant to be: a trace of God acting in my being. Or perhaps I seize upon the God–fate notion when I contemplate whether I made a fully conscious choice. Events unfolded so quickly in Chile that I find it hard to remember who I was before this story marked my life.

I grew up in South Bend, Indiana, a mid-sized city. We lived in McKinley Terrace, a development of wood-framed ranch houses, a stone's throw away from its border city, named for Princess Mishawaka, a Pottawatomie Indian. The little I learned about the Pottawatomie came through a few (in)famous mural paintings on the Notre Dame campus. The murals depicted a noble, docile people generously offering their plenty to the industrious pioneer priests and French founders of the university. As a little girl I gazed at these murals in the old South Dining Hall or in the rotunda of the Golden Dome, near my father's office.

Today, my parents' graves in Cedar Grove Cemetery on the campus lie next to those of my father's maternal grandparents, the McNamaras, and seven of their children, who died young of disease. The obelisk grave marker bears a year: 1859. Nearby, the bones of the Pottawatomie, led by Chief Pokagon, were placed in a sacred mound in Cedar Grove on September 22, 1928.[1] If I went to the graveyard on a fall day, I might see them all at rest under burnished leaves, a time of year my father relished as "Indian summer."

The truths and complexity of people and cultures meeting, suffering, embracing, loving, conquering, and even ignoring their very encounter remained buried while in plain sight. It would take many years before I understood that the ability to live unaware of the deep fiber of history, of place and plunder, marks one as privileged, even if this privilege is not sought.

I was the second child in our family, two years younger than my older sister, Julie. My birth in 1953 was followed fifteen months later by my brother, Dan, and five years later by my sister Peggy. My mother deemed me her "sociology kid," the one who questioned why. Typically, I was on call when a family dispute erupted, being the one who tried to figure out what propelled it. Facilitating squabbles seemed a natural role and lifted me out of the pack of four kids.

My ability to analyze and mediate gave me legs for small-scale leadership, the kind I first practiced in elections for class office. There I'd mostly be a second-tier leader, usually the vice president or secretary, often outspoken, but mostly organizing with others to do the grunt work. Unfortunately, as a female child I conformed myself to this helper-leader mindset all too easily.

A fixture in our town was the Kreamo bakery, which produced loaves of a spongy white sandwich bread, wrapped in a plastic sleeve stamped in a red, white, and blue pattern. Every few weeks my mom would pack us all in the car for a run to Kreamo for its sale of day-old bread. We eagerly rolled down the car windows to smell the aroma before we approached. Today, I think of my childhood as something akin to Kreamo bread. Mine was equal parts soft and homogenous, leaving me with untested substance.

Kids today would envy the independence we had. We spent hours alone riding bikes or playing kickball on an abandoned field, where some of our dads mowed the weeds to create a makeshift diamond. When it snowed, we dragged sleds over to Morris Park's "killer hill" to cascade down steep slopes unsupervised, or ice-skated after school on a makeshift rink in our neighbor's backyard. On hot afternoons my mom directed rehearsals for summer plays. Nothing topped the opening night applause we received from our parents and friends who gathered on lawn chairs to watch.

I was barely seven years old when a burst of exuberance and cheers overtook our block on the night John F. Kennedy won the presidency. When the news broke, I put on my Red Ball Jet sneakers to speed out to the street and celebrate. It seemed natural to be among Kennedy's supporters. Like Kennedy we believed in America's goodness and its capacity to change the world. That night I felt powerful, belonging to an America on the rise.

Pretty soon my eyes were opened by new encounters and experiences. At age twelve I started to babysit for the Gurdian family, who had seven children under the age of ten. I made thirty-five cents an hour. Everything about their family fascinated me. The parents were from Nicaragua and spoke Spanish. Álvaro, the father, was an architect who had graduated from Notre Dame. In spite of opportunities he might have had, he chose not to return to Nicaragua, a country ruled for decades by the powerful Somoza family. He married his high-school love, María, who left her family in Nicaragua for South Bend. In our neighborhood, their three-bedroom house stood out, with its A-frame living-room windows and modern furnishings. Their open-shelf bookcase held pre-Columbian and Mesoamerican pottery and artifacts, alongside photography books of modern architecture and design.

María and Álvaro asked me to enforce one rule. The kids could play freely in the bedrooms, kitchen, and family room, but the living room was off-limits. When the kids were asleep, I was allowed to sit on the living-room couch and page through their design books. Pretty soon I was a constant fixture in their home.

Upon entering high school, I wanted to study Spanish. Unfortunately, my freshman year teacher was our football coach, who spoke only guttural "coach," with a terrible accent. Luckily, for the next three years our Spanish teacher was a Puerto Rican, Brother Carlos L. Parrilla, CSC. Brother Carlos won our class over on the first day, saying: *"Para conocer otro idioma, hay que amar su alma."* To truly know another language, you must love its soul. He continued, "We will have no more drills! No more repetitions! No more memorization of tenses! Instead, we will recite poetry in Spanish. We will read short stories and learn the music that stirs its heart." Brother Carlos ended this litany in a firm voice, "And while class is in session, we will speak only Spanish."

Over the next three years he achieved his goal and provided me with a passport to my future. I fell in love with the Spanish language and its poetic soul. He left me with other insights too. He grew up in Lorain, Ohio, a steel town on the edge of Lake Erie. In the 1940s Lorain dealt with a severe labor shortage by recruiting male workers from rural Puerto Rico who had been displaced from their farms by the mechanization of sugar cane production. Many Puerto Rican men moved to Lorain, as part of Operation Bootstrap, only to face rental signs that said "No Puerto Ricans, No Pets" and suffer recruitment promises that weren't kept.[2]

Thinking about this I realized that the demands of industry could easily improve one community while crushing another. It was the same story my hometown was living. I was ten years old when on December 9, 1963, the *South Bend Tribune* announced that pink slips were given to all seven thousand workers at the Studebaker car plant and were let go.[3] I remember a lot of kids were crying in school that day. Our town was crushed! That night I asked my parents, "What happens when kids' parents don't have jobs?" They quietly looked at each other and said nothing.

When I was fifteen, Álvaro and María Gurdian called my parents to ask if I could accompany their family to Nicaragua as their babysitter for the summer. It would be the first time their children would see Nicaragua and meet their grandparents and cousins.

I wanted to go, but my parents said, "No. You are too young to take on a responsibility like that for the whole summer." I had a meltdown, crying, "I'll never get another chance again to go to Latin America! Never!" But they wouldn't budge.

Before the Gurdian's departure, María learned her father had a terminal illness and the slightest sounds caused him severe pain. There would have been no way for me to keep the seven children quiet and occupied as their grandfather suffered his last days. Even though I couldn't go with them to Nicaragua, they told me about the economic disparities in Latin America, such that the wealthy believed only a dictator could keep a social explosion at bay.

My first year in college I studied Spanish under Amalia de la Torre, a recent Cuban exile. Amalia shared with us her wrenching departure from Cuba and the politics that tore her away from her homeland and family.

Each of these influential people taught me things beyond the Spanish language. Foremost was their personal way of relating with warmth and respect. They were hungry to share their lives and the history of their countries. And they carried themselves with dignity, a value not always extended to them by Americans.

3

San Miguelito, Panama

I entered Notre Dame in the fall of 1972 as a sophomore, part of the first group of 362 women undergraduates admitted to a student body of six thousand male students. I spent the second semester of that academic year in Madrid, with all my college-level classes and requisite term papers written in Spanish. Even with the rigors of the program there was still plenty of time to explore every corner of Spain with a cheap student Eurail Pass.

Back at Notre Dame in my junior year, the chance to spend the summer of 1974 in Panama emerged. That spring Fr. Don McNeill drove four of us into Chicago to meet with Fr. Leo Mahon, a visionary priest from the Archdiocese of Chicago. Fr. Mahon, with a team of priests, sisters, and lay leaders, led an innovative pastoral experiment in San Miguelito, on the outskirts of Panama City. This pairing of the Chicago Archdiocese with Panama was a consequence of Vatican II's call to link First World and Third World dioceses in a mutual exchange of service, resources, and realities.

In the early 1960s San Miguelito comprised some 4,500 acres of privately owned but vacant land. Under cover of darkness, impoverished families from rural areas migrated toward the capital city seeking employment. They took over the underutilized land and fabricated tiny houses out of scrap metal and cast-off wood. They dug out primitive latrines and built outdoor ovens. Hostility and scorn often met their arrival, tagging their homes as *casas brujas,* or witch houses. From the hundreds the population grew to thousands, then hundreds of thousands, with the majority of the newly arriving population living without access to water, health care, roads, electricity, or schools. The material needs of these families were enormous, but so too was their longing for a better life.

Fr. Mahon shared San Miguelito's challenges, history, and growth with us. Key to the endeavor was developing lay leaders, initially mostly men, who led the *comunidades de base*, small faith communities. Throughout San Miguelito these small communities met weekly to reflect on the gospel and God's call to care for one another. This process created bonds among neighbors and a willingness to struggle together to improve their community and lives. As Fr. Mahon spoke, I was transfixed by the exciting and transformative work under way.

Mahon simply invited us to "come and see." The plan was to spend eight weeks, living with one of the families in the marginal communities of San Miguelito and accompanying the Panamanian lay leaders doing the pastoral outreach, learning from them how they shaped their communities, not only physically but with an alive faith. The lay leaders shared Mahon's vision of forming a people and community capable of creating their own history, built on a faith in God and living the gospel.[1]

Only a few weeks after meeting Fr. Mahon, I was living with the Uribe family in Alcalde Díaz, surrounded by Panama's lush terrain of banana, papaya, and mango trees, yucca plants, and poinsettia hedges. Leonardo and Francisca "Chica" Uribe made room for me in their already-crowded household. Their oldest daughter, Carmen, and I shared a mattress on the floor, while Antonia and Holda slept nearby on the box spring, shuffling little Yhony back into his parents' room.

In Panama I experienced the enormous contrast between the life of the poor and my secure world. One experience touched me deeply. I was walking up one of San Miguelito's verdant hills next to tired men and women returning from their arduous workday. The buses that brought them back to San Miguelito left them a great distance from their thatched homes precariously perched on the rolling hills. The climb up the hill was the final trek of a day, which had begun at 5:00 a.m., when the women and older children trudged down the hill to meet the water truck. Then they lugged gallon pails of dingy water back up for the day's use. Out of their meager earnings they had to purchase and carry the water, while in a nearby urbanized neighborhood, other families paid only one-third the price for clean water pumped into their homes.

That night I climbed the hill until I reached a dimly lit hut. Dusk settled in. There seated on roughhewn benches the members of the small faith community began to gather. A single candle illuminated the room as each person was welcomed with a hug or greeting. Antonio, the lay leader, began the evening prayer. Then he passed the candle to Victoria, a young mother, who volunteered to read aloud a Scripture passage about Jesus's baptism. Afterwards Antonio asked probing questions: Why do you think Jesus wanted to be baptized? Did he need to be baptized? What happens to someone who is baptized; what does it mean to you? Why do you think water and light are part of baptism? Are they just symbols?

As the community members shared their thoughts a palpable energy took hold. They spoke of themselves as God's beloved children and worthy of a dignified life, not the one they were living, not the one with dirty water and no electricity. If they believed that by baptism "God was among us," then how might they respond to the reality they and so many other families suffered under?

Listening, I heard murmurs for change bursting the darkness and a vision of struggle for here and now. It was a vision of God's reign and God's community. The vision was concrete: water and light, and it led to action. Within a few weeks the faith community gathered their neighbors for a street march, protesting the costly water and the lack of electricity. The street march itself was a baptism, as they dared to take their faith seriously and demand a just distribution of services. I knew their march was only the first step in a long fight for water, but it was one that illuminated for me the tremendous power of a community united by faith to transform injustice.

4

San Juan de Dios School in Buzeta

The day after my arrival in Chile, Bernadette offered to drive Rosita and me to San Juan de Dios school. Rosita took the back seat in order to work on some last-minute preparations for her first-grade class. Buzeta, where the school was located, was once a busy industrial neighborhood in Santiago's southern zone. Now it was full of shuttered factories, due to the economic collapse after the *golpe* in 1973. The school was surrounded by the marginal homes of unemployed workers and their families. The overcast winter sky matched the grayness of the faded paint on the abandoned factories and their sealed entry.

Bernadette pulled up in front of the convent, a two-story building attached to the enormous multilevel school, with its cement-colored façade. The street seemed almost empty of people and noise. Rosita rang the bell at the front gate, and we were welcomed by Sr. Helen Carpenter, a Maryknoll sister. She greeted the three of us with a loud *"¡Hola!"* and chuckled her surprise at unexpectedly seeing Bernadette, who taught at another school, and meeting me. She ushered us into a large dining room next to the kitchen, where Sr. Geraldine Doiron, known as Gerry, clicked off the hissing tea pot, promising to bring some buttered toast and jam to the table. Rosita ran off to her classroom while Bernadette introduced me to Helen and Gerry, who had arranged for me to teach in the school.

Sr. Helen Carpenter, MM, at San Juan de Dios school in Buzeta.
Courtesy Maryknoll Mission Archives.

Gerry, age forty-six, and Helen, age thirty-five, looked like two of the most warm-hearted people you would ever want to meet. Both were dressed in well-worn slacks and wrapped themselves in alpaca sweaters buttoned over long-sleeved shirts to fend off the cold. Helen was the taller and younger of the two, with an energetic, sinewy body. She spoke rapidly, jumping between English and Spanish, often laughing with arms gesticulating. She moved in a whirlwind way that reminded me of Dick Van Dyke spinning through a room. Cued by the sound of the school bell, she dashed away to complete a forgotten task.

Gerry was short, with rounded shoulders and worn, stubby hands. Her deep eyes studied you as you spoke. She would listen attentively, then share her wisdom, leaving you whole.

Over the next few hours, they asked me about Notre Dame's LAPEL program and my travels to Chile. Helen captivated me with her own story of traveling to Chile, leaving from a Brooklyn dock by freighter, making ports of call down the U.S. coast, then on to Central America and through the Panama Canal, until they reached Valparaiso, Chile. In 1964 Helen joined fifty-five Maryknoll sisters already working in Chile. On her first visit to the busy school in Buzeta, she thought, "Who could teach here with all the noise!" Nonetheless, after months of studying Spanish in Pucón, as its unrelenting rains poured, she was happy to embrace the bustle of Buzeta and returned there to teach.

As Helen Carpenter left to handle some school duties, Gerry escorted me around the school, a two-story building in an "L" shape, with classroom wings intersecting at a stairwell that led into the Maryknoll convent. Long, open-air corridors surrounded the enormous school patio and playground on one side with classrooms on the other. While today was cold and bleak, I could imagine the magic of a springtime warm-up and a bright sun pouring over the corridors as excited children ran out for recess.

As Gerry and I walked around, a few children passed us; some had been sent by their teachers to fetch supplies, while others were late arrivals. Gerry greeted each child by name, giving them a wink and a smile to "do their best today." Together, Gerry and I entered the school office, where I was introduced to Sra. Grumilda, the principal of the school. She invited us to sit down and began to scrutinize me, asking about my degree, my experiences working with children, all the while assessing my Spanish. I'm sure she was skeptical about my adequacy for the responsibilities, but she had a dire need for substitute teachers as several faculty members were out on medical leave. Sra. Grumilda asked that I shadow Srs. Gerry and Helen for the next few days. She gave me the lesson plans prepared by the teachers who were out sick, so that I could cover their classes early next week. I would be expected to turn in detailed lesson plans weekly. I also had to present my university transcripts as soon as possible.

The transcripts had to be officially translated and submitted to the Chilean consul in Chicago for certification, then mailed to me. What? I thought to myself, *why wasn't this part of our orientation prior to arrival?* This was going to take weeks.

When she stood up to end the meeting, I thanked Sra. Grumilda for the opportunity to work at the school and promised her I'd begin class preparations right away. She looked at me sternly and nodded, with a gaze that said, I'll take you at your word, for now. But don't disappoint me.

The following day Rosita and I were off by bus to Buzeta around 6:30 a.m. to arrive before classes began. The joyous screams of children playing tag in the schoolyard met us as we crossed over to the convent area for a sip of Nescafé before classes. Rosita said her hellos and gave a hug to *"Las Hermanas"* as Srs. Gerry and Helen were lovingly referred to by the children and parents alike, then cut away to prep her classroom before the bell rang.

Gerry and I lingered over our last sips of coffee as the bell clanged and kids lined up in the schoolyard patio. From afar we could hear the calls to silence, the student body pledging allegiance as the Chilean flag rose on the pulley, and the sound of their voices as the national anthem was sung. While parents drifted out of the schoolyard, the kids and teachers departed for their classrooms and roll call.

That morning, Gerry and I met with small groups of second to fourth graders in the snug tutorial rooms. It was fun to watch their faces as Hermana Gerry introduced each child to me. Shy at first, their curious eyes darted away and back again to check me out. I pulled my small chair up close to the shared table and smiled, asking Javier if he'd like to work

Sr. Geraldine Doiron, MM, and children leaving for a field trip. Courtesy Maryknoll Mission Archives.

together on some math problems. Luckily, Gerry had grade-appropriate math worksheets on hand. I started with the basics: Could Javier point to the top number and tell me what it was? And the bottom number? And what about the curious plus and minus signs, what do they tell you to do? Little by little his shyness faded, as he penciled his answers onto the worksheet.

I was no math genius, but if one of the students still lacked number recognition, I turned to a tactile approach, counting fingers on each hand, the buttons on their uniform, the lace holes in their shoes, or I had them add or take away blocks on the table. With the older children we played Bingo or counted coins to reinforce number recognition, addition, and subtraction.

Working one-on-one or in pairs, I learned that many children arrived at the school each morning hungry, not just for nourishment, but often starved for small bits of attention and praise. The hour in the tutorial room took them away from the noisy classroom, allowing time for reinforcement of difficult concepts and affirmation of their effort to learn. A smile or gleam in their eye was the best reward for the morning of work.

During the lunch break, I headed across the corridor toward the convent and walked down a flight of stairs. From a flight above, I heard someone call out, "Hello, who are you?"

I turned and looked up to the landing, where a woman, in her mid to late thirties, with short, wavy blond hair, stood dressed in a rumpled blouse, slacks, and a worn cardigan sweater. Around her neck were a necklace and cross.

"Hello, I'm Kathy," I answered. "I'm new and will be helping here at the school. And you are . . . ?"

"I'm Connie, Sr. Connie Kelly. I teach religion classes here two days a week," she replied in a friendly voice with a distinct New York accent.

I paused for a moment, noticing the expansive window behind her, where the sun had finally dashed the grayness of the morning, enveloping her in its rays. She continued down the half flight of stairs and came to a full stop in front of me.

"I know you . . . we've met before," she said confidently.

Taken aback, I replied, "No, I don't think we've ever met before, Connie. I just arrived in Chile a few days ago. But it is good to meet you."

"No, I'm sure we've met before. I know you." She uttered it again with insistence, as she stepped down the last step, now standing next to me.

I gave it another try, with hopes we could move on by asking her, "Where are you from?"

"New York. Well, Staten Island to be specific," she answered. "I am a New York Sister of Charity and have been in Chile a few years now. But I am sure I know you. I've *met* you already . . . somewhere. . . ."

I laughed nervously. Still puzzled, I tried a final time saying, "Well, who knows? But I'm heading into the kitchen for lunch with Gerry and Helen."

To which she replied, "Me too! I need to catch up with them about some things."

Connie conversed with Gerry in the large kitchen as she heated soup for the rest of us. Meanwhile, Helen and I set the table.

As the food was brought in, Helen said, "Kathy, one of the things you need to do as soon as possible is to bring your passport down to the U.S. Consulate and register your contact information."

"Really?" I asked, surprised. "Is that required?"

Connie offered, "It's advisable, given the situation. It's just a precaution. In case something happens, they will have a record of you being in the country."

"Oh," I said, still dubious, thinking I never did this when I studied in Madrid or was on the summer service project last year in Panama.

Gerry's tone sounded serious as she chimed in, "It's a good idea, Kathy. All our Maryknoll sisters are registered with the consulate. There is a lot of tension in the country. Just bring your passport, your street address, and house phone number. It doesn't take long."

Connie jumped in. "You know, next week I have to do an errand near the consulate. If you like, after school I could show you how to get there on the bus and afterwards you could go with me on some family visits in the *población*, where I live. What about next Thursday afternoon?"

That caught my attention! So, I replied, "Visit some families? I'd love to, and I'll bring my passport along too."

5

Los Desaparecidos—"Where Are They?"

Over the first weekend I was in Santiago, Isabel invited the three of us, Bernadette, Rosita, and me, to attend a special religious service in downtown Santiago on August 5, at the Basilica of Lourdes, sponsored by the *Comité Pro Paz* for those "disappeared" by the Pinochet dictatorship.

When I asked more about what the event was intended to commemorate, Isabel's answer was bewildering. She explained that early in 1975 the *Comité Pro Paz*'s legal department submitted affidavits to the Chilean court with the names of 119 persons who had been detained and held in custody by the security forces but were now missing or disappeared. The legal filing was known as a habeas corpus request. It literally meant "produce the body," by physically bringing the person named before the court or documentation about their death.

Family members of missing loved ones had given the *Comité Pro Paz* detailed information about them: name, age, height, weight, hair color. They answered questions like, Where were they last seen? What were they wearing? Did anyone witness their capture? What segment of the security forces detained them? Had anyone seen them in jail?

These sworn statements were then submitted to the court. But the affidavits and habeas corpus filings went unanswered. Without a response, public pressure mounted. Then some odd things happened. Isabel told us that during the past weeks there were news reports of mutilated corpses found on the streets of Buenos Aires, Argentina; many had Chilean identification cards on their person.

In one newspaper report, two of the deceased were said to be Wendelman Wisnick and Jaime Eugenio Robastam Bravo, whose Chilean identity cards and bodies were found inside a car in Pilar, Argentina. They were said to be leftist militants from the Movimiento Izquierdista Revolucionario (MIR) in Chile. Next to their bodies were written messages saying "MIR traitors" or "Killed by MIR."[1]

Not long after, *LEA* and *O Dia*, two suspicious magazines, circulated with partial lists of the 119 disappeared Chileans. These lists matched all but four of the 119 names of the disappeared persons documented in the habeas corpus filings prepared by the *Comité Pro Paz*, down to the filing's original misspellings.[2] However, none of the deceased bodies found on Argentina's streets fit the descriptions of those who had been disappeared in Chile. For instance, their hair color didn't match or their height was wrong.

The dead bodies were ultimately discovered to be Argentinians murdered by their own security forces. It then became clear that both the DINA in Chile and the Triple A (AAA) in Argentina were colluding to cover up the kidnapping, torture, and assassination of their own citizens. This had been suspected. But now it proved the two governments were sharing intelligence, tactics, and strategies to eliminate those opposed to their regimes.

Having learned about the disappeared, I was nervous as we traveled to the prayer service, not knowing what to expect. Rosita and I stepped off the bus and joined the enormous crowd of Chileans streaming into the Basilica of Lourdes. People walked in reverently, hushed by the sacredness of the event. In the front rows of the basilica were many members of the Families of the Detained and Disappeared, who were supported by the *Comité Pro Paz*. Seeing their faces, I sensed their anguish and suffering for their missing loved ones. The church lights were dimmed, befitting a service focused on the persecution and likely deaths of so many. In the sanctuary only a few stands of burning candles penetrated the darkness.

Some people called it the "Mass of the Forgotten Ones." It was an ecumenical service for those Chileans who had been arrested, then were disappeared by the authorities.[3] The liturgy was officiated by two notable founders of the *Comité Pro Paz* and defenders of human rights, Lutheran Bishop Helmut Frenz and Enrique Alvear, a Catholic bishop. To open the prayer service Bishop Frenz read from the Gospel of Luke recalling the story of the two disciples of Jesus walking away from Jerusalem after they witnessed his public execution by being nailed to a cross. But soon the resurrected Jesus appeared to the disciples on their journey and joined

*March of Women and Families of the Detained and Disappeared
(AFDD). Victoria Díaz Caro, Artisan, Collection of Isabel Morel de
Letelier. Museum of Memory and Human Rights.*

them for a meal. "Then they told what had happened on the road and
how he had been made known to them in the breaking of the bread."[4]

As Bishop Frenz finished the Scripture reading, no one could miss the
allusion to the mutilation and possible executions of the missing Chilean
men and women, cruelly disappeared while in state custody. In the hom-

ily that followed, Bishop Alvear looked out over the crowd of some four thousand people and spoke to the fears that those in the basilica might harbor as they contemplated whether it was safe to attend this service.[5]

Bishop Alvear spoke of his own concerns, saying, "We were fearful about calling you to this evening of prayer." He paused, then added, "But your *presence* is your response!" He prayed for unity among the faithful and enlightenment for those who govern. The Families of the Disappeared responded, "May the dark shadows part, and the light shine to illuminate the whereabouts of our loved ones." When the service ended the celebrants and family members processed out together, embraced by thunderous applause.[6] I was struck by the power of this massive event, learning that it was the largest public event since the 1973 *golpe*.[7]

Two months later, on October 3, 1975, the Pinochet dictatorship denied Bishop Helmut Frenz's re-entry into Chile. Frenz was accused by the Chilean government of "involvement in activities against the nation and gravely compromising public security and tranquility."[8] Cardinal Silva and the bishops immediately joined the international outcry. They understood the dictatorship's decision to bar Frenz's re-entry was part of a strategy to dismantle the *Comité Pro Paz*'s human rights advocacy and a step closer to targeting the Catholic Church directly.[9]

6

In the Población and Los Chicago Boys

Connie met me at my classroom door when school ended on Thursday. We took the bus from Buzeta to the Parque Forestal, a park that bordered the Mapocho River. I felt queasy as we walked toward the ornate American Consulate, seeing armed U.S. Marines near the portico entry. To me it was a clear reminder of the U.S. government's collusion in the overthrow of Salvador Allende. Once inside the consulate's busy lobby, I joined the requisite line to fill out the registration form with my personal data, residence, phone number, and next-of-kin information.

Afterwards Connie and I caught another bus to Buen Consejo, a *población* in Quinta Normal, part of Santiago's western zone.[1] We walked into a vast shantytown of *mediaguas,* small wooden shacks, without running water or sewage lines. A few sturdier homes were constructed of cement corner posts and wooden walls. I felt overwhelmed seeing the pervasive poverty. As we walked, Connie explained how the economic conditions in the community had worsened since the coup, describing the deteriorating health, unemployment, and hunger it precipitated among the poor.

In 1971 when Allende assumed power, he faced a slowed economy and a public with high expectations for increased wages and buying power. Allende tried to deliver on his promises. In his first year, the factories were humming, unemployment was low, and the economy grew by 8 percent. But this growth was unsustainable. The financial reserves that had boosted the economy were now depleted.

At the same time, President Richard Nixon sought to eviscerate Allende's socialist vision. He directed Richard Helms and the CIA "to make the economy scream."[2] To this end they rallied a powerful cohort of multinational corporations to destabilize Chile.[3] By 1972 Chile's vanish-

A street in the población.

ing credit lines and hyperinflation stoked chaos, work stoppages, hoard-ing, and truckers' strikes. By 1973 the political choices and production lines were at a standstill.

In the wake of the coup, Pinochet embraced Milton Friedman's eco-nomic theory. Friedman, a University of Chicago economics professor, was the guru to a group of Chilean economists, nicknamed *los Chicago Boys*, because they had studied under him. Friedman advised Pinochet to "impose a rapid-fire transformation of the economy—through tax cuts, free trade, privatized services, cuts to social spending and deregulation."[4]

But under Friedman's "shock treatment," Chile's economy fell to new depths. In 1973 the economy declined by 15 percent, while unem-ployment reached a high of 20 percent. In 1975 cuts to public spending reached 27 percent, while five hundred state-owned companies and banks were privatized, with massive job losses.[5]

In this *población*, the deprivation wrought by the loss of work was depressingly obvious. Yet, in Buen Consejo as in so many other *poblacio-nes* the effort of the *Comité Pro Paz* across Santiago to assist families was also evident. I trailed Connie as we walked through the parish property of San José, where a patio pavilion had been converted into a "*comedor infantíl*," a communal kitchen to nourish children. Three women were stirring an enormous pot of *avena*, oat porridge, cooking under a gas-fed burner.

Connie called a warm hello as she approached the three women stirring the pot. *"¡Hola mujeres! ¿Cómo están?"*

"¡Hola Hermana Connie!" they replied, stepping forward to embrace her, as she introduced me.

"Did you have milk today for the porridge?" she asked with a hopeful tone.

"¡No! ¡No hemos recibido leche por tres días!" they exclaimed.

"No milk for three days? What is going on?" Connie asked.

The conversation was sobering. This *comedor* was only meant to serve 80 children a day, but 127 was today's count. The food supplies could hardly be stretched further.

While they talked, I went over to a table and sat next to a mother with five children, including a small baby. I asked how she became involved with the *comedor*. She told me all the women were volunteers. Three women would come early each day to start the cooking. By ten o'clock other women arrived, fulfilling their commitment to take a weekly shift. They'd peel and cut the vegetables for soup, wipe down the tables, and set out bowls and spoons. They'd make sure the children scrubbed their hands before eating, then washed the dishes and swept up afterwards. In order to augment the meal, some women would volunteer to go to the *mercado central* every few days to ask for leftover produce or purchase it for the *comedor* at a reduced price.

Many situations kept the children from showing up for the meals. To protect the health of everyone, the children had to be up to date with their immunizations. Shame kept some families away. Unemployed and unable to provide food for their family, parents didn't want others to see their plight.

Connie jotted down a few notes and said she'd check with the *Comité Pro Paz* to see if more food and the ever-scarce milk could be garnered. Saying goodbye, we left that corner of the parish property and walked to a classroom building where a meeting of the *bolsa de trabajo*, a day-labor cooperative, was just ending.

The labor-union movement formed the backbone of support for President Allende's government, so much so that it was crushed in the aftermath of the September 11, 1973, *golpe*. Labor leaders were key targets of the military regime. Thousands were rounded up, tortured, and killed after the military takeover.

Many who escaped being detained were nonetheless *"fichados,"* or blacklisted, by their employers as troublemakers and supporters of Allende, effectively barring them from employment elsewhere. With factories closed and the economy crushed, they had nowhere to turn. Local *bolsas de trabajo* enrolled men and occasionally women in a shared effort to find employment. The members filled out cards with their name and skills, and attended weekly meetings, which allowed them to be called when temporary jobs became available in construction, road repair, carpentry, or demolition. Since many of the local coordinators of the *bolsas de trabajo* were former union leaders, they were skilled at running meetings, planning agendas, and handling conflict.

While we were at the *comedor*, Connie learned that a regular volunteer had not shown up for her shift, and the women were worried about her. Connie suggested we stop by her house to see how she was doing.

Hearing a knock and Connie's voice, María came to the door. She was a very young woman and a mother of three children. I was startled to see bruises across her face, as she tentatively cracked the door. Trembling, María pulled Connie to the side whispering that her husband had beaten her the day before, angry with her for leaving the house to volunteer at the *comedor*.

Trying to give them some privacy, I stepped a few paces away and saw three broken windows toward the back of the house. There was only one small table, covered by a grimy tablecloth, and almost no other furniture. María was shaking, telling Connie how she loved going the *comedor*, because it gave her something to do and kept her away from the desolation she felt in her home. Her unemployed husband was jealous of the time she spent volunteering. He controlled whatever money they had. She had nowhere to flee nor the means to feed their children. Now with broken windows, she couldn't even protect them from the cold.

Connie spoke with María compassionately, but had few means with which to help her. She urged her to return to the *comedor*, so that her children would have a daily meal. She told María that the women from the *comedor* were worried about her and missed her presence. Connie knew shame could overwhelm a young mother, and situations like María's were all too common.

As we left and continued walking, I noticed that many houses were fenced in. We encountered a grandmother who spoke to us quite readily, all the while telling us she didn't trust her neighbors. I thought it was strange, this level of suspicion between neighbors whose houses were so close together. At first, I didn't understand her fears, until I realized how the *poblaciones* were filled with Chileans who had recently migrated into Santiago from all parts of this enormously long country. But as we walked away, I realized all the houses had one thing in common. Outside every front door were tin cans of various sizes, filled with dirt and sprouting plants, eager for sunshine and growth, a sure sign of home.

We walked further on through the *población* to Flor's house. She eagerly welcomed us, though her home had almost no furniture. It had been sold off to survive. She had two immaculately dressed children. Flor was an active volunteer at the *comedor* and participated in a knitting group Connie fostered, crafting items later sold through the *Comité Pro Paz*, with the proceeds shared among the women knitters.

She seemed happy enough chatting, until Connie asked her, "How is your husband?"

"Madre Connie, no sé nada de él. Hace tres meses desde que huyó a Argentina. Ya los vecinos están hablando mal de mí. ¡Dicen que estoy maldecida!"

Suddenly, she convulsed into sobs, panting out the story that her husband had fled to Argentina and she hadn't heard from him for three months. Her neighbors, seeing that he wasn't around, began gossiping viciously about why he left, accusing her of being cursed. She was a woman anguished and alone with no family in Santiago, no money, left without support or affection to care for their children. Any dreams or hopes she had for their future dissolved in her despair.

It was extremely painful to step away from María's and Flor's homes, unable to share anything beyond a willingness to listen—*apoyo moral*. They epitomized the lives of many women around the world. They were hemmed in by a patriarchal culture, alone and isolated, responsible for their own well-being and that of their children. Too often they were reproached and their lives threatened when they displayed initiative or acted on their hopes and dreams.

I thought about my own awakening to feminism in high school and the first U.N. Conference on the Status of Women held in Mexico City, which had just ended in July. On a very deep level, our lives and challenges were the same. We had to break with and redefine the psychological and cultural demands forced on us by patriarchy in order to find ourselves and our voice. And we needed safe spaces to do so.

Our last visit was to see Marta, a lovely thirty-three-year-old woman who for the past year had been afflicted with cancer. As we sat in her bedroom, she told us how her husband kept trying to lift her spirits. He said hopeful things, but avoided talking about her impending death. Connie and I listened carefully as she shared her intense loneliness and fears. We sat with her for a long time as she cried, knowing she would not see her children grow up. Connie promised we'd be back in a few days.

A week later Connie asked me to visit Marta, because she had a meeting to attend. When I knocked on Marta's door, her husband answered. He seemed shaken. Marta was in the hospital with an infection. For the first time, he was in the house without her. He admitted there was little hope that she would live, saying mournfully, "I feel abandoned in the house. We used to take short business trips all over Chile together, but now I will have to care for our children alone." He went on, "The only thing I can do to distract myself is to play solitaire." Then he asked me, "May I walk you back to Sr. Connie's house? I just feel so low."

I felt uneasy walking through the *población* with the husband of a dying woman, seeing the neighbors glancing at us, calculating.

7

Weekends

Everyone had been so welcoming to me, offering me opportunities to learn the realities of Chile and see various parts of Santiago. Bernadette suggested we take a drive and stop by the house of Fr. Phil Devlin, CSC, a member of the Congregation of the Holy Cross. He was the point person for the Notre Dame program, and in another week Bernard and the LAPEL students were expected to arrive from their overland journey. As we drove up to Phil's house, Bernadette pointed out the nearby Pirámide at the curve of Av. Américo Vespucio. It was an overlook point, from where one could see Santiago's northern zone. Phil was outside his home, about to leave for a commitment. He was tall and wiry with a weathered complexion, dressed in blue jeans and a frayed shirt, a crucifix from a worn leather cord hung around his neck. I noticed his fingers were long and thin, and with one hand he was waving a cigarette. Somehow, I wasn't surprised to see a motorcycle parked outside his house and a helmet at his hip.

He was happy to see Bernadette, since they had taught together at Colegio St. George until 1973. When I was introduced, he welcomed me, but there was only time for a little small talk before he departed.

A week later, on Saturday, August 16, I traveled by bus to the Pirámide. Bernard and the Notre Dame students were now living with Phil Devlin. They told me about their experiences traveling: they'd been robbed in Peru, gone through an earthquake, and their train had derailed on the way to Cusco. They had stopped to visit the Notre Dame students, who for the next year would be working with Fr. Roberto Plasker, CSC, in Chimbote, Peru.

Our first meeting in Santiago went well. Fr. Phil spoke about the ideas he had for the program and possible service opportunities. He gave us a primer on the tense state of affairs in the country. Besides the political moment in Chile, all of the Holy Cross priests had heavy pastoral commitments. He let us know that not all of the priests in the congregation supported the idea of hosting the LAPEL program, when there were so many other needs among the Chilean youth and the families they served. Those concerns felt reasonable to me, and we would need to respect them.[1] When the meeting ended, the five of us agreed to meet up weekly on Sunday evenings for prayer, dinner, and talks by the Holy Cross priests.

The next Sunday I joined our Notre Dame group for the celebration of Jerry Barmasse's ordination as a deacon. The Mass was held in Santa Rosa Parish in Lo Barnechea, an area of Santiago skirting the Andean peaks, full of shady trees—an almost rural feel. It was home to many artisans, professionals, and poor people too. Santa Rosa was a small, beautiful church constructed with boulders retrieved from the Andean slopes, literally grounding the sanctuary to its mountain terrain. The faith community was joyful and welcoming, as was the pastor, Fr. Fermín Donoso, CSC, who invited us for lunch at the parish house the following Saturday.

After the luncheon with Fermín that next Saturday, Bernard suggested we visit Fr. Gerardo Whelan, who lived with a group of seminarians in an area called La Ponderosa. Upon the mention of Whelan's name, I recalled a long conversation I had with Fr. William Lewers and Fr. Richard Warner at the Holy Cross provincial office in South Bend before I left for Chile. They wanted to meet me and orient me to the realities of Chile. That day I heard an awful lot about Gerardo Whelan, who in 1970 had become a Chilean citizen. I learned he was from a working-class family in Detroit, a Notre Dame graduate and priest. After his ordination he was sent to Chile to teach and be the prefect of discipline in a school with 1,800 boys. I was warned that he could be stubborn and gruff, but soft on the inside. Whelan fiercely motivated his students to discover their talents, dreams, and convictions—and to live up to them; *ser consequente* was his motto. When he was named the rector of Colegio St. George, he pushed the school to open its doors to the children from the surrounding *poblaciones*.

Bernard and I found Whelan outside his house busily tending a flock of strutting peacocks and peachicks. The peacocks were noisy but beautiful to watch as they scratched the ground for feed and fanned their

Fr. Gerardo Whelan, CSC, in La Ponderosa.

tails. At first glance, Whelan did seem a bit gruff, but I felt his warmth and acceptance when he gave me a hug, welcoming me to Chile. He was almost as colorful as his brood. His stocky body was draped in a worn but brightly woven Chilean poncho. His uncombed graying hair and full beard matched his earthy presence. He was clearly absorbed with his peacocks, and I wondered what they meant to him.

Later, Sr. Elizabeth (Liz) Gilmore, a Holy Child sister who worked in Santa Rosa Parish, told me that Whelan received his first brood of peacocks as a gift from a family. He raised them for sale, sharing the proceeds with families in need. Liz would know, since she worked among the poorest families in the parish, who lived precariously on the nearby slopes of the Mapocho River.

By Monday morning I was back to work in Buzeta's tutorial rooms, where the school day ran from 8:00 a.m. to 12:30 p.m. For a new teacher like me this was a great schedule, allowing sufficient time to develop materials and fine-tune lesson plans for the next day. That week Sra. Grumilda called me into her office and asked me to take on the art and music classes for a teacher out on medical leave. Fortunately, the teacher left behind her lesson plans. When she returned to work, I was assigned to be the full-time teacher for the fourth- and fifth-grade math, science, and art classes, which was a much bigger challenge.

The ability to leave school on Fridays in the early afternoon left time to explore Santiago and some of the nearby towns. Soon after Bernard and the Notre Dame students arrived, a few of us traveled up to Farellones, famous for its ski slopes in the high Andes. We had no plans to ski, but wanted to see the picturesque mountain village, hike a bit, and spend the day outdoors. We enjoyed a picnic in the snow, with wine, cheese, and bread, perched on the back side of a rock ledge that overlooked a deep mountain gorge. Sitting there I wondered if the kids from the *poblaciones* ever had a chance to see Santiago from these peaks.

Not too many weeks later, Rosita, Bernard, and I traveled by bus to Algarrobo, a coastal city. We spent the sunny part of the day walking on the beach, then donned our ponchos and took a bus to Isla Negra, to see the home of Pablo Neruda, Chile's lauded poet and the 1971 winner of the Nobel Prize for Literature. Jutting out toward the ocean, his

Kathy Osberger and Bernard Nahlen—a snow picnic in Farellones.

weathered stone and wood-slatted house rose above the beating waves. The front windows glistened with the ocean spray, and one could imagine the life of the poet who once lived inside. A rustic wooden fence surrounded the house, and each plank was filled with lines of poetry inked or scratched into the wood, dedicated *to* Neruda from his devoted countrymen. The three of us were mesmerized as we walked around the fenced perimeter reading the sentiments. As the ocean waves crashed upon the rocks below, a salty mist enveloped me; the moment felt profoundly moving and holy.

Pablo Neruda died on September 22, 1973, just days after the *golpe*, which left many wondering if he had died of cancer or been poisoned in the hospital. The Pinochet dictatorship attempted to silence those who loved Neruda. Public gatherings were banned on the day of his funeral; nonetheless nearly two thousand workers and activists poured out into the streets to honor him.

8

Full House on Orellana

I had already been substituting in various classrooms for two weeks when Srs. Helen Nelson and Paula Armstrong returned from visiting their SSND community in Wilton, Connecticut, and their families in Boston and New Jersey. They had been missed during the past month at Buzeta, where Paula taught eighth grade and Helen worked with the school's leadership, supporting Sra. Grumilda, the principal.

I was anxious to meet them. During the final weeks of my senior year, I'd exchanged a few letters with Helen about my interest in coming to Chile. She invited me to live with them in Santiago and arranged for me to teach at the Maryknoll school in Buzeta. Their welcome home party on August 17 was fun, an evening of festive food with sips of cherry brandy. They arrived with suitcases overflowing with household items, chocolates, packets of letters, and give-away clothes. Even I received something special that evening—news from my mother—as Helen had thoughtfully called her before flying back to Chile.

Of the two, Paula was the exuberant one, approachable, full of warmth, and chatty. Helen seemed more reserved. They both dressed in slacks and sweaters and wore a simple cross on a chain. They were younger than I had imagined. Paula was thirty-five years old and Helen, thirty-six.

Paula was tall, heavier-set, and endearing. Shortly after her arrival in Chile she was baptized by friends with a string of diminutive nicknames: Paulita, *la gordita*. She smiled brightly upon hearing them. Paula had a round face and thinning brown hair and deep-set eyes; her gait, an ambling shuffle. The depth of her spirituality seemed boundless. She was open, honest, and a careful listener, loved by her middle-school students.

Helen was petite in stature with thicker brown hair, cut short in a perky style. Whenever she entered a room, you could see her absorb

41

the atmosphere, contemplating everyone around her. But it wasn't long before her sly smile and quick wit filled the room. When she spoke, she was direct and to the point, a skill seemingly honed as a grade-school principal.

Paula and her twin brother, Robert, were born in Roxbury, Boston's Irish enclave. They were the second set of twins born into the family, which grew to eleven children. Right out of high school she joined the SSND community, known for its excellence in teaching.

A New Jersey girl, Helen grew up second to last in a family of seven girls and two boys. Educated in SSND schools Helen loved learning about faraway places. Early on she knew she wanted to be a missionary and serve others.

Radical change and turmoil were everywhere in the 1960s. For Catholics, ground-breaking changes began early in the decade, when Pope John XXIII convened Vatican Council II (1962–65) to envision how the church could serve the modern world. Rather quickly, rituals once performed in Latin were set aside, enabling the faithful to worship in their own language and participate more fully in worship. This shift in vision called the church to see itself as the inspired "People of God" transforming the world by drawing the laity and religious into new roles with a responsibility to respond to the "signs of the time."

As I got to know Paula, Helen, and Bernadette, I realized that in the same era they were professing their vows and earning their teaching degrees, I was growing into a Vatican II kid. When I was little, the church was where the school bus dropped us off for morning Mass. The church was where Monsignor Bonk blasted a righteous sermon at his captive audience, while the ritual moaned on in Latin, interrupted only by the faithful standing and kneeling at the right times.

Over my middle school years changes happened before my eyes. Our teachers, the Sisters of St. Joseph, showed up with trimmed hemlines and modified habits. We saw they had ankles! Some wore no veils. Guitar Masses replaced organ music. Pretty soon, the entire Mass was said in English. In eighth grade we read the Documents of Vatican II, where I learned that young people like me had a voice and a role in the future breaking out all around us. By high school we were seeing priests and nuns on television joining hands with the civil rights marchers and pro-

Sister Helen Nelson, SSND, Chilean Independence Day picnic in Pirque.

testing the Vietnam War. I can't claim to have fully understood all the struggles, but something about the witness given by these audacious religious resonated with me.

The morning after Paula and Helen's arrival, Rosita and I piled into the Peugeot with them and headed over to Buzeta. Chile's gray days and chill continued to hang in the air, as did the looming second anniversary of the *golpe,* falling on September 11, with high unemployment, scarcity, and strife marking everyone's lives.

Helen jumped back into her responsibilities at Buzeta. Refreshed by her few weeks away, she took the pulse of the faculty. Sensing something was needed to shake things up, she announced to the staff that she was planning *un asado*, a beef barbeque for the upcoming *Dieciocho*, Chile's Independence Day, on September 18. Helen promised to provide the beef for the outdoor roast, and soon the party planning was under way.

The two-day Independence celebration fell on Thursday and Friday, creating a four-day holiday weekend. During recess the teachers agreed that Pirque was the best site for a picnic in the Andes, then planned who would bring what dish, and figured out how to transport everyone there.

On September 20 we packed the Peugeot's trunk full of food, brought along a small grill to lay over an open fire, with some wine and extra blankets to sit on. As each carload of teachers arrived, the happiness increased. Everyone came dressed in layers of turtleneck shirts and alpaca sweaters, which aided the warming brought by the sun in the higher altitudes. There was lots of food to share and time to relax on the boulders above a rushing mountain stream. For me the day couldn't have been better.

PART III
A NEW CONSCIOUSNESS
AND A COUP
1968–1973

9

A New Consciousness

Tuesday nights in the house were set aside for communal prayer and a shared meal. Over dinner household business would be discussed and chores divvied up. I looked forward to the meal and the free-flowing conversations that followed. The stories I heard gave me a window into how my housemates' lives were shaped by the social, spiritual, and political changes around them. The mosaic of those years came into focus, as did the profound disruption they experienced on September 11, 1973.

In the household, Rosita was the closest in age to me and *bien amigable*. So friendly, she took it upon herself to help me. During my first week teaching at Buzeta, she spotted a teacher coming down the corridor and whispered, "Don't worry; she looks strict, *pero es cariñosa*." She's a dear! Or knowing we'd have no ride home after school, she'd say, "Meet me at my classroom at four, and I'll show you how to get home by bus." They were simple touches, *toques*, but so comforting knowing I didn't have to go it alone. We'd ride the bus into downtown, and before we jumped off, she'd suggest, "Let me show you my favorite place to eat. We can have *once* there and it's cheap!" Hanging out with Rosita I learned the colloquial names on menus, the best prices, and a lot about her life in both Peru and Chile.

Rosita grew up in La Punta, Callao, in a family of thirteen siblings. Her brother Alberto was the jokester in the family. He teased their father, a professor of civil engineering who consulted on governmental projects *and* taught full-time at the university, by saying: "Papá, couldn't you use some more night work?" Rosita's parents were active in the post-Vatican II progressive faith movement. She told me their nightly prayers always ended with her father happily asking God for more priest and religious vocations. Deeply intuitive, Rosita sensed her call early. Asked in first grade to step onto a stool and tell the class what she wanted to do when she grew up, she proclaimed, *"¡Yo quiero ser una monjita!"* I want to be a nun!

Hearing this, I wasn't surprised to learn that both she and Isabel had, up until rather recently, been part of the same religious community, the Immaculate Heart of Mary (IHM) Sisters from Philadelphia, Pennsylvania, as both attended IHM high schools, where the majority of their subjects were taught in English.

In 1965 Rosita was sixteen when three IHM novices from Chile visited her school, among them the slightly older Isabel Donoso. They were promoting religious life during a school assembly. These young religious women, all Latin Americans, made quite an impact on Rosita and her friends.

"They were so pretty, friendly and young!" Rosita told me, and they weren't North American sisters making the vocation pitch. As graduation approached, Rosita shared her desire to enter religious life with her parents, who approved. But not all of her IHM teachers were convinced that Rosita would fit in. Stinging her with a question, one sister sniped: "Why would *you* want to join the IHMs, when you *detest* speaking in English?"

Rosita dished back angrily, bristling at the imperialistic tone of the question. Defending her culture and language, she retorted, "I don't want to speak English every minute, because we are living in Peru, and it's unjust to demand that we do so!"

Undeterred, in the spring of 1967, Rosita and four of her high-school friends left for Chile to join a dynamic group of thirty IHM novices from Chile, Peru, and Bolivia motivated to serve and claim their voice in a changing Latin America.

Like Rosita, Isabel grew up secure in the love of her family; she was the youngest, with two older sisters. She, stricken with diphtheria, came close to death at age six. Only her mother, fearful as Isabel lost weight and her fever rose, was able to enter her isolation room. When Isabel started to feel better, she said, "My first word was 'sandwich,' and my father ran to my favorite restaurant to bring it home to me!" Telling me this story, Isabel laughed, delighted by her family's frenzy to pamper her.

Isabel loved school, excelling in her classes at Villa Maria Academy, surrounded by a bevy of friends from her middle-class neighborhood. She was barely aware of the hardships around her until she participated in her school's outreach and catechetical missions in the *poblaciones* surrounding Santiago. Remembering the experience, she told me in breathless horror, "All of a sudden, I saw *poverty*. It grabbed my heart! I started questioning. Why me? Why do I have a home, a good place to live, a good school, and the ability to go out and enjoy parties, while others live in squalor? This moment was pivotal for my option for the poor."

After her graduation in 1964, Isabel joined the IHM novitiate. She embraced the discipline of religious life, rising at five in the morning for silent prayer, a ritual that would anchor her life. "For me it is so important to have internal peace, to have moments of quietness for reflection and prayer. If I have the possibility to encounter the God within, I know I can survive whatever comes."

Prayer was just the prelude to her other passion, theological studies at the Pontificia Universidad Católica de Chile. She entered the university in 1965, as the final documents of Vatican II were published, and was taught by theologians steeped in the preparations for the groundbreaking Latin American bishops' council to be held in Medellín, Colombia, in 1968.

Isabel was a natural leader, and though she would never say it, I could see she was a stand-out student. Besides her great intellect, she could synthesize complex discussions and convert ideas into practical actions. In the wake of the publication of the Medellín documents, she was selected as a delegate to the Archdiocese of Santiago's synod, tasked by Cardinal Silva to apply the conclusions of Vatican II and Medellín to the Chilean reality.

Isabel's university studies coincided with the presidential term of Eduardo Frei Montalva, the leader of the Christian Democratic Party, who won the 1964 election with 59 percent of the vote, defeating the Socialist Party candidate, Salvador Allende. The mid-1960s were a time of ferment in Chile, and Isabel was highly attuned to the moment. The political stakes between Frei's and Allende's visions were ratcheting up not only in Chile but across Latin America, where intellectuals, labor movements, and the populace were clamoring for greater control over their rich natural resources and against the foreign-owned enterprises profiting from them. While Frei believed in policies of incremental change to increase economic growth, Allende posited the need for a radical structural shift to control the nation's resources, especially Chile's prized copper.

Like the unrest in the United States during the 1960s over the issues of income inequality, urban poverty, racism, civil rights, and the Vietnam War, which often tore families apart, the unrest inside Chile couldn't be confined to the political realm alone.

Isabel and her convent friends tracked the revolutionary movements occurring across Latin America. What she was seeing and learning started to provoke a *conflict* with her religious life. Inside the convent she had a stable, safe life with many comforts. She had health insurance, plenty of food, heat, and even an electric blanket. The disparity between her life and that of the Chilean poor tore at her heart. It didn't match the life she felt called to lead, and she wasn't alone in feeling the conflict.

She shared with me, saying, "Among us, the young Latin American sisters, we started to do a critique of our religious life, realizing that it was imperialistic and coming from a North American model of formation. We wanted to have a more committed living situation, one that resembled the life lived by the poor and those in need."

The young sisters pressed their superiors to allow them to move into the *poblaciones* to live more simply and more genuinely serve their neighbors. The struggle inside the IHM community reached a pitch in 1971, coinciding with the year President Salvador Allende assumed office and when their IHM superior in Philadelphia came to Santiago for a visit. Convening a meeting of all the members, the young religious pressed their concerns, but let it be known that many, if not all, were prepared to leave the community if no changes were made. Isabel recounted that the superior responded in anger to their requests and wouldn't budge. "Within a few months," Isabel said, "twenty-five of the thirty of us left the IHM community to begin new lives."

As I listened to Rosita's and Isabel's stories, I was astonished by the depth of their convictions. By the time I met them, neither were religious sisters, but each continued to live out her commitment to serve the poor and persecuted.

10

Touching the Soul

One Tuesday night, only Helen, Paula, and Bernadette were home for the community dinner, as Isabel and Rosita had other commitments. It was a chance for me to learn more about their first years in Chile. In the late sixties the Holy Cross priests asked the SSND sisters to collaborate with them in their educational endeavors at Colegio St. George in Santiago. Helen, Paula, and Bernadette immediately volunteered.

During January and February 1968, Helen and Paula completed eight weeks of Spanish language classes in Puerto Rico, then flew to Santiago, arriving a few days before the school year started. In 1970 Bernadette, who had taught in Puerto Rico for six years, would join them as part of St. George's faculty. Their CSC colleagues, Fr. Gerardo Whelan, the school's rector, and Fr. Roberto Plasker, prefect of religion, welcomed the religious women, quickly incorporating them into the leadership of the school.

Paula moaned when I asked her about her first year of teaching. "It was terrible!" she said, describing her struggles to speak Spanish. She had made a pact with herself: "If I don't understand Spanish within one year, I'm going back to the U.S." Helen struggled too, but didn't set the bar so high. Trying to learn the language, they each faced tough headwinds. Fully half of the curriculum of the school was taught in English, polishing Colegio St. George's motto: "To Educate the Future Leaders of the Country." This meant that their students knew far more English than the sisters knew Spanish. Determined to master Spanish, Paula spent her after-school hours with the kids in the schoolyard, enduring their incessant laughter at her verbal mistakes. Over time Paula realized that the children saw her as their teacher, but loved that they could teach her too.

Likewise, Helen's frustrations soon melted away, uplifted by the welcome surrounding her. By her second year she felt more relaxed, having a better grasp of Spanish, Chile's history, and the complexity of the growing political ferment.

The sisters arrived at a unique moment in history, one of convergence and profound challenges. Colegio St. George was preparing to relocate to an enormous new campus, with breathtaking architecture and a pastoral location in the foothills of the Andes. Along with the new facility, the shaping of a new vision for the school would require the religious, faculty, parents, and students to wrestle with the painful social realities in Chile and Latin America. This task was made more pressing by the conclusions of CELAM II: the Council of Latin American Bishops held in Medellín, Colombia, which took place during August–September of 1968.[1]

The priests and sisters were attuned to the prophetic nature of the bishops gathering in Medellín, given that 90 percent of the population in Latin America considered themselves to be Catholic.[2] Draft documents were openly circulating among the bishops and in the general public two months before the assembly opened. For centuries the church in Latin America aligned itself with the traditional power structure. But by 1968 the Latin American bishops could no longer ignore the grave social inequities, where the vast majority of people lived in poverty. Medellín's conclusions arrived with the force of an earthquake.

With ear-shattering clarity, the bishops announced their commitment to the needs of all, but most especially to the poor.[3] The bishops asked themselves and the faithful to undertake a process of personal and societal critique, *concientización*, in order to give birth to a church that "heals and elevates the dignity of the human person," and lives and acts in solidarity with the suffering People of God.[4]

Among the many recommendations offered, Medellín spoke directly to the inequities in education, calling for *educación integral,* a holistic process of socio-economic-cultural integration in the schools with an emphasis on youth involvement in service to others.[5]

Quite readily the CSC priests embraced Medellín's challenges, which sharpened the vision and pedagogic foundation for St. George's new school. The priests understood that you don't easily take a school serving Chile's most privileged families on a journey to live in solidarity with the poor. Instead, to realize the school's new vision, the priests, teachers, parents, and students needed to engage in their own, personal and

*Sr. Bernadette Ballasty, SSND, Fr. Gerardo Whelan, CSC,
Sr. Paula Armstrong, SSND, and Sr. Helen Nelson, SSND,
were all part of Colegio St. George's faculty.*

collective *concientización* process, dialoguing honestly about their doubts and fears of "socio-cultural integration" as well as pondering how such an endeavor could occur in Chile, a society with rigid class, political, racial, and gender boundaries.

To prepare parents to engage more deeply with the school's new vision, Fr. Roberto Plasker led a mandatory course on the teachings of Vatican II and Medellín. Imagine, for a moment, a Friday night where you and other school parents were asked to reflect upon this one small kernel from the Medellín documents:

> Thus, for our authentic liberation, all of us need a profound conversion so that the "kingdom of justice, love and peace" might come to us. . . . The uniqueness of the Christian message does not so much consist in the affirmation of the necessity for structural change, as it does in an insistence on the conversion of men

which will in turn bring about this change. We will not have a new continent without new and reformed structures, but, above all, there will be no new continent without new men, who know how to be truly free and responsible according to the light of the Gospel.[6]

Discussing the Medellín documents often provoked heated exchanges among the parents over the proposed vision of holistic integration for the school. Fr. Gerardo Whelan relished the debates, believing that change and crisis ultimately breed growth. As participants in these parental meetings, the SSND sisters came to experience that they and the entire school were undergoing a conversion process and trusted the spiritual force under way. In spite of the moments of flaring political passions and the resistance to change voiced in the meetings, innovative ideas surfaced.

Helen reflected on those pivotal years (1968–70), telling me, "I could see more clearly the need to be among the poor, the contradiction of working in a rich school of all boys and training only them as future leaders."

For Paula, the challenge was daunting. St. George's could no longer teach only the children of the elite. It needed to be a new experience in education, open to children from all social and economic groups. Still, many parents remained skeptical.

Paula and Gerardo Whelan visited the nearby *poblaciones*, inviting parents to enroll their children at St. George's. Some parents were afraid, uncertain whether they could trust the offer. They worried about how their child would fit in with upper- and middle-class children.[7]

A key concern was how to cover tuition costs. On a large part of the school's property, Fr. Phil Devlin developed a truck farm, allowing children and parents to work together taking care of the chickens, eggs, beehives, honey, rabbits, and produce, which were then sold at a market stand at the school's entrance. Tending to the farm was woven into the curriculum, as part of valuing both manual and intellectual work. Priests, parents, and high-school students staffed the farmstand at the school's entrance to raise the funds to subsidize the tuition.

The Parent Council developed a sliding scale for tuition and a commitment to volunteer monthly in beautification and school upgrade projects. This enabled parents from different backgrounds to get to know one another, and it helped lower the expenses.

The teachers engaged in new ways too, opening a night school for the school's clerks, groundskeepers, cooks, and janitors so they could earn their high-school equivalency certificates. At the prodding of Gerardo Whelan, many teachers went on to attain their college degrees at Universidad Católica or the Universidad de Chile, the top institutions in the country.

Though some would claim otherwise, Paula believed, "In the end, St. George's education wasn't ideological, it was pretty normal. In fact, our rallying cry at school was, 'There is room for everybody here.'" The new school opened in 1970, with the faculty, parents, and students deeply involved in making Medellín's call for socio-cultural integration and service to others a success. In 1971 girls joined the student body.

11

The Allende Years until the Coup

I was always eager to hear about the experiences that the sisters, Isabel and Rosita, faced when Allende assumed the presidency. I wanted to know what their lives were like in the lead-up to the coup. So, I'd pepper them with my questions, whether it was over meals, in the car, or out on errands. Little by little I began to piece together these momentous events.

Without a doubt, 1970 was a pivotal year for them and for Chile. For Bernadette it was her first year in the country, after having taught in Puerto Rico for the previous six years. The three SSND sisters would no longer be living near the school; instead they'd be bussing to the new school campus in Vitacura, crisscrossing Santiago's busy downtown. Nor had the sisters experienced the fervor of a presidential election cycle, which took place every six years and was now set for September 1970.

By July 1970 the relocation of the entire student body to the new school, in tandem with the integration of students from the *poblaciones*, was achieved. Bernadette recalled that school year, telling me, "I felt a sense of *hope*, especially from the parents of the children who were being integrated into the school, that we would see real changes and achieve a respect for differences."

By September the political passions were running high. The current president, Frei Montalva, leader of the Christian Democrats, was barred by the constitution from seeking a consecutive term. On September 4, 1970, several well-known candidates were running for the office. Salvador Allende, a physician, who had served in Chile's government as senator, representative, and cabinet minister, led the leftist Unidad Popular (UP) party, a coalition of the Socialist, Communist, and Radical parties. Allende won the election by a plurality in a three-way race with 36.2 percent of the vote.[1]

There were jubilant gatherings in the streets celebrating Allende's election, as he sought to make a "Chilean path to socialism," one introduced not by weapons or revolution, but through the ballot box and the levers of Chile's democratic institutions. However, for others, Allende's win made them fearful. Bernadette remembered that in the days just after Allende won the election, some school parents came up to her and asked, "Are you going to be leaving because Allende was elected?"

"Staying was a sign of support," Helen told me, "support for the people and for the options within the school to keep working toward the new vision, rooted in Medellín. It wasn't so much a sign of political support, though you couldn't escape anything being politicized during these times either."

Helen noticed tensions rising in 1971, commenting, "A lot of political movement began happening. So, you had to make a decision whether to stay and assume the risks. It was impossible to go into the center of Santiago to pick up your mail or do business without getting caught in the middle of a demonstration of one type or another. But you were risking for a purpose. You were saying by your presence that something good would come out of this. It was a *choice* to stay and continue, despite what the outcome might be."

The choices were not easy for anyone, since from almost the day of Allende's election things started to disappear from the grocery shelves. When the sisters were given a tip from a school parent about where toilet paper or meat was for sale, it presented another contradiction, that of being among those who had connections. Once in a while they purchased or were given a chicken or a rabbit from St. George's farmstand. On the whole, they just learned to do without.

Helen described the journey she and the SSND sisters were on. "During this whole time while we were teaching at Colegio St. George, we had other SSND sisters in Chile working with the extremely poor in parishes near Echeverría and the Estación Central. As a group we spent one evening a week together, which was very important in our lives. We were living very intensely, even though we lived all over the city in ones and twos, or with other religious communities, because of problems with transportation and the whole political situation. When Bernadette and Sr. Peggy Regan said they wanted move into San Luis, a *población,* it was something we talked about as a community and could say, 'Go for it.' We were able to affirm their decision, and we helped to support them financially. It meant having some things, but not having others. That level of commitment among us created a very profound feeling and shaped an important part of our lives."

I could hear the anxiety in Paula's voice when she told me about the months leading up to the *golpe*, a time filled with rumors that the Allende government would fall and a national strike by truck drivers paralyzed the country. "Trucks were vital to Chile." Paula said, "It was the only way produce and products could be moved from the provinces, thousands of miles away. It was a time of scarcity, and people were hoarding things. When President Allende took office, he increased the wages of the poor. Before, maybe poor families could eat chicken once a week, but with salary increases and new price controls on basic food items, people had more purchasing power. This fed into the scarcity. Then, inflation soared."

"The shortages and insecurity increased the tension in Santiago. Wealthy women from the Barrio Alto brought their pots and pans out to the streets, banging on them, angry about things they couldn't get in the stores. The next day there would be a mass rally in support of Allende. Transportation became unpredictable, with frequent bus stoppages. One might be at work, then learn at four o'clock that a bus strike was planned for six o'clock, and you'd be rushing, hoping to make it home."

Paula continued, "For us this was one of the most intense periods of our work at Colegio St. George. In the school we were trying to get across the idea of pluralism and the ability of a society to live together. On September 11, 1973, the school was open but only about half the children were there. That day we thought the rumors about a coup might be true. Before we heard anything on the radio, though, one of the parents, Denise Chadwick, came to take her children out of school, informing us that the *golpe* was in process.[2] We called all the parents urging them to pick up their children. It was frightening since a curfew was set to be enforced at 2:00 p.m."

Paula stayed at St. George's until the last child was picked up. Then she made her way to the IHM convent in San Francisco, where both she and Helen were then living. Of that afternoon she said, "The shooting was unbelievable!"

Isabel left the IHM community in February 1972 but taught at San Francisco, a primary school led by the IHMs, while competing her thesis and college degree. She moved into the *población* of San Luis with Bernadette and Sr. Peg Regan. They lived in a two-bedroom wooden house with no electricity, fetching water in buckets from a spigot a few blocks away. They joined the efforts of their neighbors to organize the *Junta de Abastecimiento Popular* (JAP) to obtain groceries and address the community's basic needs.

"The country was tense with constant rumors of a coup," Isabel said. "In the *población* some people were already mapping out where emergency health clinics could be located; others were saving empty bottles to make Molotov cocktails." Isabel was pro-Allende and active in Christians for Socialism.[3] At 8:00 a.m. on September 11, 1973, she learned the *golpe* was under way. Sergio Concha, a Holy Cross priest, arrived at their house in his car, telling Isabel, "We have to go downtown to the Christians for Socialism's office." They suspected the office would be raided by the military and wanted to destroy compromising material. They took the bus toward Plaza Baquedano, sitting next to laborers on their way to work, where they heard President Allende's last speech over *Radio Magallenes*:

> Workers of my country: I have faith in Chile and its destiny. Other men will overcome this dark and bitter moment when treason seeks to prevail. Keep in mind that, much sooner than later, the great avenues will again open through which will pass the free man, to construct a better society. Long live Chile! Long live the people! Long live the workers! These are my last words, and I am certain that my sacrifice will not be in vain; I am certain that, at the very least, it will be a moral lesson that will punish felony, cowardice, and treason.[4]

At Plaza Baquedano their bus was stopped by soldiers with machine guns. Isabel and Sergio tried to walk toward the office, until bullets flew pass them as they neared the UNCTAD building.[5] The two of them were forced to head back. They grabbed one of the few cabs still moving around. As they went farther north, up through wealthier neighborhoods, people were celebrating, raising flags and honking horns. Isabel's voice turned to horror as she told me, "They were partying! That is when I felt so hurt! Then all around us military units started flooding down the streets toward the Moneda Palace. It was chaos."

As Isabel and Sergio Concha got nearer to Isabel's house in the *población* of San Luis, she could see the Hawker Hunter planes bombing President Allende's home in the nearby neighborhood of Tomás Moro. They hid in a vegetable store and finally made it back to the *población*, which was surrounded by the military patrols bearing automatic weapons.

Once home, Isabel dug a hole in the back of the house, quickly burning any flyers or documents that supported Allende. When she looked up, she could see plumes of smoke rising throughout the *población*. All the radio stations had been taken over by the military, and by two o'clock the curfew was in place and no one was allowed outside their home. Isabel wanted to see the news on television so she ran through the narrow streets and ducked into a home only to hear that Salvador Allende was dead.

That afternoon the military junta promulgated new laws, called *Bandos*, listing forbidden activities. Over the radio she heard the names of people, many of whom were known to her, cabinet ministers, leaders of unions and political parties. Days later the curfew was lifted for a few hours so that people could go out to the stores. When she reached the store Isabel was shocked, saying, "Suddenly the stores were *full* of groceries! That was another sword in my heart! It was obvious proof that all these products were held back in order to provoke the *golpe* and bring down the government."

Over the next weeks Isabel said, "I felt like I was walking through a desert. I was thinking of this utopia, this dream of constructing a more just, humane society with workers and the poor, a socialism done in the Chilean way, with the reform of institutions, but never in this violent way. That beautiful dream came to end. It was a death, and the death was inside me too."

Many of her close friends were planning to leave the country. Some came to her and said, "Isabel, you have to leave! Why aren't you in an embassy? Go on!" In spite of her bereft state, Isabel felt certain. "No. No, I have to stay. This is my country and I have to stay."

In 1973, due to the constant disruption in transportation and the need to live near Colegio St. George, Helen and Paula moved into the IHM Sisters' convent in San Francisco. As night fell on September 11, Helen grew fearful. She said, "I remember feeling scared a bullet would come through the window. On television I saw the bombing and people being picked up. It was brutal. But in spite of the fear, people risked being outside and came to the IHM's convent to check on us. That night the IHM sisters sheltered a couple who feared arrest because of their well-known support of Allende." Paula vividly recalled the days after the *golpe,* saying, "People came every day to the convent to tell us that one of their sons or daughters was missing."

In the days after the *golpe*, Chile's top universities were "intervened." The rectors of the universities were ousted, and military officers were named in their place. A month later, on October 10, Paula arrived at St. George's early, just as a truckload of soldiers parked outside the school's gate. In short order Paula was called to the school's office. There she was informed that Air Force Commander Osvaldo Verdugo Casanova was now in charge of the school. Accused of "Marxist indoctrination and political activity," the Holy Cross priests and the religious were "asked to resign" their leadership roles. The sisters had three hours to remove their belongings.[6] Remembering the day, Paula was emotional, saying, "Being thrown out of the school by the military was infuriating, but at the same time it was the only primary and high school in the entire country that was intervened. It meant that St. George's vision was as dangerous as the universities were to them."

Paula felt especially sorry for the children from the *población*, who were promised something that didn't happen, like so much else in their lives. She said, "Most of them never returned to St. George. The children whose families were in the political center or on the left never returned either. Many of their families went into exile."

After being expelled from St. George's, Helen, Bernadette, and Paula worked for several months with CIME, a UN Committee that was aiding those in hiding, detained, or seeking asylum in a new country.[7]

"I never considered leaving Chile," Paula said. "Though I knew I had such an option, I felt strongly that if the people we worked with couldn't leave, you don't leave just because you are afraid." Paula's motivation was clear: "I never saw myself as a radical or political activist. I saw myself as a Christian. My motivation didn't come out of belonging to a party or a particular political view. When faced with a situation like Chile's, one which I never would have chosen, I would first ask myself, what would Christ do in this situation? I was not looking for situations that were conflictive, but I was also willing to confront a situation, if I found myself in the middle of it."

"Part of that would be that in the two years after the *golpe* (1973–75), many lay and religious received people into their homes. People who had been tortured, shot, or imprisoned. I realized in making this decision, I was not far out or on the fringe. We felt strongly that we had the support of the church in accepting people into our homes. Cardinal Silva once met with the religious, and as plainly as he could say without really saying it, he asked us 'to help in any way we can.' As a foreign religious, this had a slightly different meaning for us than it did for Chileans. You always thought anyway, that if you were a North American, Canadian, or European and were picked up by the security forces you would have more of a chance to survive, because someone would protest."

PART IV
IT HAPPENED SO FAST

12

A Visitor Arrives

During my first few months in Chile, it was hard to grasp something so essential to Chilean identity: its highly political culture. Coming from the United States, I experienced politics more as a procedural exercise one geared up for every four years, not a lifetime of participatory practice and personal identity. Strongly contesting ideologies and social-political movements were the norm in Chile over its nearly 130 years of democratic government—until the military overthrow of Allende in 1973.

The power of the highly organized and politicized working class in Chile was impressive. They had a strong sense of their rights and fought for them. The military regime viciously targeted, imprisoned, and killed their members and leaders. This political reality played out in a country that was quite small and somewhat provincial—where three million people lived in the industrialized capital, Santiago, and seven million more were dispersed in smaller cities and rural communities along the thousands of miles of coastline from the northern desert to the southern ports.

Helen and Paula had been back in Santiago for several weeks now, and tonight was our community night for dinner, prayer, and reflection. I'm not sure if Bernadette had informed the others that she had spoken to me about "Juan" on the day I arrived. But during our conversation Isabel brought up a new topic. She asked the group if it would be alright to allow Normita, a colleague she knew, to stay with us for several weeks.

Normita was a young professor at the University of Valparaiso, located two hours north of Santiago. Reading between the lines, I sensed that Normita might be coming into Santiago to do some political work or that she needed to be less visible in Valparaiso for her own safety.

The motivation for her visit wasn't touched upon. No one voiced objections, so Helen turned to me, asking, "Kathy, would it be all right with you if Normita stayed in your room and slept on the empty bed?"

I answered with a quizzical, "Sure."

A few nights later Isabel arrived home with Normita. She joined us for dinner, listening to our chatter about what happened at work or school that day. Normita took it all in. After dinner I showed her our shared bedroom and made some space in the closet for her belongings. She hadn't brought much with her.

If one word could describe Normita, it would be *dulce*. Sweet. She was in her early thirties and had the most beautiful complexion. I noticed with a little envy that she always seemed to articulate her thoughts as if she just touched upon a deep and pure interior recess. Her authenticity marked our conversations. After spending all day alone in the SSND convent, she was always more than eager to talk, telling me about the hardships of her family and her quest to become an educated woman.

One day as I left school, I saw a few flowers blooming and cut them to give to Normita. Receiving them, she said, "Do you know, you are only the second person in my life who has given me flowers?" She told me that when she announced her engagement, her mother reacted furiously; undeterred, Normita left home and married.

Only her eyes gave away the pain she carried and the treacherous ledge she walked to fulfill her political commitments. A few weeks later she returned to Valparaiso, leaving behind a goodbye note for me. I read it once, then twice.

Then I tore it up, because *no conviene,* it would be dangerous to remember Normita.

13

Dinner with Isabel

One night in October, Isabel was home early from her work at the *Comité Pro Paz*, and for some reason we were the only two around for dinner. She was a food enthusiast, especially if she prepped the meal. She'd taste the soup, saying, "Ohhhh, this is good! *¡Bien sabroso! ¿No?*" Anxious to eat, she'd place the food on the table and exclaim again, *"Súper good, ¿no?"* Then, she'd pause. "Let's say a prayer." And it would always be a long prayer, long enough to cool down the food. This particular night, her prayer revealed the concerns from her work-day. She meditated for a time, then spoke profoundly about the suffering mothers with disappeared children, the detainees in Chacabuco, the families volunteering in the *comedores infantiles*, and the increasing numbers of sick children. All of it deeply pained her, especially the Chile that cast off the poor and persecuted after the *golpe*.

Finishing the prayer, we dove into a dinner of crusty bread, melted butter, and bean soup with nuggets of salty ham. Chit-chatting for a while, Isabel steered the conversation, saying, "Kathy, you've been here for over a month now. Tell me, what are your impressions of each one of us?"

I was taken aback. I hesitated, trying to formulate a reply, saying, "It's really all so new to me. I had a great talk with Helen last week and appreciated her openness and support. Rosita is a phenomenal teacher and so willing to help me with ideas for lesson plans; Paula and Bernadette . . ."

Isabel drew back in her seat; her brown eyes intensely focused on me: "Are you CIA?"

"What?" I croaked out, as if a dagger had pierced my rib.

"Are you CIA?" she repeated, her gaze unremitting.

I slumped back into my chair, thinking, there is no believable answer to this question. The question itself reveals distrust. What trained CIA agent would answer yes to such a question? Of course, they would deny involvement. My no would mean nothing.

Instead, I said something that sounded equally ludicrous, but was true: "Isabel, I'm not CIA! I'm a feminist! I'm against the Vietnam War. I came here wanting to understand the realities of Latin America."

Somehow, I thought these U.S. college-age identities of mine and the inherent values behind them would be obvious to Isabel and help her see me in a different light.

"Isabel, what makes you think I am CIA?"

She didn't stumble in her response: "Philip Agee. Tom Dooley. Notre Dame." Adding after a pause, "And besides your Spanish is too good."

"Philip Agee?" I said aloud, vaguely remembering the mention of his name in the newspapers last spring.

Isabel pounced. "He is a CIA agent and just wrote a book about how the CIA has spied on and destabilized countries in Latin America. They go to countries like ours, inserting themselves as 'volunteers,' just like you."[1] Then she readied the final punch. "He graduated from Notre Dame too."

I listened and felt sad. What Isabel said was true. She was right in making the connections to the devastating reality of Chile. The U.S. government, pressed by U.S. corporations operating in Chile, colluded with factions of the Chilean military to achieve the brutal overthrow of Allende.[2]

In fact, I had just read reports in *El Mercurio* that the Senate Select Committee on Intelligence Activities was now holding closed-door hearings on the "Alleged Assassination Plots Involving Foreign Leaders." Senator Frank Church was investigating the clandestine intelligence units operating in Chile, Vietnam, Congo, Indonesia, and Cuba.

Besides that, Notre Dame was indisputably known as recruitment territory for the Defense Department and the CIA. But I was adamant that she should understand, I was *not* one of their recruits.

Somehow the tension between us softened enough that I dared to ask her a question on my mind. "Isabel, what really happens when the DINA comes to a house?"

She pulled her chair closer to the table and leaned toward me.

"Look," she said sighing, "They come dressed in civilian clothes, Levi jackets and jeans, carrying machine guns. They drive white Fiats, four doors. Sometimes they bring other, less educated soldiers along, often giving them drugs before an *operativo*. They search the house and take people away blindfolded. They shove them onto the floor of their cars. They drive around trying to disorient their captives. They do horrible things to them in the secret torture centers. The interrogations are brutal. Those who are detained try to hold out, not naming names so others can flee."

Chills went down my spine.

14

Twilight

A memory came to me in the dawn hours. I bolted awake. My heart raced. What I saw was as vivid as day.

Or was it a dream?

I had gone to the hospital again to visit with Marta, my friend from the *población*. Weak and even sicker on this visit, she barely spoke a word. Her cancer was advancing. I never knew anyone so sick, even though as a teenager I had worked one summer as a nursing-home aide. The afternoon's light grew dusky as I approached an intersection near the Plaza de Armas. I was coming back into the central city by bus. I got off the bus and began to walk through the plaza, packed at this hour of the day with people finalizing errands and moving quickly to nearby intersections to catch their buses home. My mind was flooded, thinking of Marta, aware of her approaching death, and her fears for her children and husband. Everything felt very heavy and insecure.

I was only a few blocks away from La Alameda; it was around 6:00 p.m. I was about to cross an intersection when a car whipped past me and careened into the narrow cross street on my left. There, a stone's throw away from me, I noticed a man walking. He was about a quarter of the way into the block. He didn't seem to hear the car. He didn't sense its acceleration. His head never turned. In an instant the car doors flew open; two men in suits grabbed him from behind, pulled him expertly without a scream or a moan into the car. The car never stopped moving. Shoved inside, the doors slammed and the car accelerated out of eyesight. Another man came out of a storefront and looked. The street was empty. He turned his head, saw me, and ducked back inside.

Did I just see a man vanish? Was that a kidnapping? I'd have to tell Isabel.

Why didn't I do anything, why didn't I scream?

It happened so fast!

No! It happened with precision.

Did the man in the store see it? Was his heart beating as fast as mine? Would he tell someone?

Or was he the informant? Was he just checking to see if anyone saw it too? Did he think I was part of it?

My hands turned to ice. I kept walking. A few blocks later I crammed aboard my bus home, but I didn't really know where I was.

PART V
THE CHURCH BEARS WITNESS
OCTOBER 15–31, 1975

15

Malloco

I'd been in Chile for almost three months. Downtown the sidewalks and plazas were jammed with itinerant street vendors crowding the corners next to newsstand kiosks. On this particular day, October 16, my eyes grazed the offerings for sale—trinkets, purses, and books—spread out on the pavement. My mind wandered as I did along La Alameda, flowing more easily with the crowds and the bustle. I felt a bit more rhythm and routine to my life. I wasn't getting lost as often when I ran simple errands. I enrolled in an evening theology class at *Centro Bellarmino*, a Jesuit institution. Sometimes I'd meet up with Rosita or another new friend, sharing a bite to eat in one of the cafes before nightfall. The inkling of fitting in was comforting, not to mention that a hint of spring was in the air.

I was feeling a little more secure with my teaching. But some days had been tough, like the days before Chile's Independence celebrations last month. That week during recess the kids came running toward me, pointing out the military guards standing on the roof of the nearby Soco-agro, S.A., slaughter-house plant. They had their machine guns drawn as they surveilled the school's patio and neighborhood. The kids were scared because some of their fathers worked there. I quickly lined them up, and we went back into the classroom.

This week the kids were playing dodge ball during recess. I noticed that instead of ducking the ball, they'd run pell-mell toward the thrower. They wanted to be hit by the ball, so they could be the lucky one to move to the center and be noticed by everyone. Honestly, I couldn't seem to give them the individual attention they craved and keep up with the teaching objectives and lesson plans.

As I strolled along the Alameda something else caught my attention. I passed a newspaper kiosk where the vendor cried out the headline:

"*¡Malloco!*"

Curious about this word, I drew closer. By now a small crowd gathered around the newsstand—like bees to the hive—when some shocking news was announced. Everyone shuffled up to read the headlines of the dailies hung by clothespins on strands of horizontal wires. Several evening newspapers were stacked underneath ready for sale, each crowned by a rock to prevent them from blowing away. I stood at the back of the assembled crowd. It took me a while to comprehend that Malloco was a place, a rural town southwest of Santiago. The people around me stared mutely at the headlines while the vendor's bellicose voice chanted: *¡ENFRENTAMIENTO EN MALLOCO!* Shoot Out in Malloco! One MIR militant killed and two police wounded in the overnight armed confrontation with MIR commandos![1]

MIR, the Revolutionary Leftist Movement, was the number one enemy of the Pinochet dictatorship. Instantly the spring air grew chilly. I noticed that no one reached to purchase the papers. How odd, I thought. No one spoke. People stood still, their faces stiffened as they grasped the stakes and the ratcheting up of fear in an already tense country. Killing or wounding a member of the security forces would unleash a relentless manhunt. It would include locking down all entry points into Santiago, a course of action already under way. No mercy would be shown to those who fell under suspicion. The crowd's pulse of danger ricocheted through me. Even standing by to absorb this evening's news felt like an act of complicity. I backed away from the crowd, then darted toward my bus stop, where a cloak of darkness fell.

When I got home Rosita and Helen were in the kitchen. Helen set the table while Rosita dropped a hambone into the bubbling *porotos*. It would probably take forty-five minutes for the beans to cook, so I asked them if they had picked up an evening paper. Both said no. I told them about the headline and the fear it seemed to strike. Helen's head twisted toward me as she bent to lay the plates on the table.

"A shoot-out with MIR? It happened last night? There will be hell to pay for that!"

Rosita chimed in, "This is really bad. The military will never tolerate that some of their own were wounded!"

In the two years since the dictatorship had been in power, everyone in the house had seen reports about these skirmishes between MIR and the security forces, knowing their terrible consequences. Seldom reported in the official news were the stories of raids during curfew hours on private homes, resulting in warrantless detention and disappearance. By morning as the curfew lifted, a sobbing wife or distraught father would seek out a person of trust, often a priest or sister, and tearfully reveal the events with a plea for help. It was the enormity of these experiences after the *golpe* that led to the formation of the *Comité Pro Paz*.

While the *porotos* cooked we turned on the news. The programming of Chile's National Television station was woeful. The nightly news came on the air at 8:00 p.m. If you popped the television set on a minute or two early, the snowy screen with an irritating, distorted sound would be blaring. At the start of programming a loud, prolonged buzzer rang. Then the national anthem was played as the Chilean flag came on the screen. The buzzing sound made my stomach churn. I was told this was the sound and format that interrupted programming on September 11, 1973, when the dictatorship ushered itself into Chile's living rooms. By 1975 the dictatorship controlled all channels and every television newscast.

The television anchor breathlessly led with the story of Malloco, explaining that the police had been tipped off by a neighbor of suspicious movement or a possible robbery in progress on the adjacent property. The police notified the DINA, which was already tracking rumors of a secret meeting of MIR's Political Commission. When the security forces entered the property, the MIR lookout alerted the assembled MIR leadership and a firefight began, lasting past midnight. One member of MIR was dead and two *carabineros* were wounded. The other members of MIR's leadership reportedly fled.

The government announced that every roadway into Santiago and all the highways of the country would be patrolled. Every car would be stopped and searched in its pursuit of the hated MIR militants. Clearly, it was presumed that the MIR leadership would try to enter Santiago and secure themselves in safe houses. No measure to safeguard the country would be left undone until they were captured.

There wasn't much conversation as we watched the broadcast, and pretty soon the power of the story and my uneasy feelings began to fade. We clicked off the television before the soap-opera *novelas* came on and retreated to the kitchen to taste the steaming ham-and-bean soup. By then, Bernadette and even Isabel had arrived home to share the good food and a few moments of conviviality before the urgency of sleep took over.

Our weekends were always busy. Saturday mornings were full of household chores, which rotated among us: shopping for the week at the enormous outdoor *feria*, scrubbing the bathroom, mopping the floors, washing and hanging the laundry. I had helped out on previous shopping trips, but today was supposed to be my job to do the *feria* shopping on my own. For this task there was no firm shopping list or week's menu to guide the purchases, just an intuition of what was needed for six people, what would be healthy and taste good. As I was still used to the minimal responsibilities of dorm life and cafeteria food, I had little confidence in being able to pull this off by myself.

Fortunately, Rosita took pity on me. She liked haggling over the produce and prices, something I shied away from. Being from a very large family, Rosita was a *feria* wonder. I was only too happy to be her understudy. We took the four-wheeled wire cart and grabbed some *mallas* before heading out the door. Six blocks away the outdoor market appeared like a phoenix, rising and falling every Wednesday and Saturday with the vibe of live theater. Vast lanes of squawking chickens in crates were piled next to tipped produce carts where nearby, unhitched mules nibbled on debris. There were rows of stalls selling shiny fruits, toys, folded jeans, and sweaters. It was all there to savor, shoulder to shoulder. We pressed through the crowds. I loved the lilting sounds floating in the air. The indigenous Mapuche women vendors were easily identifiable. Their dark, shiny hair, braided and trimmed with ribbons, was offset by tiered silver earrings

Rosita Arroyo and Sr. Bernadette
Ballasty, SSND, on the patio at
1128 Calle Orellana.

dangling from their ears. On top of layers of sweaters, they wore rick-rack trimmed aprons with multiple pockets to store change and kerchiefs.

Although we weren't in a hurry, the shopping took quite a while. Helen's birthday fell on October 20, so we needed to pick up extra items for the celebration. Rosita decided that we should serve hamburgers, which Helen liked. Ridiculous as it may seem, that sounded fabulous to me. Months had passed since I tasted a hamburger. We returned our empty soda bottles, purchasing refills, a bottle of *Pisco,* and a jug of Chilean red wine. After a couple of hours, we pushed the wire cart back to the house and filled the refrigerator with the items for the week and Helen's party.

On Monday when I arrived home after school, the buzz of party preparations greeted me. I hurried into my room to dump my school papers and freshen up so I could help out.

The doorbell rang a few times as more friends arrived. Helen intercepted me in the hallway outside my bedroom. She wanted to let me know that we were going to be having a visitor for a few days, coded language for someone whose life was in danger and needed a safe place to stay. I nodded, learning that her name or pseudonym was Mariana, and she was in the kitchen. Helen cautioned that we not share too much about ourselves or ask many questions. Her tone and body language betrayed that somehow this "case" diverged from others. I absorbed something I couldn't accurately describe. I felt tense and uncertain. We were walking toward the kitchen, where Helen was going to introduce me to Mariana, when Paula arrived. Paula seemed flustered and asked to speak with Helen right away.

Entering the kitchen alone I noticed the ceiling light was already on, though a strip of daylight still hung over the patio garden outside the window. Mariana stood at the sink, gazing at the falling shadows with her back toward me, her hands soapy from rinsing a few dishes listlessly. I said hello, told her my name, and welcomed her to our house.

She turned her head only slightly to say hello; her face appeared tired. Rather tallish for a Chilean, she was a slender young woman with long hair, dressed in blue jeans and a white knit turtleneck shirt covered up by a folkloric short-sleeved red top with bright flowers embroidered around its square yoke. I remember all these details, but when I try to think about the characteristics of her face, the color of her eyes, the shape of her brow, the curve of her chin, I see only a blur. She has no eyes or brow or chin. I am not supposed to remember her.

She seemed ill at ease. So was I. I tried to tamp down my curiosity, straining to find something to talk about. Beyond the swinging door, we could hear the happy sounds of arriving guests and music. Rosita and Bernadette entered with last-minute purchases, which I helped to unpack and assemble on a tray.

Rosita sensed Mariana's unease and said in an aside to her, "Don't worry, even though there are a lot of people, they are all trustworthy." Rosita's voice was low and firm, lending authority to her message. Mariana didn't know that this is a voice honed to reassure small children.

The majority of the guests gathered for Helen's party were religious sisters and priests, mostly North American missionaries and Chilean clergy, who were friends or worked with the sisters. I had already heard stories about how their lives were intertwined through friendships formed while teaching at Colegio St. George, Buzeta, or the primary school in San Francisco. Several were colleagues of Isabel's, from the *Comité Pro Paz*. To a person they were dedicated to helping improve the quality of life and education of poor families. The guests had a dizzying array of affiliations through their religious communities.

Isabel and Paula soon asked people to gather for a prayer and Scripture reading to give thanks for Helen and her life. Mariana stepped into the living room at Bernadette's invitation and stood next to her on the far side of the room near the phone. Not everyone could sit down, since the room was ringed with over thirty people. Many expressed their gratitude for Helen's friendship and presence in their lives. Helen smiled shyly as her friends spoke about her.

I was struck by how this moment offered a necessary spiritual balm in the often-harsh reality of Chile. The comments were sincere, lifting up the gift of good friends and the recognition of one's commitment and sacrifice.

The telephone rang, abruptly ending the prayer. Bernadette answered it, then walked out to open the garage door for Fr. Gerardo Whelan and Fr. Patricio Cariola, a Jesuit priest. Rosita and I moved toward the kitchen to fry the hamburgers and bring out the food, while Isabel broke open the jug of wine and a bottle of *pisco* to serve the guests.

In just a few minutes the mood was festive, with the music back on. As I moved back and forth from the kitchen, I sensed some commotion. Gerardo was coming in through the back patio doorway leading to the bedrooms. Only later did I learn that he had brought with him two more "visitors," escorting them to my bedroom at Bernadette's behest. Mariana slipped back into the kitchen and looked ashen. She showed no interest in eating.

While I was busy visiting with people and replenishing the serving trays, a current of unease coursed through the room as the arrival of unnamed visitors was observed and its potential meaning absorbed. Even so, Helen remained the center of attention until the loud party patter dissolved into quieter conversations and curled cigarette smoke. The night grew late. Several of the guests lived at the farthest edges of the city in the poorer *poblaciones* near Las Condes, Maipo, Peñalolén, and, of course, Buzeta. So, in order to safely reach their neighborhoods before the curfew, they needed to depart soon. At the front door the goodbyes and whispered "happy birthdays" were swift, and then everyone was gone.

I started to empty ashtrays and collect cake plates to bring them into the kitchen, where Rosita and Mariana were finishing the dishes. Bernadette lingered at the front door while her eyes swept the sidewalk. She secured the door with a snap of its heavy bolt and dropped the half-inch-thick iron latch into place. Then she joined Isabel, Paula, and Helen, who had gathered in the front bedroom, to debrief.

I can't fully recall how the gravity of the situation became apparent to me. But when Rosita and I finished up in the kitchen, we saw Isabel, Paula, Bernadette, and Helen enter the living room looking pale. Helen asked me if I wouldn't mind retrieving a few of my clothes and belongings from my bedroom, because we had two more visitors, a couple, who would be staying in my room. Mariana, our first visitor, would sleep in the extra bed in Bernadette's room, and I would sleep on a day bed in Isabel and Rosita's room. Under normal circumstances this would be like your mother divvying up the beds if too many cousins unexpectedly spent the night. But circumstances weren't normal; they were dangerous. Tonight, three of the top four leaders of MIR who had escaped from Malloco and were still feverishly hunted by the DINA would be in our safekeeping. Upon hearing this, the puny worries of my life puffed away.

As I went toward my bedroom, a lithe woman with long brown hair came around the short hallway. She was wearing blue jeans and a maroon turtleneck sweater. Paulita walked up behind me and stopped to introduce us: "Maria Elena, this is Kathy."

The rules of social nicety were still in place, but pseudonyms hadn't yet been devised. Of her face and this one momentary encounter I only remember that her smile was kind.

Maria Elena continued down the hallway and into the kitchen to speak with Mariana. I walked toward my room. The door was ajar. I am sure I knocked, or at least tapped before I entered. Or maybe I was thinking something crazy in my exhaustion like, "Well it *is* my room." Instead, I startled Nelson Gutiérrez, now number two in MIR's political command. He was sitting on the far bed with his back to the door. As I entered, I saw him pulling something heavy out of a pillowcase that hung nearly limp between his knees and touched the floor. He quickly shoved it back inside as he turned toward me. He didn't glare; he just looked momentarily afraid. His shirt was unbuttoned and pulled out of his jeans. Chest hair protruded out of the neck of his T-shirt.

I murmured, "I'm sorry, but I need to retrieve a few things."

I then marched through the room and opened the closet doors in front of him, pulled out my underwear, pajamas, and a few things to wear to teach in the morning and somehow backed out of the room without looking at him again until I grabbed my purse and school satchel from my desk. I departed, saying, *"Buenas noches."* He wished me a "good night" too.

Dangerous. That was the word on Isabel's lips when I went into the front bedroom to sleep. Very dangerous. She was pulling some items, possibly work related, from around the room and off the extra bed, stashing them deep in the closet as she spoke with Rosita. I could see the grimness on her face. This wasn't the sprightly Isabel, *la Pulga*, the effervescent flea. No, this was Isabel landing on a thought and burrowing down, quickly analyzing what went wrong and how to ward off catastrophe.

I dared to interrupt, *"¿Isabel, que piensas?"* What are you thinking?

From her work with the *Comité Pro Paz*, she understood the inner workings of political organizations, their platforms and goals. Day-to-day experiences documented by the *Comité's* legal department gave her insight into the DINA's mode of operation. She didn't bother to review the things she had already tried to explain to me about Chile's political parties and resistance movements.

Instead, she focused on the obvious. "There has been a dangerous breach. Too many people are hiding here, and too many people saw them tonight. That has escalated the situation for all of us. It is very unsafe."

I knew what she meant: "Loose lips sink ships."

And certainly, though it remained unspoken, there was now a hierarchy of potential consequences at play. Even though the decision to offer this house as a safe haven had been mutually agreed upon, Isabel's work and Chilean citizenship put her life at the gravest risk. I wanted to make a pledge of trustworthiness to my friend, but I didn't know what to say that wouldn't sound lame. I just felt relieved to be in their room, sensing maybe for the first time a closeness, like that forged among dorm friends. We sat on the beds for a while talking as Isabel wished aloud, "If Helen or

Paula had only called me this afternoon, maybe I could have done something."

But we all knew that was impossible. Something like this couldn't be spoken about over the phone, no matter how you tried to disguise it.

In spite of my exhaustion, I couldn't sleep, aware that only four inches of wall separated me from the darkness and empty sidewalk outside. I could hear nothing. The silence of a city under curfew haunts the mind. Your ear travels all night searching like a detective for a sound, which then rouses you in panic over the familiar: a footstep, a truck motor purring. I lay still while tears squeezed between my eyelids. I didn't know if I would live through the night and thought: if the DINA has the slightest hint, they'll shoot first and ask questions later.

I pictured my family. I prayed. "God, tonight may be my last night. You know the danger. Please tell my parents I was okay. Tell them not to doubt. Tell them it was the right thing for me to come here. Tell them I love them—Julie, Dan, and Peggy too." I spooled through the prayer over and over again, trying to make it reach them, my face wet with tears.

Daybreak found all of us drained. Helen, Paula, Rosita, and I departed in the Peugeot at 7:00 a.m. as usual. Very little was said about the night before. Isabel and Bernadette both started work a little later and remained behind. They instructed the three visitors to keep the blinds closed, not to use the phone or answer the door, essential precautions that they knew well. After all, they were trained in the clandestine life.

I wondered how I'd get through the day. But it wasn't hard. We no sooner arrived at school than a sea of children swarmed us in the courtyard, their voices lifted in happiness as they chased one another around the yard. Some teachers and parents stood on the fringes monitoring the kids at play, while others served the recent arrivals a warm cup of *avena*, oatmeal stirred with milk, from an enormous chrome pot.

The inauguration of a breakfast program at Buzeta became a necessity after the coup. So many parents were without work in the crushed economy and could not feed their families. Even though the school was surrounded by factories, many fathers had been fired for their union activism. Other parents were jailed or disappeared, though no one at the school spoke of this openly. Gerry and Helen Carpenter, the Maryknoll sisters who ran the school, depended on parent volunteers for the breakfast program. They especially cultivated the participation of mothers, who were often isolated in their homes by poverty and machismo. I loved passing by the women in the morning to hear them chatting and laughing.

Rosita Arroyo celebrates the Week of the Clown on the playground of San Juan de Dios School in Buzeta.

Pretty soon the school day started. Upon hearing the bell, the smallest children ran back toward their mothers to reclaim their notebooks and pencils, getting a final hug. The older ones sauntered through the cement schoolyard into the required line formation for each class: boys on one side, girls on the other; short in front, tall in back. I stood at the front of my fourth–fifth grade homeroom and took in the faces of my forty students. We stood at attention for the flag raising and sang the national anthem, which I'll admit I was never able to sing. Instead, I thought to myself, why must all anthems be so impossibly difficult to sing? A few announcements followed before Sra. Grumilda, the principal, signaled us to proceed to our rooms.

Inside the classroom, teachers and students alike wore long-sleeved smocks over their uniforms, which were washed weekly at home. Their use seemed peculiar to me, until I realized how much they protected your clothes from grime and wear. Their utility hid another fact. Many teachers and children had few changes of clothes, and there was no money for new ones.

The theme for the week was "Flying Kites!" Over the weekend I had asked the children to bring to school sticks suitable to build a kite and some string. I was surprised on Monday when several kids arrived with stalks of *colihue*, a type of Chilean bamboo, and the perfect wood needed to build their kites. During the math hour we measured and cut the stalks into the proper length for the kite frame. We didn't have enough supplies for everyone, so they worked in groups of three, cutting and gluing on the newspaper, then adding strips of ribbon to decorate the kite tails. Watching the kids, I realized they were seasoned builders of kites, and I was learning a lot from them, since my knowledge of kite building started with a five-and-dime store's kite kit. On Thursday we would test them out. I was hoping there'd be enough wind that day to lift the kites into the air.

The morning passed quickly. When we finally broke for lunch, I headed over to the convent attached to the school to eat. I was glad to see that Helen and Paula were there, since their administrative duties often kept them busy through the lunch hour. I hoped to get their sense of the situation. I no sooner sat down when Helen said, "Kathy, we want you to make a list of things you need us to bring from the house. We've decided that the situation is too dangerous for you, Rosita, or Isabel to be there. For the time being, only Paula, Bernadette, and I will sleep there. Gerry and Helen Carpenter have offered for the three of you to stay here in Buzeta."

Paula stressed that the fewer people in the house, the safer it would be. They explained how, the day before, their communication around these matters had broken down. Two trusted contacts had spoken separately to each of them late yesterday. Each agreed to house one person unbeknownst to the other. Then, by nightfall, the placement for the third person had fallen through, with the curfew looming. They were extremely nervous about the situation. Since the house was rented in the name of the SSND religious community they felt that only they should be in the house.

Clearly, they expected some fallout and knew that if any protection from their SSND community or the U.S. Embassy should be needed it wouldn't cover us. I felt relieved. I understood that my presence would only add to the risk. Yet I felt bad that I could not share their burden.

Our lunchtime conversation ended with new boundaries drawn. Now our conversations in public would be guarded, superficial, and light. In private they might pulse with anxiety or be crisp like the one we just finished. Paulita left for her afternoon position at CIDE (Centro de Investigaciones y Desarrollo de la Educación—Center for Research, Development, and Education), and Helen slipped out of school to return home. After a few listless hours of lesson planning and grading papers I decided to go and help Gerry prepare dinner and set up the bedrooms.

Gerry seemed relieved to see me and drew me into the tasks at hand. I peeled a few vegetables with which she concocted the evening's soup. Gerry's persona felt grandmotherly and cozy. She was small in stature and dressed like many of the Chilean mothers, always in a heavy knit sweater. Forever self-deprecating, she'd call herself "an old shoe" and laugh aloud about her "worn-out self," while being the first to rise at daybreak to tend to her vegetable garden and see to her chickens and dogs, which she kept in a scrappy yard off the convent's kitchen. Often, she had completed a couple of hours of chores before any children peeked through the school-yard's gates.

Gerry grew up in a rural community near the seaport villages of Prince Edward Island in Nova Scotia. She had been in Chile for nearly twenty-two years and had a deep respect for the culture and psyche of the people. Most of the families who lived in Buzeta had migrated from coastal towns and rural areas to seek employment in the adjacent fac-tories. During the school day she was often sought out by a mother or father, who shared their troubles with her.

Today I found her fretful and anxious, talking aloud to her dogs in the patio garden and fussing at her cooped-up chickens for not laying enough eggs. We were both thinking of Helen, who by now was back at the SSND house on Calle Orellana with the visitors. We spoke obliquely about the situation, then Gerry went into the living room and pulled out a few LP albums. Somewhere tucked in the back of the cabinet she had music by Violeta Parra, Victor Jara, and Mercedes Sosa, music that pulsated with poetry, protest, and Andean rhythms. But she didn't pull these records out, because if the DINA searched your house, this music might signal antipathy toward the dictatorship. Instead, she reached for the LPs of Chilean folk music, the lyrical *cantos* from the rural south and fishing ports, the *cuecas* and *marineras* that make one want to dance. My favorite was the love ballad "*Si Vas Para Chile.*"

16

I Was Sick and You Looked After Me

My knowledge of MIR was minimal. I assumed that their goals were paramount, and anything could be sacrificed to achieve them. Its membership drew from labor unions, university students, and leftist adherents. MIR supported Salvador Allende's government, while remaining officially outside of it. MIR concentrated instead on opposing the treasonous, right-wing factions trying to destabilize and overthrow Allende. After Allende's death, Pinochet and the junta unleashed a campaign to eliminate MIR members. "In 1974 MIR bore the brunt of the disappearances by . . . the DINA."[1]

Even knowing of MIR's armed militancy, I was certain that "no weapons" was a pre-condition for the three visitors to be sheltered in the SSND convent. The sisters had no role in selecting the cases they took. Instead, they made the decision to shelter people when circumstances permitted. Their desire was to save the lives of those who faced torture or death at the hands of the authorities. The decision about *who* needed their safe haven was made through the *Comité Pro Paz* and key bishops or clergy, often with the knowledge of Cardinal Silva.

The SSND sisters were very modest women. Yet they lived their faith prophetically. Faced with a moral order of systemic repression, they were willing to act boldly. They weren't alone; almost everyone I met through the church in Chile was living with some level of risk as they ministered to others. From what I could see, the church was part of a massive act of faithful disobedience, against the dictatorship's death-dealing tactics.

I trusted the role models around me, but honestly, I wasn't fully there yet—asserting this choice as mine. I was still partially puffed up with ideas, trying them on and off for size, a set of choices, unavailable in a situation of systemic death. Neutrality wasn't an option. Go home? I didn't consider it. I had come to Chile for a two-year stay and wanted to be here.

Deep inside me there was a current, an intuitive connection I couldn't fully comprehend. I couldn't turn away from it: the dark cloud of energy that passed through me when my mom read aloud the *Time* magazine article, then learning that the tortured man named in the article, Sergio Zamora Torres, had been hidden in the SSND convent until the morning of my arrival in Santiago. I sensed it again when the bolt of fear pulsed through the crowd at the newsstand.

When I learned the identities of the three visitors the night they arrived, I felt overwhelmed. The reality was too much to take in. I tried to push back against my fears, knowing I would need reserves to react and survive. Up until that moment my energies had been spent on teaching, building friendships, observing and learning from an intensely political culture. I wanted to emulate the radical Christian values being lived out by the people around me. But I hesitated to voice my questions, fearing that it might be seen as a betrayal of good people and good ideals. Most of all, I hadn't had a chance to fully absorb and grow into this fight.

Can a day be both empty and intense, void and vortex? That is how I felt over the next several days. Every morning a pallid swath of light came across the dull concrete walls of the Buzeta convent. I'd climb out of bed and skip the wait for the water to warm in the gas-fed *califón* heater, preferring the icy splash on my face. I had only a change or two of clothes, making do by hand-washing underwear and blouses at night, hoping they would dry in spite of the damp air.

Within a half hour of getting up, I could hear the voices of children playing in the school yard. Gerry would have a kettle steaming with water ready to mix with the powdery brown Nescafé, a product Bernard jokingly referred to as "*no es café.*" In the kitchen Gerry would place butter and jam on the table and pull the bread, sightly hardened overnight, from a crinkled plastic bag to toast.

Those days wore on with heaviness in the air. I pulled myself together to teach, and the hours in the classroom were all absorbing. At the end of classes I would head back over to the convent dining room, occasionally spotting Helen Nelson. She looked nervous and drawn as she spoke softly with Gerry about the current state of affairs. I didn't want to intrude or eavesdrop, but I desperately wanted to know if she believed they could get through this without detection. Each day, when Helen and Paula arrived at school, I felt utterly relieved to see them alive.

Throughout these days information was being shared on a need-to-know basis for everyone's safety. Isabel, who was residing at Buzeta with Rosita and me, threw herself into resolving the crisis alongside the sisters. The overriding priority was to make a very unsafe situation more secure. Isabel took nothing for granted. She understood that this would require the MIR leaders hiding at our house to seek asylum in a foreign embassy. But for MIR leaders to seek political exile through an embassy would be an act of cowardice and disloyalty.

Nonetheless, the top four members of MIR, Nelson Gutiérrez, Maria Elena Bachman, Andrés Pascal Allende, and Mary Ann (Mariana) Beausire, were in a vise provoked by the surprise shoot-out at Malloco. The rural areas were scoured for the militants' presence. The DINA waged a full-court press in Santiago, anticipating that the MIR fugitives would try to slip into their urban safe houses in the capital and its shanty towns. The news of the Malloco shoot-out triggered the immediate abandonment of MIR safe houses and disrupted the militants' internal communications. Suspected MIR members were being tracked by *soplónes*, a network of paid "whisperers" who hung out on the buses and street corners observing, listening, and informing.

I learned parts of this story from the news, but other parts were shared by the MIR visitors in their conversations with the sisters, and later the sisters' own descriptions of events. This is how it unfolded.

On October 15 several members of MIR's Political Commission had assembled at the clandestine headquarters of MIR, an estate and farm property known as Santa Eugenia, in Malloco, to plot the next phase of their resistance. An armed lookout was positioned outside the farmhouse, ready to alert the members meeting inside to any danger. The DINA and the military were also on the lookout, having learned that a meeting of MIR's Political Commission was in the offing.

In an apparently routine call to the local police, a neighbor reported seeing some unusual activity on the Santa Eugenia estate. The police alerted the DINA, who arrived and surrounded the property, which was located a kilometer away from the police-controlled road stop at Padre Hurtado. The firefight broke out around 8:30 p.m. between the MIR lookout, Dagoberto Perez Vargas, and the DINA. In the firefight Perez, then number two in MIR's line of command, was killed.[2]

The burst of gunfire caused a scramble inside the farmhouse as members of MIR took up positions to return the fire, reportedly wounding two *carabineros*. During the firefight two bullets lodged in Nelson Gutiérrez's leg.

Ultimately, the MIR combatants inside the farmhouse broke through the DINA's encirclement and escaped into the surrounding fields. Gutiérrez and his *compañera*, Maria Elena Bachman, would later tell the SSND sisters how they fled with their ten-month-old daughter, Paula. They ran through the fields and hid with her in ground troughs, camouflaged by shrubbery. They had almost no food, except for a few candy bars and breast milk for the baby.

Pascal Allende and his *compañera*, Mariana, also fled under cover of darkness, hiding in the same fields. News reports said five other MIR members, four men and one woman, fled but were later captured, one seriously injured.[3] The firefight ended sometime after midnight on October 16.

According to what the MIR members shared with the sisters, after dawn on October 16, DINA patrols combed the farm property, unwittingly standing over the hole where they hid. Their greatest fear at that moment was the inadvertent cry of their infant. Sometime on Friday, October 17, with little food left and Gutiérrez's wounds festering, their options were shrinking. They decided to make a run for it. As they ran through the field a woman called out, "*¿Compañeros, les puedo ayudar?*" Sympathetic to their plight, she offered to help. Instinctively, Maria Elena thrust her infant daughter into the woman's arms.

On October 19, the Sunday news reported four attempted hijackings between October 17 and 18. The final hijacking reported in the article was done by two women and two men, around 9:30 p.m., near Padre Hurtado. That report noted that the four assailants not only robbed the owner's car but carried away two suitcases with men's and women's clothing, toiletries, and food.[4] The newspapers also reported that two vehicles, a red Volkswagen and a Cintroneta, had been used in their escape, then found abandoned in Santiago.[5]

According to what the MIR members told the sisters, when their stolen car eventually approached the highway checkpoint on the outskirts of Santiago, a distracted patrol officer waved them through.

Once inside Santiago, Gutiérrez sought medical help from a doctor, who he believed was sympathetic to the left. The doctor cared for him as best he could and called upon a priest friend to help secure a safe haven for them. Without further treatment Gutiérrez would likely die. Two Jesuit priests, Patricio Cariola and Fernando Salas, worked together with Gerardo Whelan, a Holy Cross priest, to secure safe houses among their contacts.

On the night of October 20, during Helen's birthday party, the sisters discovered that two weapons had been carried into the convent. Fr. Salas, the former executive secretary of the *Comité Pro Paz*, demanded a piece from each weapon to disable them. The next evening, Salas returned. He wrapped the remaining parts of the guns in pillow cases and drove off with them in the trunk of his car. He scouted a remote area on the northern edge of Santiago, then tossed the dismantled weapons into the shrubbery.

In addition to no weapons, the agreement allowing the MIR to shelter in the convent included that no one could leave the house, no one could answer the door, and absolutely no visitors, telephone calls, or messages could be received or sent. But from the first day the sisters were suspicious that in their absence these agreements were being broken.

Helen, Paula, and Bernadette were greatly relieved when Sr. Peg Lipsio, a Maryknoll sister, offered to stay in the house while they were at work to help monitor the situation. Peg soon spotted another weapon in an unzipped bag in Gutiérrez's bedroom.

Even though I saw Nelson Gutiérrez turn ashen when I entered my bedroom on October 20 to retrieve my clothes and school gear, it never occurred to me that the heavy object he dropped back into the pillow case might be a weapon. In my naiveté this act seemed incomprehensible. How could anyone seeking refuge presume to put others at even greater risk?

When Peg informed Helen, Paula, and Bernadette that she had seen another weapon in the house, a very tense confrontation with Gutiérrez and Bachman followed.

"No weapons. That is the condition," Bernadette said bluntly. "Or you leave." They were given the night to make their decision.

In spite of these terse encounters, the sisters never lost sight of the human crisis their visitors faced. In the evening they sat with them in the living room, listening to the story of their escape from Malloco. With the stress and abrupt separation from her infant daughter, Maria Elena spiked a high fever. Paula accompanied Maria Elena to see a doctor, a former student from Colegio St. George. He provided Maria Elena with medicine, urging her to see a doctor immediately should she enter an embassy. The sisters also made inquiries to see if anyone had approached the *Comité Pro Paz* with information about the baby.

For greater safety, Mariana, whose given name was Mary Ann Beausire Alonso, was transported a day or so later to a safe house where her *compañero*, Andrés Pascal Allende, was hidden.[6]

On Wednesday, October 22, Paula left school to check on things at home. She was drained and anxious as she stepped off the bus on Av. Matta. She knew that Fr. Patricio Cariola had found a doctor to treat the worsening sepsis infection in Gutiérrez's leg. Helen would be bringing the doctor to the sisters' convent that afternoon. Approaching the house, worrying thoughts ran through Paula's mind. She told herself that when the doctor arrived, she had to remain alert, guard her words, and not reveal names. Why, wasn't it just a few days ago when she bumped into a friend of a friend, Dr. Sheila Cassidy, a British physician working in a poor community clinic, who told her that all medical clinics were under surveillance?

With these thoughts running through her head, Paula entered the house and informed Nelson Gutiérrez that a physician would be coming to see him. She no sooner left Gutiérrez's bedroom when she heard the front door open and Helen's voice. Upon seeing Helen with the doctor in the vestibule, Paula's stomach roiled. It never occurred to her that the doctor would be Sheila Cassidy. As far as Paula knew, Sheila had never gone out before to treat someone in hiding.

Sheila grasped the stakes too. This was yet another serious breach of anonymity, endangering everyone. No words were spoken, as Paula walked Sheila into the back bedroom to examine Gutiérrez's wounds. Though Sheila tried to excise the bullets, they were too deep and the sepsis pervasive. She administered more antibiotics, but said Gutiérrez needed to have surgery immediately or he would die. She could do nothing more.

A few hours later the sisters met with Gerardo Whelan and Patricio Cariola in the convent's living room to discuss the escalating situation. They urgently needed to find an embassy willing to accept Nelson and Maria Elena. Since an embassy is the sovereign site of a recognized foreign government, it would have the freedom to assemble medical personnel and equipment to treat someone on their premises. But, as of that moment, the delicate inquiries Gerardo and Patricio had made with their diplomatic contacts had gone nowhere.

17

In the Trunk of the Peugeot

Given the politically volatile case of the MIR leadership, larger questions loomed. Even if an embassy could be found, how would Nelson Gutiérrez and Maria Elena Bachman be safely transported there? It was known that government agents monitored the embassies. They might try to identify the driver, trace license plates, or breach protocol and demand to inspect the cars entering the diplomatic preserve. The most tormenting concern was Gutiérrez's deteriorating condition. What if he died at the convent on Calle Orellana?

Gerardo Whelan and Patricio Cariola left the convent and drove to the *Nunciatura*, the diplomatic seat of the Vatican State, where they met with the papal nuncio, Monseñor Sótero Sánz de Villalba, the representative of the Vatican under Pope Paul VI. The papal nuncio could not have been at ease with what he heard, but reluctantly agreed to give the two MIR members asylum. He asked that they be brought to the *Nunciatura* during daylight hours to reduce suspicions.

The move was arranged for Thursday, October 23. Fr. Phil Devlin agreed to transport them. But that morning, he fell off his motorcycle, injuring his leg. Another plan had to be put in place.

Learning about this mishap, Helen left work immediately to phone Fr. Humberto Muñoz, the pastor of San Andrés, to ask if he would allow her to use his garage the next day. He agreed and asked no questions. On October 24, Helen arrived home and drove the Peugeot into the garage from the street. She closed the garage door and exited through a service door into the backyard of the parish property. She walked through the parish patio alongside a high wall that divided the parish and convent properties. She reached the convent's patio door and slipped into the house through the kitchen.

Within the hour, Gerardo and Patricio arrived and spoke with Nelson and Maria Elena, finalizing their plans. The couple slipped out the kitchen door with their few belongings, crossed the secluded patio, and went through the back gate into the parish property. Nelson's movements were slow and pained; his gait and grimace could have easily drawn attention. Inside the garage, Gerardo opened the trunk and waited as they secured themselves inside, then pressed it closed. Patricio took the passenger's seat as Gerardo grabbed the steering wheel.

The *Nunciatura's* property backed up to the French embassy and abutted a portion of the Turkish consulate. Gerardo anticipated a twenty-minute drive through increasingly heavy traffic, as the sidewalks filled with school kids and their mothers on late-afternoon errands. At a stoplight Gerardo straightened his clerical collar and brushed his black suit jacket, hoping that all would go smoothly.

Paula always joked that Gerardo was a terrible driver, a comment he knew was true enough to deserve a laugh, but not today. By now they had crossed through the busiest section of Santiago, traveling on tree-lined streets shading the immaculately landscaped estates. Now, only a block away from the *Nunciatura,* Gerardo prepped his maneuvers. At the next corner he would turn onto Montolín, a one-way street, and approach the *Nunciatura's* guarded entrance. Patricio was well known to the guards from his previous meetings with the nuncio. They both hoped his familiarity would smooth their passage.

About to turn, Gerardo spotted the guards at the gate. He then glanced toward the opposite end of the street, where another car appeared, going the wrong way! Seeing the errant car, the guards abandoned their posts and ran into the street waving their hands to stop the driver. Gerardo hit the accelerator and slipped into the driveway that led to the covered back entry. They had made it without detection. For the moment they were beyond the reach of the junta.

As evening fell, the house on Calle Orellana was still, now emptied of any MIR visitors. Paula and Bernadette had already made their way home from work to join Helen. They sat in the living room and talked softly, contemplating all that had transpired in the five days since October 20, Helen's birthday. Almost four hours had passed, and Gerardo and Patricio had not returned. The tension in the room swelled as they waited.

Suddenly there was a tremendous pounding on the door, and their eyes darted from one to the other.

Bernadette walked slowly toward the door, opening it carefully, then saw Gerardo's and Patricio's flushed faces. They were elated. Shooing them into the house, Bernadette smiled with delight. She grabbed some glasses and found a bottle of liquor left over from Helen's party. They all had a stiff one while they heard the details from Gerardo.

Relief took over for a good while, until they considered what would come next. Patricio said the papal nuncio would soon inform the government, as required, that he was providing asylum to Nelson Gutiérrez and Maria Elena Bachman. Hearing that, all of them had a single thought: What reprisals would the church face?

Five days later, Helen, Paula, and Bernadette thought it was safe enough for Isabel, Rosita, and me to come back to the house. All clear would be overstating it, but after several uneventful days, there was no obvious reason to stay away.

Over the nights we spent at Buzeta, I experienced a greater sense of friendship with Isabel and Rosita. We stayed up late, talking endlessly, and grew closer. While none of us had the whole picture of what was happening, we wove our impressions together, trying to understand the dramatic events as they were disclosed.

We came back to sleep at the house on Thursday, October 30. My room looked the same, as I put away my few clothes. Most likely one of the sisters had already checked the room for any telltale signs, stripping the beds and washing the sheets. Nonetheless, the tension and suspense of the past days still hovered over us. We agreed that on Saturday morning we needed to thoroughly clean the house.

18

El Día de Todos los Santos

Throughout Latin America, November 1 is All Saints' Day, observed in Chile as a national holiday. In keeping with the reverence for deceased loved ones, the day is celebrated in the cemeteries with entire families bringing flowers to their tombs. Often the family stays long enough for a springtime picnic on the gravesite or gathers at home around a candlelit altar, adorned with photos, flowers, and memories of ancestors.

The sun was shining warmly that Saturday morning as we were up early and began to clean. We had the patio doors open to circulate fresh air and some LPs playing in the living room to keep us motivated. The fussiest and best cleaner was Isabel, even as she laughed at her outsized priorities for spotlessness, honed by her years of convent training.

"Do you know what? I love to clean the bathrooms!" she would tell us to our shared incredulity. But in spite of the kidding and chatter that went on all morning, she chided us with orders from the bathroom as she scrubbed the floor: "Wash everything; we can't have fingerprints anywhere! Wipe down the dresser drawers, closet doors, and desktops. Wash the windows, the sills and walls, bedposts, and frames. Clean the kitchen sink and refrigerator and burn the trash!"

We worked for four or five hours mopping and dusting, meticulously erasing any evidence of the visitors. Rosita cleaned at a pace of one who had grown up with thirteen brothers and sisters. By the time I surveyed my bedroom in its now pristine state, she had already finished cleaning several rooms, hung out a few loads of wash on the patio clothesline, and prepared a snack for us. Just as she called us to come and have something to eat, the phone rang. It was for me.

On the other end of the line was Sheila Cassidy. She introduced herself in a pleasant but slightly hurried way. I had never met Sheila, but Connie Kelly had mentioned her name to me, hoping we could meet each other. Sheila asked if I was free to come to her house that afternoon. She explained that today was Connie's birthday; she'd be turning thirty-eight, and she thought it would be good for Connie to have a visitor to cheer her up. I hadn't seen Connie at school for more than a week, as she had been out sick.

Sheila proposed that we meet at her house for a late lunch, then I could accompany her up the block to the Columban Father's Center house, where Connie was recuperating. She said she would brief me on Connie's condition prior to our visit.

Sheila was a confidant and friend of Connie and recently assumed the role of her medical doctor, as Connie spiraled downward with exhaustion. Given Connie's condition, Sheila was limiting her visitors. Sheila asked that I not mention my visit to anyone else.

"Come around four," she said. Then she gave me her address and phone, which I scratched on a slip of paper under her name, folded it, and put it in my pocket. I walked away from the phone rather bewildered. I couldn't put a name on it at first, but the whole thing seemed quite strange. Why me? Why am I the friend Sheila wants to visit Connie? After all, I had known Connie only for a few months, while Paula had been friends with her much longer and certainly had a better grip on her situation than I did.

Feeling kind of sheepish, I returned to the patio table and said, "That was Sheila Cassidy." Isabel's eyebrow rose and curled.

"I don't really understand, but she asked me to visit Connie for her birthday. I'll be leaving around three or so."

Rosita started clearing away the plates and silverware, while Isabel called out from the kitchen, "I'm going to the *feria*; is there anything special I need to pick up?"

Although we spent the morning trying to get things back to normal, a collective unease had snuck back in. After showering and changing into clothes more suitable for a social visit, I left for Sheila's house. Closing the door behind me I felt a bit of relief—being out of the house and on my own. The sun warmed my shoulders as I walked toward Av. Matta to catch the bus. The street was humming with signs of spring: homeowners sweeping their patch of sidewalk, guys at the curb oiling a two-seater *moto*, and clutches of families out on errands. I took two bus rides toward downtown Santiago, getting off in a neighborhood of grand old homes, many secured behind decorative wrought-iron fences. I walked a few blocks from the bus stop a bit mesmerized by the beautiful surroundings, so different from the uniformity of my block and the dull industrial gray of Buzeta, where I taught. The neighborhood felt friendly too. I paused a few times to ask passersby for directions, pulling Sheila's address out of my pocket for guidance.

Sheila's home was very near the intersection of Bilbao and Manuel Larrarín Gandarillas. Two-storied and painted white, her home was set back from the sidewalk by ample shrubbery and tended flower beds. The gardener was in the yard clearing away debris when I approached. I rang the doorbell at the front gate, smiled at the gardener, and then heard the housekeeper.

I introduced myself in Spanish and my purpose in coming: "Hello! My name is Kathy, Dr. Sheila invited me . . ."

But, before I finished, a matronly Chilean woman wearing an apron said, "Yes! The doctor is expecting you. I am Mercedes."[1] Then she ushered me into the house.

Sheila appeared wearing blue jeans, sandals, and a striped, comfy knit V-neck sweater over a collared blouse. Her sandy-brown hair was hooked over her ears and touched her shoulders.

"Hello, Kathy! I'm so glad to meet you," she said as she reached to embrace me. "Connie has mentioned your name to me often. I told her of course I'd love to meet you, and now we finally are."

"Sheila, I'm glad to meet you too." I said, a bit taken aback by her effervescence and sparkly blue eyes. To tell the truth, when Connie suggested that Sheila and I should meet, I really never gave it a second thought. Why would Sheila, a busy, established British doctor who had been living in Chile several years and probably more than fifteen years older than me want to meet me?

I felt a bit shy at first, but there was nothing pretentious about Sheila. She was immediately warm and open, even familiar. She asked Mercedes to prepare some tea and sandwiches for us—speaking in Spanish—and then switched to British-accented English.

Sheila showed me around the first floor of her home apologizing along the way for how sparse it looked.

"I'll be moving soon, and I've been giving away many of my things," she said, adding, "I'll tell you more about that when we sit down for tea."

Actually, I hadn't really noticed that it was emptied out. Instead, I was taken with the openness of the house, its brightness and large front windows, and her garden coming to life with spring buds and green shoots. We entered the kitchen, where Mercedes had the hot kettle and tea cups laid out on a tray.

"I'll take the tray, Mercedes," Sheila said, without pausing to notice Mercedes's exasperated look.

Quite naturally, Mercedes had her way of doing things, which Sheila in her helpful exuberance had just short-circuited. In most Chilean homes of means, household help was a given. Typically, a housekeeper like Mercedes might live in, and in addition to cleaning, shopping, and food preparation, be the loyal guardian of the home. She may have cared for more than one generation of the family. Many homes also employed a male *cuidador,* who served as a full-time caretaker of the property. Many housekeepers and caretakers had lost not only their employment in the economic crisis provoked by the coup, but with it lost a piece of identity and status nurtured by years of faithful service. The coup and its socialpolitical rifts barreled through the country's living rooms and kitchens, bringing at a minimum new secrets and often open family warfare. While the homeowner and employer might have supported the coup, believing it was necessary to restore order, a housekeeper might have more leftist sympathies, aligning with one of the household's younger children, known to be politically active in support of Allende. Conversely, some politically active employers might have hidden their involvement in the opposition to the Pinochet dictatorship from their more conservative household help out of the fear that their sentiments might be inopportunely disclosed.

Sheila held the tray and empty cups aloft while calling back to Mercedes, "We'll be at the table by the window."

As we sat down, Mercedes quickly appeared with a plate of petite, squared sandwiches filled with sliced cheese, ham, and an assortment of mayonnaise-based spreads. They looked delicious.

After pleasantries I asked Sheila, "Tell me, how is Connie doing?"

Sheila told me that Connie was better, but still quite exhausted. When she improves enough to travel, Sheila believed Connie should return to the United States to recover. At the moment, Connie was residing in one of the guest rooms at the Columban Center, instead of her home in the *población*. Sheila wanted me to visit with her, but asked me to avoid topics that might be upsetting.

"Okay, I'll give it a try, Sheila. But tell me, is she seriously ill?" I asked, feeling uncertain about what to expect and concerned that I might not see Connie again for a long time.

"I'm not sure if she will come back to Chile, though I know she wants to," Sheila answered. "The Sisters of Charities, her religious community, will have to evaluate with her the feasibility of returning, especially if Sr. Marie Tolle, the only other sister from her community, decides to leave. These have been difficult years for them, and both are run down."

I contemplated what Sheila was saying and realized Connie's departure from Chile was a *fait accompli*.

"So, you work with Connie at Buzeta?" Sheila queried to pump the conversation.

"Yes, I see her several times a week, when she comes to teach her religion classes. Right now, I am substitute teaching several subjects to fourth and fifth graders. To tell you the truth I'm not much further ahead than the kids. I am preparing lesson plans or grading homework all the time.

"A couple of afternoons a week I've gone to the *población* where Connie lives to visit with the women involved with the *comedor infantil*. The visits with Connie have helped me understand the hardships the children and their families face."

My introductory chatter seemed shallow and spent. In spite of this, Sheila continued to ask me about my university studies at Notre Dame, what I majored in, and my goals. But topic number one when you are getting to know someone anywhere in Latin America is to ask in depth about their parents and siblings. In some ways this patter was odd, since in all likelihood if we were meeting for the first time in London or Chicago, this might never come up until much later in a developing friendship. Nonetheless, the Chilean customs already had their grip on us, and I was glad to turn more of the talking over to Sheila.

She quickly traced her roots for me.

"I was born in Lincolnshire, England. My father was an air vice-marshal in the Royal Air Force, and when I was twelve we emigrated to Sydney, Australia. When I finished high school, I began my medical studies at the University of Sydney, and two years in, I transferred to Oxford to complete my medical degree. There I became great friends with Consuelo Silva, a Chilean physician, who was doing advanced studies in plastic surgery and always encouraged me to come and visit her country."

Then, for all the casualness of our conversation and the sunlight in the room, the house began to feel hollow, and I became anxious. I noticed her gardener was now crouched below the window just beyond the tea table where we were sitting.

As I glanced toward him, she said, "No need to worry, he is trustworthy."

I gulped, not knowing for sure if Sheila knew that I knew she had secretly treated Nelson Gutiérrez on Calle Orellana. It occurred to me that Sheila may not have known that I lived with Paula, Helen, and Bernadette on Orellana. No matter what, I definitely didn't want our conversation to hint at that while someone was within earshot.

Before she could go on, I interrupted her, asking, "Sheila, you said earlier that you are moving? Why is that? Where are you going?"

"I've decided to leave Chile and join a contemplative order of religious women."

Her answer took me aback. What? How does a doctor from England, working in Chile, decide to join a cloistered community? Sheila could read the incredulity and puzzlement on my face, but held back, perhaps unready to share something so deep and personal.

Pivoting, she continued, "When I came to Chile, I really wanted to pursue intensive training in plastic surgery. When I learned that Chile had one of the most highly regarded training programs, I thought, *why not?*

"I arrived in 1971 and lived here with my friend, Consuelo. But by 1973, with the strikes, shortages, and transportation collapse, life deteriorated. Then came the coup, the mass arrests, killings, and torture of Allende's supporters. Consuelo's sister Claudia was active in opposition to Pinochet. She and her friends hid out here with us during those terrifying days. Claudia eventually had to go into exile."

Her voice became more somber with each recollection. Sheila sighed deeply and said, "A few months later, in early 1974, Consuelo fell ill and in March she died. This is her house. But with all of her close family in exile, she left the house to me."

Sheila paused quietly, not minimizing the deep loss of Consuelo, but seemed to be mentally quilting together all that had transpired in those few short years.

She admitted that she knew very little about Chile before she arrived in 1971, including the political situation. She was never accepted into the plastic surgery program, but became credentialed as a medical doctor in Chile. She started working at Posta Medica No. 3, the medical clinic where Consuelo had worked. She was inspired by the dedicated doctors serving the poor, but always with inadequate supplies. Through her clinic work with patients from the *poblaciones*, she began to meet some of the foreign-born religious women and men working in the area. Some were from Ireland, Spain, and the United States. She marveled at their lives and their incredible dedication, saying, "Something deep stirred in me. I can't fully describe it."

As she spoke about her personal journey, the atmosphere around our tea table changed. The pattern of her life story evoked kindred emotions in me. The struggle of being a foreigner in another country, both being single women, not nuns—though Sheila was aiming for that now. My twenty-two-year-old eyes were trained across the table on her expressive face, listening intently as she began to divulge the poignant details about an early relationship with a man who abruptly left her behind for another woman. Rejected, she despaired of ever marrying and having a family. This powerful feeling collided with an incessant spiritual call by God. During a recent retreat, she decided to leave everything behind to become a nun.

Sheila spoke on without pause, telling me about the devastating moments in her life. Each story poured out with incredible emotion: wrenching anguish, loneliness, and utter solitude, seemingly compelling me to merge and dissolve inside of her almost trance-like state of self-dissolution and knowing submission to God's call.

Dazed by her confidences, I pulled back, asking myself, "Am I being cursed? Am I doomed to live a similarly anguished life?"

I tried to shake my head to clear these thoughts, telling myself: "Don't be crazy!" But the intensity of her story kept pressing against me. Across the table it came toward me, this purging of pain that seemed to physically plunge into me. I didn't want to accept it, but it flowed in.

I had become a receptacle. But why?

Suddenly Sheila stopped, and the trance-like energy vanished. She abruptly glanced at her watch and was surprised at the hour, closing in on 6:00 p.m. "We should probably get over to see Connie soon, since it is later than I thought. But first I want to show you quickly around the house."

I was more than relieved to push back from the tea table. I followed Sheila up the unadorned wooden stairs. A crackling sound shot out with each of our steps, reverberating against the hollowed-out interiors of the packed-up rooms. A feeling of tenderness entered her voice as she pointed out Consuelo's room and her favorite possessions, now in the process of being wrapped up.

"Come in, this is my study . . . ," Sheila said, ushering me forward toward another room.

I laughed to myself, thinking, "Why do the British always get to have illustrious studies, and we Americans only have dumpy dens?"

"I just can't believe how empty it is," Sheila remarked, her eyes a bit sorrowful. "I've been giving it all away. Do you know what has been the hardest part to relinquish?"

She paused, staring around the room and over her scattered desk, before she answered her own question. "The books! The books! It's been anguishing to relinquish them. I've cried and cried. Now, I only have a few more to give away before I join the cloister."

She walked across the room toward her desk and picked up a worn, palm-sized booklet, maybe eight to ten pages thick and said, "Here, please take this. It is something precious given to me by a dear friend."

Sheila handed me the booklet. I glanced first at the upper-right-hand corner and saw her meticulous signature, Sheila A. Cassidy, penned Palmer smooth in blue fountain ink. Below I saw the title of an unfamiliar, long poem, "The Hound of Heaven," by Francis Thompson.[2] It would be days before I would read the ponderous, mystical opening lines.

> *The Hound of Heaven*
> I fled Him, down the nights and down the days;
> I fled Him, down the arches of the years;
> I fled Him, down the labyrinthine ways
> Of my own mind; and in the mist of tears
> I hid from Him, and under running laughter.
> Up vistaed hopes, I sped;
> And shot, precipitated,
> Adown Titanic glooms of chasmèd fears
> From those strong Feet that followed, followed after.
> But with unhurrying chase,
> And unperturbèd pace,
> Deliberate speed, majestic instancy,
> They beat—and a Voice beat
> More instant than the Feet—
> "All things betray thee, who betrayest Me."

Then, before I could say thank you for the booklet I was holding, Sheila said, "We'd better hurry! Connie will be waiting and wondering where we are."

She dashed down the stairs, calling out to Mercedes that she'd be back shortly. Mercedes emerged from the kitchen as I reached the bottom step. I thanked her for the tea and sandwiches and waved to her as I walked through the front door and out the garden gate. As we crossed Bilbao and walked up the short block of Manuel Larrarín Gandarillas to the Columban Center, Sheila asked, "You know what else will be the hardest to give up?"

"No. What?" I asked.

"My blue jeans!" Sheila said, laughing.

I started laughing too, because I was pretty sure that the cloistered nuns weren't expecting their new recruit to be tethered to her blue jeans.

The Columban Center house was on a lovely street. As we walked up the block, I noticed that the street was narrow and the lots were small-ish for the breadth of the gracious turn-of-the-century brick homes. Yet the snug lots made the street feel intimate, especially as the late after-noon sun trickled through the budding leaves. When we approached the Columban Center, I was startled by the diamond-cut leaded glass win-dows arrayed on either side of the entry door. As Sheila rang the bell, she reminded me to keep my conversations with Connie on "light" topics. Sheila planned to say a quick hello to Connie, then return sometime after 8:00 p.m. for a longer visit.

A petite woman peeked out the front window and waved at Sheila. She opened the door smiling, saying,

"¡Ay Doctora Sheila! How are you? We've been waiting for you!"

As we were ushered into the foyer Sheila introduced me to Enriqueta, the Chilean housekeeper for this large religious community. You could immediately feel her warm enthusiasm. I smiled and reached my hand out toward her. She quickly removed the dish towel from one hand to the other, holding out her right arm with her fist closed. It wasn't an affront, but a deferential signal to shake her "hand" above the wrist, since her hands had been recently dipped in dishwater.

She looked down shyly and said to Sheila, "Let me take you upstairs to Sr. Connie's room. She's anxious to see you."

Enriqueta darted into the kitchen to wash her hands. Next to the kitchen was the dining room, which could seat fifteen to twenty people around its oak table. On one side of the foyer was a hallway with offices. I peeked into the room with the diamond-cut windows, seeing a parlor with comfy furniture and a colorful Oriental carpet.

Before Enriqueta could usher us upstairs, we heard Connie calling, "Are you coming up?"

We found Connie in bed in one of the guest rooms. For all she wanted to mask it, I saw a weariness and strain on her face. Over her nightgown she wore a thin cotton flowered robe that touched the top of her knees.

As we entered the room, she tried to swing her pale legs over the edge of the bed to sit up, stretching her feet out toward the cloth slippers on the floor.

But Sheila would have none of that, firmly saying, "Back in bed, Connie. Remember you are here to rest!"

I stood behind Sheila and tried to interrupt the upcoming tug of war between patient and doctor, cleared my voice, and said, "Connie, it is so good to see you. We've missed you so much at Buzeta." I moved forward to give her a hug as she slumped back onto a stack of pillows. "Happy birthday! I'm so glad I could come and visit you. How are you doing?"

I was trying to pump some effervescence into what was an awkward and embarrassing situation, seeing Connie, my mentor over these past three months, dressed only in thin pajamas.

Connie smiled wanly, saying, "I'm glad you are here, though I didn't expect to celebrate like this." Her voice dropped as she spoke, but brightened a bit as she saw her agency in the gathering. "I am so happy you and Sheila have finally met! I've wanted to get you two together. Have you had time to talk yet?"

Sheila jumped in, seeing her chance to leave. "Yes, we have! Kathy can tell you about our visit. But I have to run now. I'll be back in a few hours. We'll say prayers together and chat a bit more before bedtime."

Turning to me, Sheila asked, "Do you think you will still be here?"

"I don't know, Sheila. I told the others in my house I'd be heading home by then. I'll try and stay as long as possible and hopefully see you to say goodbye. Thanks again for inviting me for tea."

Sheila turned and met Enriqueta coming in through the bedroom doorway, saying, "Enriqueta, don't worry about me. I'll see myself out the front door."

"Of course, doctor," Enriqueta replied. "But I'll go with you to lock the door."

She turned to Connie and me to let us know she'd be back shortly to see what we would like to eat or drink. Sheila descended the staircase at a lively pace with Enriqueta behind her.

From upstairs, we heard Sheila depart. *"Adiós, hasta pronto, Enriqueta!"* she called out as Enriqueta latched the door.

Enriqueta returned to the bedroom, smiling and saying, "Sr. Connie, I have a surprise for you."

Connie smiled and answered, "You have a surprise for me? What is it, Enriqueta? Yes, please bring it!" Enriqueta slipped out, then walked in with a cake she had baked with lit candles. I cleared the bedside table and helped Enriqueta lower the cake and joined her in singing: *"Cumpleaños feliz, te deseamos a ti. . . ."* Then, with hardly a murmer, Connie made a wish and blew out her candles.[3] Enriqueta deftly arranged the cake plates and poured soda into petite glasses, then gazed happily at her handiwork.

Connie sipped from her glass, then sputtered, "Enriqueta, you've only brought two cups and two plates! You must stay and have some with us!" Enriqueta demurred, saying she had more work to do, but Connie prevailed.

I joined Enriqueta downstairs in the kitchen, helping her retrieve an extra place setting and a folding table. Enriqueta looked so tiny in the expansive kitchen with its broad counters and industrial-sized oven. As

Sr. Connie Kelly, SC, on a trip to Southern Chile. Courtesy Sisters of Charity of New York.

she leaned over the sink, I wondered how she managed to prepare meals for such a large religious congregation with their constantly shifting schedules and roster of guests. When she turned from the sink and took off her apron, I realized she was more than happy to cease her chores and have some company.

"Enriqueta, shall we go up now?" I asked as I picked up the folding table and followed her.

Connie had moved from the bed and was seated in a side chair, where we scuttled the furniture into a cozy circle. Enriqueta seemed to relax as we cut more cake and passed around the soda.

"Enriqueta, tell Kathy and me more about your children," Connie urged.

With a little more prompting Enriqueta spoke in a lively voice about her hometown of Rengo, a rural community, two hours south of Santiago, near Rancagua. She was a middle child from a large family of twelve brothers and sisters. Her parents were traditional farmers, who raised chickens and tended large animals needed for milk and plowing. They grew onions, potatoes, and squash on their own land as well as farming rented acres nearby.

Enriqueta, who was separated from her husband, came to Santiago leaving behind her four children in Rengo, watched over by her extensive family. I remember moments of pained longing in her voice as she spoke about each of them. It was as if by describing her life, she could bring her children closer than the miles and her days off allowed. I could not fathom being in her shoes.

I remember being entranced by her story. In some ways it was an introduction to family life in rural Chile, which I had yet to visit. And it mimicked what I knew of Chile's rural-to-urban migration story, including that of the children I taught.

The house phone rang. Enriqueta excused herself and hurried down the stairs to catch the call. The telephone nook under the stairwell functioned as a bit of an echo chamber, such that Connie and I could hear her greeting the caller, politely promising to deliver the message. When she hung up, she climbed a few of the stairs and called out,

"Sr. Connie, I'll be back soon. I have to do a few things in the kitchen."

After a pause, I turned to Connie and said, "How are you really doing, Connie? We've all been worried."

"Kathy," she said, "I'm just exhausted. I've needed this rest, and Sheila has been great. I really don't want to leave Chile, but I may have to for a little while."

She described how run down she had become, coughing as if to prove it. She went to see a doctor about ten days earlier, saying she was having trouble sleeping, and was prescribed something to help her rest, but she kept spiraling down.

"I'm so sorry that happened to you, Connie. Sheila mentioned to me that a doctor you saw might have given you the wrong medicine." But, frankly, even as I spoke, none of these ill effects, except a verifiable tiredness, were evident to me.

Connie moved the conversation to other topics, wanting to know how the classes were going at Buzeta. I told her about the twenty-fifth anniversary celebration in honor of the Maryknoll Sisters' arrival in Chile. For the celebration each class had been asked to prepare a *baile tipico,* a folk dance. Because the Maryknoll sisters, Gerry and Helen, were from North America, the teachers wanted to include an American folk dance in the ceremony, so Gerry asked me to teach my students the Virginia Reel. She gave me a record of the music while the dance steps were printed out on the back of its cardboard jacket.

"Connie, you wouldn't believe it! We practiced the line-dance steps in the schoolyard, with its twosome's twirls and sashays down the center, for two weeks straight. On the night of the performance, the principal directed the kids to enter from the wrong side of stage, placing the lead couple at the end, not the beginning of the line. When the music started with its do-si-do rhythm, the kids panicked. Some began the routine on their own, bumping and crashing into each other as they sashayed down the line in opposite directions. I felt so bad for the kids and was mortified in front of the parents."

Imagining the scene Connie couldn't repress her laughter, nor could I. Relating a few more stories from the anniversary performance was my way of keeping things light.

Due to her illness, Connie hadn't been in school to notice the early-afternoon departures of Helen or Paula, their drawn faces, or the aura of consternation hovering over the place. She didn't know that Rosita, Isabel, and I had been staying over in the convent bedrooms at Buzeta. She most certainly didn't know that Sheila had been the physician sent to our house to treat the festering bullet wounds of Nelson Gutiérrez.

I wasn't supposed to know these details either, but I did. They slipped out in fragmentary ways during some of those whispered conversations *de confianza* that were held late at night between Isabel, Rosita, and me, or sometimes after school over tea with Gerry and Helen Carpenter, who kept tabs on what was happening. "Keep that confidential," someone would say after uttering a dangerous detail. Or, "No one should know about this." I would gulp and plunge the data down. But deep inside, the terrifying unknown remained. If the DINA gets wind of this, will we survive?

Yet, oddly, when I heard these small, even dangerous details, I felt calmed. Little fragments of knowledge provided a bit of microscopic mastery, some tangible content within the void. I needed these morsels to serve as an antidote to that void, to be like the fairy-tale bread crumbs dropped on the forest floor, magically secure markers destined to guide one to safety.

"What time is it, Kathy?" Connie asked. Before I checked my watch, I peered over her shoulder to see the dimming sky outside her bedroom window.

"It's well after eight already," I answered. "I'll have to be going shortly."

"But you haven't told me much about your conversation with Sheila yet," Connie said, urging me to stay a little longer.

Hearing Connie mention Sheila's name, my stomach flipped. Too much felt covert. Under no circumstance did I want to venture into the connection of Sheila coming to our house to treat Nelson Gutiérrez's wounds. Nor could I adequately convey the mystifying experience I had over lunch, as Sheila described her life.

Dodging the uncomfortable parts I said, "I really enjoyed meeting Sheila. We had a powerful conversation. She's lived an amazing life. But I had no idea she was going to join a cloister of nuns and leave Chile! Had you told me about that and I didn't remember?"

Connie laughed and said, "No, I probably didn't tell you about that; she hadn't really made it public until just recently. I just wanted you two to meet, since I thought you might have something in common."

In common? I thought to myself again, wondering how to piece together the meaning of the afternoon's experience.

Connie's energy seemed to sag. I left the room to call our house. Enriqueta heard me coming down the stairs and showed me to the phone. I was surprised to hear Paula's voice answering it, since she had planned to be at a retreat overnight. I told her I was visiting Connie, and I'd be home soon.

Connie came down the stairs to say goodbye. For a few moments Enriqueta, Connie, and I stood near the telephone nook chatting and laughing. I thanked Enriqueta for our conversation and the delicious cake, hugging her and Connie goodbye.

Just then Sheila rang the doorbell. Sheila was surprised to see us and began to chide Connie for being out of bed.

"I was just leaving," I said, "and Connie came down to say goodbye."

"Kathy, why don't you stay a little longer? Come upstairs and visit awhile more with Connie and me," Sheila asked.

"I'm sorry, Sheila, but I've already called to say I am heading home. I'd better go. It is already getting dark."

Just then, upon hearing Sheila's voice in the foyer, Fr. Bill Halliden, the superior of the Columban community, came out to greet her. He said hello to Connie, and I was introduced to him. I felt edgy as more chatter ensued, detaining me longer. I looked for a polite way to exit. When Fr. Halliden said he needed to work on his sermon, I said I'd be leaving too. After another round of goodbyes and hugs, Enriqueta escorted me to the door. Fr. Halliden returned to his office. Meanwhile Connie and Sheila started up the stairs to say their evening prayers.

"*¡Adiós, Enriqueta!*" I called back as she closed the door behind me. The warm air from earlier in the day had dissipated, and a slight breeze brushed pass me as I stepped out on the front walk. Enriqueta waved her goodbye from the diamond-cut window as I secured the gate. I turned left on the sidewalk and walked back toward Bilbao, cutting diagonally across Manuel Larraín Gandarillas to the other side of the street.

Suddenly, as I stepped into the street, a car accelerated, flashing its headlights and weaving side to side. If I hadn't known better, I would have thought it was aiming for me.

I barely reached the opposite sidewalk when it passed by.

What is this? I thought. *It's way too early for a bunch of guys to be out driving drunk!*

After making it to the sidewalk, I paid them no mind. Strangely, no street lights came on as a bluish darkness fell quickly over the street. Behind me I heard a car door snap close. I picked up my pace, knowing I still had two buses to catch.

I was barely five houses away from the corner of Manuel Larraín Gandarillas and Bilbao, catty-corner from Sheila's house, when a tall slender man, between twenty and thirty years old, dressed in jeans and a denim Levi jacket, came running through the side yard of the home on my right. He raced out from the shadows, and before I knew it, cut directly in front of me, gliding past at an angle only four to five feet away.

He didn't seem to see me, but as he stepped into my view, I saw his left leg and arm bend, propelling him forward in a runner's stride. Meanwhile, he kept his right arm straight, stretched backward and taut against his leg. Above us, a passing cloud parted, releasing the shimmery glow of the crescent moon, illuminating the *metralleta,* machine gun, at his side.

An intense fear seized me. My eyes darted right and left. I saw other figures running in the shadows; some were across Bilbao, possibly near Sheila's house. *Is this a DINA undercover operation?* I asked myself. *Is this MIR? Who were those guys in that car I saw weaving and flashing their lights?* My mind sprinted from question to question. If there was a legitimate police operation under way, how come there are no sirens and no one shouting orders? I didn't dare break my stride.

Suddenly, I heard footsteps behind me. They were heavy steps, a man's footfall. Had someone gotten out of that car to follow me?

As I reached Bilbao and turned right, I started to seize up in panic, but refused to look back to see what was happening. If I showed curiosity, I might be suspect. I sensed that whoever was behind me was not out for an evening stroll. He made no noise, never coughed or jiggled coins in his pockets. While I judged he was taller than me with a larger stride, he kept an even pace a few steps behind me.

I reached the bus stop as quickly as I could, stepping into the small crowd of people nestled there waiting. The moon shifted back under the clouds, making the huddle of people nearly indistinguishable. I wished for the darkness to hide me. I stole a furtive glance at the man who trailed me. He nonchalantly strolled over the curb and stood aloof at the far edge of the crowd. Tallish, as I suspected, he wore a shiny brown suit and tie, which seemed rumpled and ill fitted. He never looked sideways to see if his bus was coming.

A bus pulled up to the stop, and several people hopped on. As it wasn't my bus, I didn't board it; but then neither did he. When my bus pulled up to the curb, I tried to tuck myself into the middle of the crowd to board. The bus was already packed with people, so I pushed my way toward the back. I couldn't see if he got on too, until a stop or so later, when a seat opened up and I sat down.

There he was, up ahead; my stomach churned. I did *not* want this man to know where I lived. A few stops more and I would need to get off and transfer buses. Just as the bus slowed toward the transfer stop, I stood up and pushed toward the back door. When I jumped off, he was practically behind me. Seeing my second bus approaching a few lengths away, I lunged into the street to flag it down. I was lucky enough to grab the first seat across from the driver. The man was pushed farther in by those who boarded behind him. He took an aisle seat four or five rows back. I could feel his eyes boring into the back of my head.

When the driver's assistant called out "Portugal," my stop along the broad Av. Matta, I didn't flinch. Several people got on and off. Then just as the driver cranked the door closed, I jumped up, saying *"Perdón"* to the driver, who fortuitously cracked the door back open.

I leapt onto the sidewalk, hearing the closing slap of the door, as the bus immediately accelerated away from the curb. I ran a few steps alongside the bus, saw the tall man inside, looking for me. I darted behind the bus directly into oncoming traffic, picking my way between the coursing headlights driving up and down Av. Matta. I kept running until I reached my street. I was panting, but pretty certain that I had shaken my brown-suited "tail."

At the corner of Av. Matta and Calle Orellana, a number of parishioners from San Andrés Parish were milling around after Mass. I waded through them, hurrying toward my house a few doors down. I rang the bell and pushed my key into the lock. But before I could unlock it, Paula pulled the door open from the inside, took one glance at me, and said,

"What's the matter with you? You're ashen! You look like you've seen a ghost!"

"Inside the house I started to tremble. I followed Paula back into the kitchen, where Isabel and she had been having a bite to eat and talking. They prepared a little food for me as I told them about my experiences.

"*¡No! ¡No puede ser!*" Isabel exclaimed, before switching back into English, saying, "That can't be! Something is up!"

Isabel started to shoot questions at me in rapid fire. She raced through scenarios, trying to make sense of the events. "Do you think it was the DINA? Maybe they were not in uniform? Were they were dressed in blue jeans? Levi jackets? Were they pretending to be militants?" "Or was it MIR? Are they out on an operation tonight? No, that would be crazy given all the pressure on them!" "Were they at Sheila's house, or just nearby?" "Are you sure that guy did not get off the bus and follow you?" "How sure are you?"

None of my answers were definitive, except I was sure the man did not get off the bus. I barely eluded him. They told me there were rumors that a statement by Nelson Gutiérrez was supposed to be released, as early as tonight. If this was true, they speculated that he had smuggled a statement out of the *Nunciatura*. According to the information they had, he and Maria Elena had not yet left Chile under the Vatican's diplomatic auspices. Any statement by him would surely escalate the danger for anyone found to have aided him.

Paula hadn't planned to be home tonight. Weeks ago, she committed to attend a retreat, but during the day she had a gnawing feeling that she should go back home. So, she did, arriving only a short time before me. As she talked, I glanced around the room. Above us the kitchen ceiling lamp threw off an eerie fluorescent glow, starkly illuminating us, while outside the walled-in patio filled with matted darkness. For a moment we sat quietly, three silhouettes around a table.

We took no actions that night. Without the actual knock of DINA at the door there was a certain kind of denial, maybe a sense that fate would decide. On the practical side, our telephone line might be tapped, and any calls we would make about staying elsewhere might snare someone else. Gerardo Whelan had the sisters' car in *Lo Barnechea* in case it had been traced when he visited the *Nunciatura*. Without a car it was too late to depart for anywhere before the curfew as the buses would be shutting down shortly. Even so, where would we go?

Just then Rosita popped in the kitchen. She had been in the front bedroom preparing materials for next week's classes.

"*¿Oye, quieren mirar las noticias?*" Would you like to watch the news? she asked.

It didn't take much to encourage us to shove back from the table and turn off the lights. Isabel pushed the square portable electric heater into the center of the living room near the television, hoping to warm the atmosphere. We watched the news for fifteen or twenty minutes, but nothing of note was reported.

"Maybe I'll try the radio?" Isabel said. "Just in case."

The phone rang, startling me. Maryknoll sister Peg Lipsio was on the line when I answered it. We chatted for a moment. She told me that Helen and she were spending the night at Buzeta, so that the convent wouldn't be empty. All the Maryknoll sisters who worked in Santiago were in El Quisco for a weekend meeting.

Since Peg was calling to speak to Paula, I passed the phone off to her. Feeling totally drained I went to my room to get ready for bed.

What a day! I thought to myself in exhaustion. *But at least this room is spotless.* Mindlessly I pulled my keys and the slip of paper with Sheila's name and address on it out of my pocket, dropping them on the empty desk next to "The Hound of Heaven" poem she had given me. I thought, *I'll take a look it tomorrow*, then plopped my purse on the chair.

In just a couple of motions I drew the drapes, pulled off all my clothes, and didn't even care about how cold the room felt tingling against my skin, until I found my nightgown and pulled it over my head. Too tired to light the gas water heater in the bathroom, I splashed icy water over my face and hands, then quickly brushed my teeth. Back in my room I grabbed an extra thick wool blanket and threw it over the bed, sinking under a pile of heavy covers pulled up to my nose. Even so, I shivered.

19

El Día de los Muertos

Something woke me up. A soft rumble. A motor purring. The clank of chains. Murmurs. I heard feet shuffling just outside my bedroom window. My room was pitch black. A tremendous pounding on the front door shook me out of my bed. As if in a dream, I walked dazed down the corridor toward the door, my heart pounding. Deep, muscular voices shouted repeatedly, *"¡Madres! ¡Abren la puerta!"*

I stumbled backwards in fear. Paula with her slippers sliding against the floor came up behind me as the pounding and shouting continued.

"¡Madres! ¡Abren la puerta!" Sisters! Open the door!

I glanced at Paula. I saw in her eyes the thought, *They know who we are.* She whispered, "It's the DINA."

Escape? I looked past her shoulders toward the patio, visible through the living room window. Not a chance. The night's curfew still hung over a hazy dawn. Paula spoke decisively to me in a low, flat voice. "Open the door."

I pulled up the iron latch, and six to eight men shoved their way over the threshold into the narrow vestibule hallway. For a moment, Paula's girth detained them and their pointed machine guns. A few of the conscripts blinked glassy-eyed at her belly, partially visible under a gaping robe. For an instant they hesitated, apparently not wanting to disrespect a nun, especially one this unveiled.

Rosita and Isabel emerged from their room next to the front entry just as the squad leader shoved his way through the door, demanding, *"¿Quién es Helen Nelson?"* Which of you is Helen Nelson?

"She is not here," Paula retorted.

"Where is she?" he said, eyeing Paula.

"Away at the coast," she replied.

"What town? Where?" he commanded, staring at Paula.

Rosita broke in, startling him by saying in her earnest and emotive voice, *"O, eso sí, no lo sabemos. . . ."* Oh, we don't know where.

He unlocked his gaze, turned away from Paula to look down at Rosita's petite figure, illuminated by the dim hallway light. Wrapped in a heavy robe with her mussed hair springing in all directions, Rosita continued talking in this mesmerizing voice, as if they were her first graders assembled for their story hour.

"We don't know where Helen is. She is our mother superior," she said, using a ruse to cover the three of us who were not SSND sisters, then continued, "She left last night to go to the coast for the weekend, on retreat."

"Well, you must know where she might go," he insisted.

"Pues, sí. Pero no lo sabemos de verdad. . . ." Well, yes, she said, agreeing with him. But no, we really don't know where she went.

Rosita continued, "Honestly, Helen really enjoys the coast, and it is just so immense! She could be anywhere, maybe in Viña del Mar or Algarrobo? They are such beautiful places! But really we have no idea." Rosita hummed along, dappling the story with some likely possibilities for a getaway.

"What does she look like?" he asked.

"She's not too short or too tall. Her hair is a little long," Rosita said, touching her shoulders, then adding, "She has a nice smile."

Briefly, she had the squad leader under her spell. Then, as if seized by an idea, he yelled, "Which bedroom is hers? Do you have a picture of her?"

Paula pointed to the first room down the corridor to the right.

"Search it!" he said to the guards next to him. "Search the whole house!"

As they darted away, we exchanged grim but grateful looks. So far, they were looking only for Helen, who fortuitously was at the Maryknoll convent next to the school in Buzeta. In other words, both she and Peg Lipsio were far away in one of Santiago's forgotten industrial neighborhoods. We could cling to the story, continue to weave the thread, delay, and not contradict one another by repeating: "She is not here. She's at the beach. We've already told you we don't know where she is."

Still, we didn't dare move, given the machine guns pointed at us. Rather quickly, the guy searching Helen's room came back, holding a Hallmark card taken from her dresser top, sent for her birthday. The front of the card had a blurry black-and-white photo image of a woman looking dreamily out an open window, framed by fluttering curtains.

"Is this her? Is this her photo? Is this what she looks like?" the squad leader asked demandingly.

Taking the card carefully into her hands Paula examined it, ignored the absurdity, and answered with all sincerity, "Yes. Almost. It is almost like Helen."

Then she gently handed the card back to him, maintaining a sober look on her face. Paula contemplated the situation before her. Clearly some of these guards were scarcely educated men, harnessed to do the DINA's dirty work. Two other guards returned after their bedroom searches, having found nothing but an empty, crate-sized corrugated packing box. He kicked it into the front bedroom where we were standing. On one side it had a thick black arrow pointing upwards with lettering saying "This side UP." It was the box Helen's family used to mail her birthday gifts from the United States.

An edgy conscript pointed at the box with the nose of his machine gun, raising his voice, asking suspiciously, "Why do you have this? It says, *¡UP! ¡Unidad Popular!*" Unidad Popular, referred to as the "UP," was the political movement and governing coalition of President Salvador Allende.

Alarmed, Rosita piped up, attempting to overcome this serious misunderstanding. *"No, no. ¡Esta caja tiene letras en inglés! ¡Vea Ud.! ¡Y esta flecha indica la posición en que se debe mantener la caja!"*

Once again, Rosita was the soothing teacher unpacking a mystery for a confused learner. As she spoke, she crouched down and touched the box, explaining how the letters were in English and that the arrow pointed up, to keep the box upright. The conscript eyed the box, then eyed her, uncertain whether he was being played the fool in some sort of cross-cultural game. Shades of humiliation began to surface on his face. He stepped back, said nothing, but looked at her warily. To him the box proved our sedition.

The squad leader then ordered us to get our *cédulas de identidad,* our Chilean identity cards. After a few minutes we were all corralled back into Isabel and Rosita's bedroom, half-sitting, half-standing in a semicircle against their two tossed beds. In front of us the phalanx of machine guns in their arms were at the ready.

Paula was seated to my right. I could feel her body heat, even though it seemed she wasn't breathing. I glanced to my left, where Isabel sat slightly bent forward, her shoulders dropped as if she were relaxed, her folded hands resting on her knees. Her skin was clay colored and looked moist. Her brown eyes were focused intently on the men before her. Rosita was to Isabel's left; her face reflected a seemingly practiced nonchalance. *How could she be so detached and calm?* I wondered. Then I realized she was silently praying. Behind us was the large closet, partially open but not yet searched.

Out of view, in the entry vestibule the guards were talking with someone who just entered. A commander arrived, checking the status of the operation. We could hear an exchange of information in low voices. The squad leader came back into the room and was handed our *cédulas* by an underling. He lifted the first one, studied the picture, perused the rim of faces in front of him, and began the roll call, nodding toward Rosita. "*¿Arroyo?*" he asked.

"*Sí,*" Rosita answered.

Oblivious to the fact that her *cédula* indicated she was a Peruvian citizen and possibly merited further investigation as a foreigner, he placed it back in the pile. He picked the next *cédula*, looked it over carefully and stared at Isabel. Then in a serious and knowing voice he asked her, "*¿Ud. es alemán?*" Are you German?

"*Sí, soy alemán,*" she answered, without a blink.

What? I thought. *You told him you are German but your last name is Donoso?* Undoubtedly it was my last name on the *cédula* he was holding. I was the only one in the room with a German-sounding last name. *What was I going to say when he got to me?*

But I was learning the lessons of power and survival quickly by watching the guards' missteps and the counter moves made by Isabel, Paula, and Rosita. Isabel seemed to be saying, "Stay calm and give them what they want." But, I thought, what if this guy figures out Isabel lied to him? She is a Chilean citizen and comes from a distinguished family, evidenced by her last names. She is the person *most* in danger here, not to mention that they will discover she works for the *Comité Pro Paz*. I knew

I couldn't do or say anything that would risk exposing her. Perspiration started trickling down my sides as I pressed my arms even more tightly against my body.

Suddenly the roll call was interrupted. The squad leader ordered Paula out of the room and into the living room for a one-on-one interrogation with the commander. We could hear his aggressive tone, but couldn't distinguish what was being said. Paula returned to the bedroom after her interrogation with a grave look on her face, but we had no idea of what was unfolding. Right behind her the squad leader pushed back into the room past his conscripts, clearly agitated.

He stared at each of us demanding, "Who here knows Sheila Cassidy?" The cascade of events from yesterday coursed through me. The mere mention of Sheila's name meant she was in imminent danger; so were we. A long silence filled the room.

"I do," I said.

I surmised that during the house search they had found the slip of paper with Sheila's name and address, which I carelessly pulled from my pocket before bed and had left it on my empty desk.

"Come with me!" the squad leader demanded.

I followed him mutely into the living room, my blue flannel nightgown billowing around my calves. The commander of the operation, wearing snug blue jeans and a Levi jacket, stood gripping the telephone with his back to me, listening to a final set of orders. He placed the open telephone receiver down on the round ottoman and turned. He was tall and light-skinned. His blue eyes scrutinized me, and I him.

The eyes of the DINA, I thought. He had soft, light-brown hair. He was young, maybe thirty or a little more. He wanted to know my name, wanted my *cédula*, wanted to know how long I'd been in Chile. He switched easily between Spanish and English. I answered the questions curtly, matching the language used to ask them. His English was perfect, too perfect. I watched his eyes and demeanor, experiencing a devastating truth.

He was an American.

He grabbed the phone and shouted all my data over the live line and waited. I drew back, not able to fully take it in. Naming it would come later. Was he a double agent? CIA or U.S. military special ops? Military trainer? Mercenary? I could see the collusion of forces that deposed the democratically elected Salvador Allende was still in full force.

His connection on the other end shouted something through the phone, which he lifted off the ottoman and pressed to his ear. He grunted agreement. "You are coming with us!" he said to me, slamming the phone and clutching his gun upright in one fluid movement. "Go and get dressed."

I moved a few steps backward, realizing I had to obey. I walked back to my bedroom, pulled tights and slacks out of the closet, insanely thinking of ways to delay, and of feeble attempts to protect myself. I know they will rape me, I thought, but at least I'll make it harder.

I even grabbed makeup, thinking it takes time to put on. I can stall. I went into the bathroom to wash and dress, leaving the door slightly cracked as he ordered me to do. I could hear Paula in the corridor.

"Why are you taking her?" she demanded of the commander. "She's done nothing. She's only been in Chile a few weeks."

"*Madre*, hurry up!" he screamed at me through the bathroom door.

"No more time! You are going!" he yelled from outside the bathroom, ignoring Paula's pleas. I dropped the blue eye shadow into the sink, realizing to delay more was futile. Then I heard him cock his gun.

Behind the bathroom door and in answer to his shouts, I hurriedly threw my toothbrush, toothpaste, a hairbrush, house keys, and *cédula* into a small, woven string purse, an expandable bag made of agave fibers. I had purchased it along the *Ticabus* route from two indigenous women in Panama only three months earlier. For centuries these women survived by pounding the pulp of the succulent plant to harvest its fiber threads, later drying and knotting the threads into nearly unbreakable, ingeniously expandable bags with which they hauled their goods on foot to market.

The brief memory of the women and their arduous survival gave me a touch of courage. I hooked the bag on my shoulder, looked in the mirror one last time, then opened the bathroom door. I was determined to whisper something to Paula before I left. I saw her down the hallway, still arguing with the commander. Her eyes were filled with terror as she looked at me. Her fear ricocheted inside my ribs.

My body was numbing, my spirit detaching. The squad leader started hustling his crew, calling out orders for my departure.

"No! You cannot take her!" Paula said vehemently and squared off against them.

"You cannot take her until we pray over her! This is our sacred Sunday, and you have interrupted it! We are going to pray over her!"

Amid the fury around us, Paula pulled me to her side and maneuvered me around the corner, past the American commander with his gun, into the small chapel. Acting in concert, Rosita and Isabel stepped in, leaving a wake of nervous quiet in the hallway, allowing the hit squad to ponder their nightly deeds, while peering at us through the chapel doorway. Rosita gazed at them disarmingly and said, waving her arm, "You can come in and join us in prayer. But you must leave your machine guns outside."

Feet shuffled, but no one moved.

I had only stepped into this room once; it was on the day I arrived in Chile. Of course, I was free to use it, but I thought of it as the nuns' space, a spot reserved for their private prayer in a home where they welcomed me as their young guest. Now, inside it I felt more than ill at ease. The carpeted room was no bigger than a storage closet, illuminated only by a small table lamp. Centering the room was a low table draped with a woven cloth. A crucifix hung on the wall with an open Bible on the table below. Next to the Bible was the Blessed Sacrament inside a copper box adorned with the lapis lázuli stones.

Having accomplished her daring maneuver, Paula released a long sigh and then began to string loving words into a heartfelt prayer. She poured them forth like frothy water, trying to calm the feverish nerves pulsing under our skin. Paula prayed like a charismatic evangelist. She prayed fervently in Spanish, caressing its poetic soul. I knew she believed in the words she spoke. She believed in a prayer's fruition in spite of the surrounding futility. She knew this might be the last moment we would all be together.

She ended her prayers with, *"Padre Nuestro que estás en los cielos. Santificado sea Tu Nombre . . . ,"* and we joined her in saying the Our Father.

Memorized, rote, familiar, and often soothing, the prayer is full of complexities, of duties, of anguish and longing for nourishment of daily bread, of confidence that both bread and forgiveness will be given if we willingly give of ourselves, of hope for a reign of justice on earth as it is in heaven, and of restraint in the face of temptation. All of us gathered knew the prayer was spoken and shared from the depths of Jesus's own inner experience and relationship with God.

I felt dazed. The DINA were restless. They weren't going to let us linger. I wanted desperately to whisper something to Paula before I was pulled away. Calmed somewhat by the prayer and the momentary presence near my housemates, I tried reciting it along with them, but my thoughts kept darting around until I heard the thudding pulse of the prayer's finality—"Deliver us from evil."

Evil. The word rang in my ears as Paula stepped toward the altar and opened the copper box. She lifted out a Communion wafer and placed it in my opened hands. I took it and swallowed it, then embraced her and whispered, "They have Sheila."

If she heard me, she didn't react. Rosita and Isabel followed me and received Communion too.

Paula had barely swallowed her host, before we heard the commander yell, "That's it! You are leaving now!"

I was ordered out of the room and pushed out the front door, separated from my housemates, surrounded by guards with their machine guns pointed forward. I tried to steady myself on the sidewalk. I scanned the block, wondering if there would be a witness. But I could see only the emptiness perfectly imposed by the curfew. Up and down both sides of the block, there were no signs of life. Heavy curtains fully drawn covered nearby windows. Almost no cars were parked on the street.

"Great," I thought. "Nighttime in a national security state. No one dare notice."

A half block away, nothing moved on the broad Av. Matta either. Always frenetic by day, now it seemed like a glowing, distant mirage, where streetlights cast shadows on shuttered storefronts, then spilled down onto the opaque asphalt, creating glinting pools of light.

In front of our house sat a convoy of vehicles. There were at least three white, unmarked four-door Fiats and a military truck or two. The back hatches were being shoved closed, disturbing the night with their clanging chains.

The commander gave his last orders, "Lock this door. You are not to leave." Then he added cynically, speaking in a mocking voice to Paula, "Don't worry, *Madre*, I'll bring her back."

I didn't turn to look at their faces. I was a prisoner in the hands of the DINA now. There was nothing anyone could do.

"Get in the car!" came the command. "Behind the driver."

Escorted off the sidewalk and around the Fiat, I folded myself into the back seat, driver's side. My hands gripped my woven purse. Doors started to slam. The military truck at the front of the convoy revved up and headed off. The Fiat in front of us loaded up. Four guys. Four machine guns. Three guys with machine guns filled in the seats around me. The DINA squad leader, seated in the front passenger seat, turned to look at me and propped his weapon over the seat pointing it at me. Ditto the guy to my right. Keys turned in the ignition in a kind of clumsy symphony of fired-up Fiats, each motor of the convoy synced with the others, as they lurched away from the curb. They sped up to the corner of Av. Matta and swung to the right without the need to stop, check traffic, or sound a siren. They ruled the night and the road.

I wondered where were they taking me, then realized I should watch for landmarks and street signs. No sooner had we made the turn when a *venda*, a kerchief blindfold, was tossed over the front seat. I was gruffly commanded: "Put it on! Tightly!"

I did as I was told, leaving only a sliver of space between my lower eyelids and my cheeks from which to orient myself. Blindfolded, I barely moved or breathed. I didn't talk. I acted compliantly. So far no one had touched me.

Blindfolded I spoke to God with a directness and sincerity I had never conceived of before, tasting in my mouth the host barely swallowed. Silently, I prayed:

God, I don't think I have much longer to live.
You know the situation and reality are grave and dangerous. I have
    absolutely no knowledge or power to act or change this destiny.
I surrender.
I surrender myself to you.

Only you know what is needed now. I may only be able to speak a few
more words. Make them your words, true words.
Speak through me. Save my friends. Help my family understand.

Upon uttering the words "I surrender," I felt for the first time in
my life an immediacy, a depth of communion, as a profound consola-
tion spilled over me. In that moment, I experienced God. I experienced
an inviolable knowing of God, infinitely present to me. A precious calm
soothed me. The physical sensation lasted long enough for me to intuit
that God encompassed all of me. It lasted long enough for me to express
gratitude. Whatever might transpire, I knew God would not depart. In
surrendering I was joined. That the physical sensations did not last long,
or that mentally I might soon dissolve into a bundle of legitimate fears,
didn't matter. The unshakable knowing undergirded everything.

At the moment of this brimming, luminous awareness, I felt a clamor
inside my head telling me that if I had any chance of getting out of this
alive, I needed to stay alert. I tried to press every sensation into a memory,
squeeze it to help orient me and keep me safe. Unable to see, I could feel
my eyelashes bent against the cotton blindfold, while my eyes remained
open staring into darkness. My ears attuned; every sense heightened.

The car had traveled only some distance when it jerked, making me
slide toward the gunman on the seat beside me. I righted myself and
scooted back quickly to my spot, touched my blindfold to secure it against
any accusations that I was trying to see where we were.

I had no idea where this car could be headed. But, sensing the intensity of the driver in front of me, I knew he was speeding toward a known
destination. We traveled a few more miles on an expansive and eerily
silent street. I heard only the friction of the convoy's tires on the pavement, sounding as if it were a night breeze. No one spoke directly to me,
but the tone of some muttered words between the driver and the gunman
in the front seat made me clench my teeth.

Before long I heard the driver of the first car in the convoy grind
the brakes as it veered off the asphalt across a short cinder drive, and up
onto an embankment. The car I was in followed, abruptly crunching its
wheels to a stop on the rocky ground. I could hear several guards greeting
the men from the convoy when a few of them stepped out and slammed

their car doors shut. The sound of breaking gravel underneath their feet allowed me to trace each footstep. They didn't take many steps.

From the back seat of the car, beneath the blindfold, I heard the loud scraping of a heavy metal gate as it was manually pulled open over the cinders. Several of the men from the lead car continued talking and entered the gated area on foot, their voices evaporating into the interior enclosure. My heart palpitated. I suspected we were at the infamous Villa Grimaldi, an old estate on the far edge of Santiago, near *Peñalolén*. It had been commandeered after the *golpe* as a torture center—a place known for its barbaric treatment of political prisoners who were held *incommunicado* in decrepit conditions.

A guard from the car I was in got out and walked away, leaving the car door wide open. A chill air entered. I could hear footsteps around the car. Maybe they were having a smoke; perhaps others were coming by to have a look at me? Then someone slid in the car and began to question me in Spanish.

"How long have you been in Chile?" he asked with a dryly curious voice, trying to warm up the interrogation.

"Only a couple of months," I replied.

"Why are you here in Chile?" he wanted to know. "You speak good Spanish," he said, half-flattering and half-impugning me. I guess he thought that if I had only been in Chile a short time, I couldn't be fluent.

"I studied it in college," I said flatly.

"So where is Helen?" he snarled at me.

I blinked, feeling the crush of my eyelashes behind the blindfold and retorted testily, "I've told you. We've all told you. She is away, somewhere on the coast."

"It is not very responsible to leave and no one knows where you are," he tossed back.

"I don't know. What can I tell you? We live together and have a lot of trust." I answered, using the ruse that I was a member of the SSND community. Then I said to him, "You have a family, don't you?"

I purposely paused, hoping the question would jolt his conscience. Then I pressed on, saying, "I suppose it is just like in your family. I am sure there is a lot of trust. You don't always know exactly where they are, but you trust them."

"She is your mother superior, isn't she? Shouldn't she tell you where she is going?"

"Perhaps you are right. But like I said, we live in a community and just like in a family, there is trust between people."

I paused again to determine if I could go on. "Most likely you are married. I'm sure your wife trusts you. Even though perhaps you haven't told her where you are or what you are doing tonight." Then I took a deep breath. I knew I was paring too close to his conscience and macho bones, but hoped he might back off.

A momentary quiet fell. I sensed the presence of the guards outside the car getting nervous. Even while I spoke, I couldn't lessen the insistent voice inside my head running on another track. *Are they going to pull me out of this car? Are they going to take me inside this place? This must be where they are holding Sheila. Is she being tortured? Will I be tortured?*

I had heard about the clandestine practices of the DINA documented by the *Comité Pro Paz,* from Isabel and others. Dissenters picked up by the DINA tried to hold out for twenty-four hours, not naming names and giving false addresses. In the same time period their family, friends, and colleagues who might be compromised by their detention would immediately take cover. Their children would be hidden, so that the DINA could not use them as pawns. When a tortured prisoner gave up a name, those they named would be swiftly apprehended, dragged into the same cell, and tortured simultaneously.

I doubted I could hold out for twenty-four hours. Especially since the DINA ratcheted up their torture swiftly, afraid that the prey they were really after would have time to get away. Then I heard several rushing feet coming toward the car over the gravel driveway. *This is it*, I thought, breathing rapidly with my heart racing.

One of the squad members ordered the guard who was questioning me to get out of the car. He slid in, leaned over the front seat, and said commandingly, "Do you know where the Maryknoll Sisters' house is in Los Leones?"

My body went rigid hearing the word "Maryknoll," fearing they could close in on Helen Nelson in Buzeta. "Where?" I answered in disbelief.

"The Maryknoll Sisters' house! Will you take us there?" he barked.

I didn't move. Obviously, they had some new piece of information. Things were unraveling. The DINA wasn't going to rest until they knew who had aided the MIR fugitives. Then I realized they were asking for the Maryknoll Sisters Center, *not* the Maryknoll convent in Buzeta next to the school where I taught and where Helen was spending the night. I remembered from the telephone conversation I had with Peg Lipsio before I went to bed that both she and Helen were in Buzeta because the rest of the Maryknoll sisters were on retreat in El Quisco.

Why not take them? I thought to myself. *They don't have the exact address, but they knew the intersection. Maybe no one will be there. But if I go, maybe one of the sisters will recognize me and realize that everyone in my house is in danger. Even if I'm captive, maybe the others can be helped.*

"Yes," I said firmly. "I will take you there."

Feet scrambled, doors slammed, and the car took off. When the Fiat hit the main road, I heard a bit more traffic around us, and from the crescent-like slit at the bottom of my blindfold, daylight emerged.

Encountering the dawn and a lifting curfew, they drove madly. When the car approached the intersection of Bilbao and Los Leones, they told me to take off my blindfold. Wasting no time, I pulled it off and tossed it on to the floor of the car.

"Where is the Maryknoll Center?" the driver brusquely asked, eyeing me in the rear-view mirror. I shook my head, trying to regain my orientation to the daylight.

"It's nearby," I said.

I had been there only once. I recalled being struck by the modernity of the neighborhood, comprising upscale homes, professional offices, and some embassies. One feature of the Maryknoll Center stood out in my mind; I prayed it would help me to pick it out again. The two-story house, used for administrative offices, community gatherings, and respite for the sisters and their visitors, had a strikingly broad frontage set behind a wrought-iron fence. It had almost no front yard. Instead, beautiful manicured hedges and flowering bushes arced its semi-circular drive, which was uniquely paved with upturned, palm-sized river stones.

Spying the stones, I exclaimed, "There it is."

The car swerved toward the driveway, but couldn't enter the partially open wrought-iron gate. Before the car came to a full stop, I jumped out and briskly walked through the gate's narrowed opening. I stooped to pick up the Sunday edition of *El Mercurio,* which lay in the driveway. I reached the front door before the DINA did. Sr. Katherine Gilfeather answered the doorbell, shocked at seeing me and the DINA.

I had met Sr. Katherine, a sociologist, who worked at CISOC, which was part of the Jesuit-run institute, Centro Bellarmino.[1] Seizing the only opportunity I had to keep the DINA off Helen's path, I blurted out, "Sr. Katherine, the DINA came to our house this morning looking for Helen Nelson, but she went to the coast this weekend." I wanted to keep the decoy going, hoping that Helen would get to safety before the DINA grabbed her.

Sr. Katherine showed amazing composure. She looked at me and said firmly, "Kathy, go inside. Go to the kitchen."

She took the newspaper from my hand and pressed me through the door, physically blocking the entryway with her body, keeping the DINA at bay as they scrambled up to the front door with their weapons.

I stepped into the hallway, where a decorative screen partitioned the entry from the living room immediately behind it. Realizing that the DINA hadn't gotten in, I ran down the hallway toward the kitchen. I said a quick hello to Angelita, the sisters' housekeeper. In the kitchen was Fr. Brian Smith, a young Jesuit priest, whom I had met once while doing home visits in the *población* with Connie.

I greeted him with a swift embrace, unleashing a string of staccato directives in a low voice: "Brian, the DINA is at the front door." He looked at me stunned. He stepped back and braced himself against the kitchen counter. I continued, speaking urgently, knowing time was precious. I told him the DINA came to our house this morning to arrest Sr. Helen Nelson. She wasn't there so they took me, because I said I knew Sheila Cassidy. Something has happened to Sheila, I told him. Everyone from our house is in danger. I urged him to call Gerardo Whelan and the Holy Cross priests in Lo Barnechea to tell them they are in danger.

I backed away from him, feeling I had accomplished my mission. Now at least someone else knew what happened and could alert others. I watched his face seeking some response. He looked back at me blankly. I felt destroyed. Nothing had registered.

I walked back into the corridor and could now plainly see the living and dining rooms on either side of the partition. The DINA had not yet pushed themselves into the house. Sr. Katherine kept stalling them at the front door, questioning them as to their business, denying their authority to enter.

At the far end of the corridor, behind the partition, I peered into a commodious living room, where against the far wall, a set of stairs rose toward the second-floor bedrooms. I saw buffed shoes descending the stairs. They were worn by two North American men, each over six feet tall. I couldn't believe my eyes.

Before I could think, one said to me, "Hello ma'am!" in the most exuberant voice.

Friendly and eagerly trying to strike up a conversation, they asked how I knew the sisters. Totally taken aback, but keeping my eye on the rising voices in the foyer. I distractedly asked, "What brought you to Chile?"

"Ma'am, we are here with our wives. We came to adopt a Chilean baby!" As they walked toward me and shook my hand, they told me they were friends of Fr. Brian, who arranged their stay with the sisters.[2] Then they stepped across the corridor toward the dining room.

Simultaneously, the DINA pushed their way past Sr. Katherine and barged into the entryway. When the six-foot-tall men saw the DINA with their machine guns, they dove under the dining room table. In the same instant, I glanced back toward the stairwell and saw two well-dressed women descending the stairs.

"She is leaving with us!" one of the DINA said angrily, pointing his machine gun at me from only a yard or so away.

I knew they would pull me out of there if I tried to resist. Sr. Katherine attempted to step in front of the DINA, but could only get so far. Blocked by them, she said to me in an insistent voice, "Kathy, why don't you go back into the kitchen? Please stay for breakfast."

She repeated it more than once, but I did not move. My brain seemed to freeze, solidify like concrete. Breakfast? Why is she talking about breakfast? I couldn't process the cues she tossed my way. Not done with the DINA yet, she was determined to keep me on the premises.

The DINA boss butted in, "No! She is coming with us. We promised her *Madre Superiora* we would bring her back!"

I moved toward them, not because I believed them, but because I was their prisoner. I had complied and brought the DINA to the Maryknoll Sisters Center. I had also delivered my urgent message and plea. At that moment I felt there was no way out of the DINA's all-powerful vise, and I wanted no one else in the Maryknoll house to be similarly harmed.

The DINA guards closed in behind me and marched me out the door and back into the Fiat. I never looked back at Sr. Katherine. I didn't want to feel her fears, see her face crumple, or her tears of defeat.

They ordered me to put my blindfold back on. I did as commanded. The driver punched the accelerator and cut out to the street. I don't remember ever hearing orders for my return coming over a radio frequency, but perhaps new orders had been given. Slumped against the back-passenger window I gave up any attempt to keep myself oriented, assuming I'd be taken again to the detention center with the iron *portón*. I expected to hear it scraping across the gravel at any minute, but this time I'd be taken inside. I felt dead.

Seven to ten minutes passed before the driver spoke to me again.

"*¡Quítese la venda! Estamos llegando.*" He abruptly ordered me to take off my blindfold. I did so as he hooked a U-turn in front of my house and, just then, I threw open the car door and jumped out!

I ran to the front door and rang the bell. No one answered. I pulled my house key from the woven purse and pressed it into the lock, turning it enough to hear the mechanism drop. The door wouldn't open. The latch bolt had been secured from inside. I instantly knew that Paula, Isabel, and Rosita had fled out through the back patio. I felt relieved that they had gotten away, but scared for myself.

Seeing my futile efforts to re-enter the house, the squad leader came up behind me yelling at me, "I told them not to leave! Where are they? They were not to leave the house!"

Anger surged inside of me and I yelled back, "Well, it is Sunday and they went to Mass! And that's where I'm going now too!"

I pulled away from the door and started to run toward San Andrés, the parish church on the corner. He jumped in front of me, cornering me against the wall, saying, "No! No, you cannot go! You have to sign this." He waved a paper in front of my face. "You have to sign this saying we did not harm you."

I glared at him. How dare he. No harm? He shoved the smudged paper with some official emblems on it into my hands. He told me to write on the other side. My eyes wouldn't focus. I couldn't sign it.

I held the grimy arrest warrant for Helen Nelson. Touching it I almost collapsed on the sidewalk overcome by the farce. To add my name to this warrant would condone it, dignify a system of surreptitious night searches, disappearances, torture, and death. What if they found Helen? Undoubtedly, they'd figure some way to use this against her. I would be betraying a selfless religious woman who had risked her life to keep others from being killed on the spot without due process or a right to defend themselves. I didn't want to add another lie to this masquerade meant to keep the dictatorship and national security state intact.

"We are not going to let you go unless you sign it!"

Three of them surrounded me now, pinning me to the wall. They shoved a pen into my hand. Touching the pen, a wave of nausea rocked me. I felt sick with betrayal and collusion. They dictated to me the words I needed to write on the warrant: "I voluntarily sign this saying I was not harmed."

I caved. I scrawled it out and signed it, guilt-ridden. They scattered hurriedly as many parishioners, leaving the morning Mass, began streaming around the corner and down the block. The DINA, a covert agency, certainly didn't want to be seen outside the convent, much less at the pastor's residence next door, where they had me against the wall. They thrust their machine guns inside the Fiat and bolted away. I ran up the block and through the crowd.

Where could I go and be safe? I had no idea how to reconnect with my housemates. Even if I could use a public telephone, I had no money on me, and all calls were potentially monitored. Moreover, I had no idea where the others might have fled. Everything—money, phone numbers, clothes—was inside the locked house. Many other religious homes, especially those in the *poblaciones*, were constantly under surveillance. Ticking off names and places in my head, I felt very scared and alone. Having been identified, captured, and released by the DINA, I felt my very presence would endanger them.

Overwhelmed with the terror of the morning, I stepped inside San Andrés for the first time, since on Sundays I mostly went to Mass in Lo

Baranechea. I was surprised by its brightness as the morning sun poured into its airy spaces. Here and there clusters of parishioners chatted quietly. Toward the right-side altar, several knelt in prayer near a stand of vigil candles. I moved toward them, wanting to pray for guidance and express my gratitude for being released.

I knelt in a pew a few rows away from the altar and vigil lights, trying to calm my thoughts. Barely beginning to pray myself, I glanced at those kneeling in front of the vigil lights and noticed the back of a smallish woman wearing a loosely knit alpaca sweater. She was praying fervently.

Utterly shocked, I recognized Rosita and ran to her, tapping her shoulder.

"¡Kathy! ¡No lo puedo creer!" she exclaimed in disbelief and joy, jumping up to hug me. We immediately hushed our voices as others turned their heads to look at us.

"Ven, ven," she said urging me to come with her to see Paula, who was down a hallway and around the corner in the rectory office.

When we entered, Paula was on the phone with her back to us, giving a detailed report to Josiah Brownell, the U.S. consul. She relayed to Brownell the DINA's dawn raid, their arrest warrant for Helen Nelson, and taking me captive. Sensing something, Paula pivoted, turning pale in astonishment when she saw me with Rosita.

Paula sputtered nearly incoherently into the phone, "Oh my God, she's here! Kathy's here. She's back!" Consul Brownell immediately asked her to put me on the line.

I drew back when Paula handed me the phone. I wasn't sure what to divulge. When Brownell began to ask me questions, all I could see in my mind's eye was the tall, light-skinned DINA commander, his soft light-brown hair, blue eyes, dressed in Levis, who spoke like an American.

What do they need to know from me? I thought in disgust. *The United States has an agent in this detention and torture game. He is making a report to someone at the embassy or the CIA right now.*

I answered the consul's questions testily: My name, where I was born. Had I registered with the embassy? Why was I in Chile? What happened this morning? What time? How many guards? Were they *carabineros*? What uniforms did they wear? What did they say? Did they harm you? Brownell kept going, preparing the incident report that would be cabled to the State Department.[3] I felt exhausted, confused, and no safer when I handed the phone back to Paula.

Paula answered a few more questions, then hung up the phone, staring at me. "What happened to you? How did you get back here?" she asked, still in disbelief.

I couldn't explain why I was brought back, but I told her the DINA kept me blindfolded, took me to a place I thought was a prison, where they had Sheila, but didn't take me inside. Then they wanted me to take them to the Maryknoll Sisters Center, where I saw Sr. Katherine Gilfeather. I hoped if someone saw me, they would realize you and others were in danger.

"Where is Isabel?" I wanted to know.

"Right after you left with the DINA, she left for Buzeta to warn Helen and Peg. I hope she got there in time," Rosita said anxiously.

Paula interrupted the debriefing. "We've got to get away from the house. Rosita, can you take Kathy and go to someone's house for a few nights?"

Rosita offered, "Yes, we can go to see the sisters in San Francisco. I think they'll let us stay."

"Good," said Paula. "I'll find a way to be in touch with you both there." And then she continued saying rapidly that she would try to send a message to Bernadette, who was in El Tabo. Now, the three of us needed to run back into the house through the back door, since the front of the house might be under surveillance. No curtains should be opened. We should be in and out in five minutes, grab a change of clothes, some money, our *cédulas,* and passports. It's going on ten o'clock; she warned, they'll be coming back.

Dread came over me as we stepped across the rectory patio and re-entered our property through the back gate. Yesterday's wash was still clipped to the clothesline, including Rosita's jeans. She snapped a pair off the line leaving the rest, then ran into the house and through the kitchen with us.

As I darted back toward my room, I could see the upheaval from the early morning raid. The living room furniture had been shoved around, the clay-colored ottoman tipped over, and the telephone was off the hook, disassembled, its mouthpiece unscrewed and missing. I rushed into my bedroom and grabbed a nightgown, some underwear, and another top. My carry-all bag was in the closet. I dumped the string bag with its possessions into it, checked for my passport and money. Fortunately, we had just been paid on Friday, so we'd have enough to move around.

I scanned the room to see if I'd forgotten anything important. There on my desk, undisturbed, was the slip of paper with Sheila's name and address on it alongside the poem booklet she had given me, her inked signature visible. I was wrong. The DINA had *never* seen them. I picked them up carefully, hesitated at seeing Sheila's signature, then hid them deep in my bag and exited the room with it over my shoulder.

The three of us met up in the kitchen, clicked off the lights, and locked both the kitchen door and back gate as we slipped over to the rectory. Back in the pastor's office, Paula reviewed the plan and promised to stay in touch. We were saying our goodbyes when the pastor, Padre Humberto Muñoz, entered. Paula thanked him profusely for the use of the phone. She introduced me as the "missing sister," informing him she had spoken to the U.S. Embassy and that we would be staying elsewhere for a few days.

Fr. Humberto responded, *"¡No, No! No es necesario! ¡Quédense aquí! Por lo menos quédense un ratito más para comer algo."* He wanted to keep us from leaving, reassuring us it wasn't necessary; we should just stay and have something to eat. Though we appreciated his generosity, we politely said we had to get going.

In a kindly voice he turned and looked at me, speaking paternally, *"¿Por qúe no viniste a hablar conmigo antes? Te hubiera protegido. ¡No te van a llevar de aquí!"* Tears came to my eyes as I listened to his kind but innocent utterance. "Why didn't you come and speak with me earlier? I would have protected you. They can't take you from here!"

He was speaking as if he still lived in a democratic Chile subject to law, or at least in a country where a pastor's persuasion held sway.

We decided to leave separately, hoping to draw less attention as we exited through streets that were filling up with families out doing Sunday shopping. Paula suggested Rosita and I leave first, through the church entrance and out on to Av. Matta, while she deliberated whether to follow us or try the back route via passageways that eventually opened out on to Av. Matta.

My anxiety was surging. I needed to get going, to move, if only to physically shed some of the tension inside of me. More quick goodbyes; then Rosita and I left via the church vestibule, slipping through the crowd of parishioners arriving for the ten o'clock Mass. We walked briskly down Matta and jumped on the first bus we saw coming, glancing around to see if anyone followed us as we climbed aboard.

So far, we had escaped. Unbeknownst to us, nearly at the same moment, the DINA returned to our house and pounded on the door, this time with an arrest warrant for Paula.

20

No Place to Hide before the Nation

Rosita and I spent the next three hours riding random buses, often to the end of their routes. Then we'd reboard them, pretending we were lost or had chosen the wrong route. We passed the time squeezed shoulder to shoulder on the bench seats with small talk and occasional whispered questions like, "Do you think Isabel reached Helen in time? Has Paula found some place to stay? How can we reach Bernadette?"

We didn't dare discuss even in whispers what had transpired that morning, fearful of being overheard by *soplónes*, the plainclothes security agents who regularly boarded the buses. For my part, I was crumbling inside and weepy, flooded by trauma. Rosita saw me tearing up and turned to me asking, *"¿Estás bien?"* Are you okay?

In the midst of all the anxiety, I felt extremely grateful to Rosita for caring about how I was doing and for her willingness to shepherd us to some safe spot, especially since by my presence I endangered her. Nonetheless, Rosita exuded cheer and confidence. As always, she had a plan in mind. We would kill time until around one o'clock, arriving at the convent of the Immaculate Heart of Mary (IHM) Sisters on the outskirts of Santiago, just after their noontime lunch. I knew enough about Rosita's history with the IHM sisters to wonder about our welcome. But Rosita remained close friends with three of the IHM sisters, Edwardina, Teresita, and Martita, who still taught at San Francisco, their primary school adjacent to the convent.

I don't think it occurred to us to stop and eat, but we were famished and depleted when we stepped off the bus. All around us the air smelled fresh, and the tree buds looked ripe, requiring only a few more days of sunshine to burst open. The convent and school were located in the eastern zone of Santiago, in the foothills of the ascending Andes.

Woodsy and secluded were the impressions that came to mind as I tried to take in the surroundings. As we walked along the road toward the sisters' house, I could see Chile's poverty hidden away among trees and down a ravine. There, children in tattered clothes played outside their roughly assembled homes, perched precariously on the sloping terrain. Looking down the hill I saw a landscape of patched zinc roofs and clotheslines stretched among the trees, which demarcated each family's lot. The smell of smoke from wood-burning fires scented the air. Tucked in here and there were a few middle-class homes with a car in the driveway.

The IHM convent was a sturdily built, honey-toned ranch house with many windows. It sat on a large lot, hemmed in on three sides by enormous pine trees. As Rosita rang the bell, she spoke to me reassuringly, "You are going to like Madre Edwardina, *es un amor.*"

Rather swiftly the doorbell was answered, and Madre Edwardina was summoned. Edwardina, a tall, slender woman in her late thirties, seemed genuinely surprised to see Rosita on her doorstep and warmly greeted us.

"*¡Tanto tiempo!*" Edwardina said to Rosita, teasing her that it had been too long.

Some of the other sisters, hearing Rosita's voice, came into the living room and gave her excited hugs. She quickly introduced me as her friend and told them about my connection with the Holy Cross priests through the Notre Dame program, layering me with some legitimacy in their eyes, as the IHM sisters had shared ministries with the priests over the years.

Rosita pushed past the awkwardness of our unexplained visit as best she could, saying her visit was overdue, but wanted to show me the school where she had once taught. The nuns looked puzzled, but let it pass as Rosita teased them about past events, leading to lots of laughter.

Sisters Edwardina, Teresita, and Martita stayed with us while refreshments were carried in by other sisters, who soon excused themselves. For most of the next hour I ate from the platter of food and watched the conversation. After a while I could see Rosita growing a bit strained, in spite of all her chattiness. She was looking for an opportunity to speak privately with Edwardina about why we were really there. "Let me take these plates into the kitchen and wash them," Rosita said, prompting Edwardina to reply, "No, no, we'll take care of that!"

"Well, at least let me help," Rosita said, standing up and gathering cups, following Edwardina into the kitchen.

When they came back into the living room, Edwardina asked Martita and Teresita if they wouldn't mind setting up the guest bedroom, since we would be spending the night. Exchanging quizzical looks, they both stood up, saying, "*¡Qué bien!*"

They acted as if it were the most wonderful, albeit unexpected, request, then left to prepare the room. We entered the bedroom with great relief, placing our bulging carry-all shoulder bags on the twin beds. Edwardina took her leave, saying she was going to rest and that she'd see us later for dinner. Thanking her and closing the door, I felt exhausted, but couldn't just fall on the bed. Instead, I asked Rosita anxiously, "What did you tell her? Is everything okay?"

Rosita answered reflectively, "Look, I didn't want to say too much, because we really don't have any idea of what will happen, and it isn't to anyone's advantage to know very much."

She thought for a moment, then listed all the unknowns: the safety of Helen and the whereabouts of Paula, Bernadette, and Isabel. She thought we might be gone for only a few days. The main thing was to figure out a way to get back in contact with them. We might hear from Paula, who knew where we were. Or Isabel might have a better handle on how dangerous the situation was from her colleagues at the *Comité Pro Paz* and find a way to contact us.

As she talked, my mind seemed to be slowing down to a freeze. I was going into a kind of delayed shock. Never in my life had I been in a threatening situation like this before, where my ability to process information or formulate a path forward was so compromised. Hearing Rosita's reflections, I recognized her intact judgment, her ability to moderate each step, holding forth the top priority: reconnecting and getting the facts of the situation before determining any other steps. I felt so indebted to her, but couldn't find a way to say it. My thoughts and speech began disconnecting. I just stared across the small, curtained room to where she sat on her bed. She tried to cheer me up, saying, "*¡Mira, es un milagro que estás aquí! ¡Te soltaron! Por ahora estamos bien.*" Look, it's a miracle you are here! They released you! For now, we are fine.

I knew all of it was true, but we weren't out of danger. In the next few hours, I showered, dressed in the same clothes, and rested. Rosita slipped out of the room to speak with Madre Edwardina, then came back to nap. When she awoke, Rosita spoke quietly across the space between our two beds. *"Oye, Kathy. ¿Estás despierta? ¿Sabes qué estaba pensando? ¿Qué va a pasar mañana con los niños?"*

Uppermost in Rosita's mind at this moment were her little students. Who would be there to teach them tomorrow? How were Gerry and Helen going to cover all our classrooms, with Helen, Paula, Rosita, and me out? How would they explain our absence?

Frankly, this was a set of worries I hadn't thought about yet. Rosita was incredibly conscientious as a teacher and so gifted, while I still struggled in the classroom. She delighted in each child and their progress, pouring out all her energy for them. She stayed late most days to work with special-needs students, talk to their parents, and revise her plans for the next day. Seeing Rosita in action, you'd wish to be six years old again to enter the fun.

We talked about school and the kids until we heard stirrings in the house as some of the sisters began to prepare supper. We hung back until all the sisters had been informed that we were staying over—and to avoid the unspoken questions about our arrival.

"Would you like to come to dinner?" Madre Edwardina called out as she tapped on our door. We sprang from our beds and entered the kitchen with her. The lights had been turned on in the house. But out the kitchen window I could see a few blinks of daylight, until dusk diminished into night.

Observing the IHM sisters, I noticed how much more North American the atmosphere felt inside this kitchen than in our home on Calle Orellana. What accounted for it? For starters, the IHM sisters still dressed in modified habits and wore short veils. They seemed to range in age from thirty to fifty and included sisters from Chile, Bolivia, and the United States. But it was something else, maybe the full sets of matching plates instead of the mixed sizes and patterns in our cupboards? Maybe the newer tabletop appliances, spices, or brand-name products that I saw on the tidy counters, most likely carried back in suitcases from the States?

I couldn't put my finger on it, but somehow it felt so familiar, yet at the same time disorienting. The dinner menu would be a special treat, hamburgers, with fries and Heinz ketchup—not tomato paste from a can—on *soft* hamburger buns. Famished as I was, I couldn't wait for them to be served.

We were invited into the dining area as hamburgers were put on to fry. The aroma from the kitchen smelled delicious. In short order, everything was carried in on platters and placed in the center of the long table, which seated about twelve. A brief prayer of gratitude was recited for the food and for "our two visiting friends." While saying amen, everyone on cue took their seats and began to pass around the food.

As our plates filled up, one sister rose to turn on the television, which started as usual with the loud, snowy noise and the blaring alert signal. The buzzer didn't even irritate me. I was so hungry and had the hamburger up to my mouth, taking the first savory bite, when the anchor shouted out the headline news: "Three Communist nuns being sought as MIR collaborators in the Malloco shoot-out case!" Up came the names and photos of Helen Nelson, Paula Armstrong, and Peg Lipsio. Instantly, the hamburger inside my mouth turned to ash.

I could barely swallow. A bolt of terror shot through me. Right before us on the television screen the outlines of the story unfolded with innuendos and lies. The report tossed wild accusations against the nuns. They were presumed to be longtime collaborators of the MIR militants. Photos posted on the screen reinforced the accusations made by the government. To wit, a photo of the locked front door on Padre Orellana was "the sinister front door to the Communist convent." Photos taken from the roof peering into our back patio "proved" the blue jeans drying on the line were worn by MIR fighters who had been hidden by the nuns in this "safe house." The nuns' names and their religious communities were repeated over and over.

The sensational report ended with a declaration by the security forces: "These nuns are on the run and in hiding! We will be going door to door, to every convent and rectory, until they are found! Anyone who aids them will be culpable and detained!"

Rosita and I looked at each other. There would be no hiding before a whole nation. For a moment we were mute, contemplating the fate of our friends, should they be detected by the security forces. The intimidating threat to search every convent was lost on no one. Our hosts, the IHM sisters, looked to us for some explanation.

After a breathless silence, Rosita broke the ice. "Let me tell you what truly happened." Then she paused. "Not everything in that report is true. It is true that we gave shelter for a week to members of the MIR. It was something asked of us through high channels of the church. It was a difficult week, but afterwards they were brought to an embassy, in the hopes that they could get medical treatment and that their lives would be saved." Rosita spoke simply and earnestly, pausing to let the sisters take it all in. "Naturally, the DINA has been looking for them and anyone who helped them. Right now, what worries me most from seeing this report are the lives of Helen, Paula, and Peg. They are in grave danger."

Then she told them about the DINA's dawn raid and the arrest warrant for Helen, who wasn't home. She described the DINA's rough behavior and the machine guns pointed at us. Then she said, "The DINA took Kathy prisoner for a few hours."

Rosita slowed as the sisters turned to look at me. I couldn't meet their eyes.

"It was horrible!" Rosita said. "We knew we had to leave the house for a few days, and that's why we came here. We didn't tell you all these details because it would be more dangerous for you to know them. But now that everything is on television and in the open, we want you to know the risk you are taking to have us here."

The sisters listened intently, sometimes shifting in their seats upon hearing a particular detail. No one ate. The dinner plates looked identical with piles of cold fries and uneaten hamburgers stacked atop them, as if they were Andy Warhol prints. Outside the dining room, the darkness blackened the trees. The curfew would be in effect soon.

Rosita spoke as a friend to trusting friends, wanting them to know she would fully understand any decision they might make. I wondered to myself, *What we would do if they asked us to leave?*

Edwardina's eyes roamed the table, taking the wordless pulse of the group, before saying, "No. Absolutely not! It is not a problem! You will be staying here with us until we can find you another safe place to stay."

This was followed by a reassuring echo of similar sentiments from the other sisters.

Before anyone left the table, a few fundamental rules were put in place. Since Rosita had lived and taught with the IHM sisters in the school next door, she was well known to the school's families and personnel. It was determined that the two of us should limit our movements in the house during the daytime, and never go outside. Under no circumstance should anyone mention that we were staying there. With that agreed upon, the sisters got up, gave us hugs and more reassurances. Then they scurried about to clear the table and quickly wash the dishes.

We slipped in and out of the common bathroom quickly so as not to disturb their nightly rituals. Back in the bedroom we whispered our fears and parsed the television news.

Terror kept me awake. My mind whirled, reeling in the darkness around me. Fears and memories of the last few days tramped around my head. In bed I pressed my tense body up against the outside wall. Inches above my face the bottom edge of pinch-pleat curtains brushed over my nose as I squirmed, drawing blankets around my shoulders. I stared through the darkness watching the door on the other side of the room, wondering if the DINA would make good on its threat to "immediately search every church, rectory, and convent for collaborators." *Will they come through the window and seize us? What if they're on their way right now?* All night, outside the window I could hear crunching sounds, the scratching and digging of night creatures in the woods, amplified amid absolute stillness.

The Day of the Dead was over.

PART VII
SOLIDARITY
NOVEMBER 3–8, 1975

21

Another Fiat and Solidarity

I awoke feeling dead. Overnight, the depth of evil crept too close. Yet just beyond the bedroom door sounds of the nuns' slippered feet swished past. The thump of kitchen cabinets, the light clatter of breakfast bowls tapping the counter, and silverware jangling in kitchen drawers reminded me it was morning. Monday. The first day of a busy school week that was not to be ours.

"Kathy, are you awake?" Rosita asked in a hushed voice. *"Dormiste?"*

"Dormí un poco no más, ¿y tú?" I slept only a little, how about you?

Madre Edwardina tapped on the door. "Rosita? Are you up? Both of you, come and have something to eat."

We readied ourselves, smelling percolated Folger's coffee emanating from the kitchen, a treat compared to the usual Nescafé. We needed to eat now because we'd be spending the day enclosed in our room.

Sunlight beamed through the kitchen window, unveiling an outpost of trees dazzling in the bright, spring green surroundings. Warm light flooded the convent's living areas, making the smiles on the sisters' faces almost as bright, as they sat at the breakfast table, eating, then dashing off to launch the school day. If last night's revelations left anyone perturbed about our presence, I couldn't detect it this morning. As the last of the sisters left, we rushed behind them to wash the dishes and finish showering before the school day started. Then, as agreed, Rosita and I retreated to our room, where we remained with the curtains drawn, dreariness creeping in behind us.

A surge of yesterday's anxieties surfaced. Were the others safe? When might we get back to school? Who was covering our classes? Every question led us around the maze with no outlet. Wait. Be patient. Stay calm. The only distraction was the delightful noise of children playing during recess, just down the hill.

Occasionally we would hear a sister or two running into the convent to retrieve some missing material for class or escorting a parent into the office for a private conversation. When we heard voices, we went silent.

The day dragged on. The shouts of the children faded soon after the last school bell. I wondered how long I could endure being enclosed in the room. By afternoon I dozed off, allowing sleep to ward off the ever-spiking fears.

Late in the afternoon, Edwardina told Rosita that Isabel had called. It took some effort to decode the conversation, but the gist was that we would be moved to another location. Perhaps as early as tomorrow someone might be coming by to talk with us or pick us up. Most importantly, it seemed Isabel had some knowledge about Helen, Paula, and Bernadette and signaled that they were safe. Edwardina assured Rosita we were welcome to stay another night or two, if needed.

Hearing about the telephone call, I felt overjoyed and enormously grateful to Edwardina for keeping us here another night. Rosita and I tried to visualize the circumstances of our other four housemates and Peg. It was as if we finally dared to lift the pause button and imagine them alive, having escaped the DINA.

"Do you think Isabel's message meant that she got to Buzeta and warned Helen in time?" I asked.

"Probably," Rosita replied carefully. "Well, at least she got word to them to get out of there. I doubt she called them. That would have been too dangerous."

"Helen didn't have the car, did she?" I asked, then leapt to my next thought. "If they went out on the streets around Buzeta, they'd be so obvious! I mean for as long as they've been in Chile and working in the neighborhood, they still stand out as foreigners, kind of like me. I mean, Peg's so tall!"

"When Paula left the parish church, where do you think she went?" I asked.

"Paulita has lots of friends! She might have gone to one of the houses of the sisters in her prayer group. Or maybe she went to the home of one of her co-workers from CIDE," Rosita ventured.

Rosita didn't think Isabel knew the name of the friend Bernadette was visiting and worried about who would warn her.

"Rosita, you know what's on my mind? Do you think Isabel went to work today at the *Comité* with everything that came out on the news last night?" I asked.

"*¡Claro, que sí!*" Of course, she did! Rosita answered, to which we both laughed. Then she added somberly, "Isabel knows. She knows she has to be careful."

The thought of being moved to an unknown place triggered my anxiety. I wondered who might come for us. Rosita told me the *Comité* usually arranged such things. Rosita's voice sagged as she took in the likelihood that she'd be leaving the security of a once-familiar home and her three IHM friends.

We had supper with the sisters. Like most Chileans, they ate late. The sisters seemed quiet, not sure of what to talk about over the meal. No one turned on the television, but before bed, one of them passed along the Monday edition of *El Mercurio*, which she'd picked up while out on an errand. The next morning, we passed the tedium of the day in our darkened bedroom reading it and the Tuesday edition, which had been left in the kitchen for us. Oddly, there was no news article similar to the Sunday evening television report about the "Communist nuns involved with MIR." Had the government quashed the story or banned further reporting about it? The story was so big Sunday night; why wasn't it covered in either edition?

Yet, one article served as a reminder of Pinochet's reach. A month ago, *El Mercurio* reported the assassination attempt on the lives of Chile's former vice president and leader of the Christian Democratic Party, Bernardo Leighton, and his wife, Ana Fresno. Today's article described the delicate neurosurgery Leighton was to undergo. The Italian authorities mandated "strict police vigilance" outside his hospital room. No visitors were permitted. Even doctors and medical personnel had to be searched prior to entering his room.[1]

At dusk we heard a knock on the front door, and Edwardina called for Rosita and me. There in the living room, a tall, lanky man, dressed in crumpled black slacks, a frayed leather belt, black-rimmed glasses, and a loose-fitting white shirt stood next to a more petite, bubbly woman. When we walked into the room, the woman greeted us, saying, "I'm María de los Angeles Marinóm, but everyone calls me Ma. We are friends of Isabel's, and this is Daniel Panchot." Her compassionate eyes seemed to peer into mine as I opened my hand to her outstretched arm.

I turned toward Daniel, a man in his late thirties. He seemed accustomed to tipping his head downward to compensate for his height. In spite of his look of consternation, there was a softness to his gaze. Immediately, I sensed his goodness. I'm not sure if Rosita knew them already, but she evidenced a slight familiarity with both of them, as did Edwardina. It took me a few moments to catch up with their chitchat and realize that Daniel was a Holy Cross priest, whom I had met only once, and Ma was a sister from the Religiosas del Sagrado Corazón.[2] Isabel had spoken of them before. They were colleagues of hers from the *Comité Pro Paz*.

"Do you have your things? Are you ready to go?" Daniel asked, glancing at his watch.

Fearful thoughts raced around my mind: Are we going outside, daring the DINA to find us? I tried to disguise my panic as I entered the bedroom to shove my belongings back into my carry-all bag. My blood was running hot, and my veins felt like streams of boiling bubbles, while my leg muscles trembled. As we departed Rosita thanked Edwardina for the kindness shown to us. Stepping over the threshold a wave of dread silenced me.

Daniel and Ma scurried down the front slope outside the convent door. At the bottom of the hill sat an egg-shaped, cream-colored Fiat 600. Ducking our heads, we slid into the back seat, closing the skinny car doors with a thud. It might carry five people crammed in. Daniel tried the ignition a few times until the engine finally purred. A get-away car this was not, but it was a luxury even to be in a car, particularly with the curfew approaching.

Daniel guided the car down the hill and onto the uneven roads leading away from the convent. Soon we were driving past the Air Force Academy. As we approached the military base, no one spoke. Ma turned her head sideways once or twice, to try to put us at ease. I didn't realize it then, but she and Daniel often helped those targeted by the DINA by ferrying them to *"casas de confianza,"* a network of trusted homes.

Neither Rosita nor I peppered them with the questions we had rehashed, such as, "Are our housemates safe?" "Is the DINA looking for us?" I could have asked Daniel, since he was a member of the Holy Cross order, "Is Gerardo Whelan okay?" Or more importantly, "Has anyone been in contact with my parents?"

Instead, we intuitively followed the Chilean code of silence, that the less we knew, the safer it was for everyone. Right now, we needed to focus on the immediate task of getting to the next secure home without detection.

Daniel broke the hush. "Listen, we are going to a house not too far from here. A very nice woman has welcomed you to stay with her. You'll be there only tonight. We won't be introducing you. It is better not to use names. It is very difficult right now. Tomorrow at 10:00 a.m. Ma and I will be back to pick you up and take you to another place. The owner of the house will leave for work before that, so you will need to be up and ready. Don't answer the door for anyone but us. Alright?"

Rosita answered swiftly from the back seat, her voice sounding a bit ashy. *"No. No hay ningún problema. Entendemos."* It's no problem. We understand. Ma glanced back again, and I nodded. She said to us, "Isabel is fine. I'll let her know tomorrow that we saw you." I heard her say the words, but I felt so numb, I didn't respond.

Daniel made a few turns after diverting off the main artery. I couldn't be sure because of the darkness and dim street lamps, but it looked like we were on Av. Américo Vespucio. Just like it wasn't convenient—*"no conviene"*—to know the names of people who welcomed you into their homes, so too it was better not to know the name of the street you were on.

Just in case.

Yet, it is hard to tame the desire to fix yourself within the universe. So, I glimpsed at the houses along this broad street, a lovely row of tidy, modernistic ranch homes, some trimmed with fieldstone and open carports, similar to ones that sat across from the entrance to St. George. That could mean we were just down the hill from Phil Devlin's house, where I would catch up with Bernard and the other Notre Dame students on Sunday nights for our meeting, meal, and prayer. My momentary circumstances remained light years away from the bread and spaghetti dinners we splashed together with plenty of red wine, conversation, and a warming fire.

Daniel pulled the car into a driveway. We all got out quickly and shimmied alongside the owner's car to a recessed door. There, away from the glare of any exterior lights, we were ushered into the home.

A middle-aged woman in professional clothing led us into her living room. I can't remember any details about her face, just that it seemed to ache with tiredness. She certainly knew the routine: the arrival of anonymous people who would sleep in her extra bedroom and evaporate from her home after she left for work in the morning. I couldn't name it then, but the weariness etched in her face reached beyond the fatigue of a long work day. More likely she still mourned the loss of a loved one, maybe a husband or a child taken from her during the coup. Perhaps in their name and memory she willingly risked her life by opening her door to those fleeing the DINA. Tonight, there would be no fleeting attachments, no names, no settling into the living room with her. As Daniel and Ma left, she showed us to our room and readied herself for bed.

Realistically speaking, I shouldn't feel afraid. This appeared to be a quiet, inconspicuous house in a middle-class neighborhood. I didn't notice anyone in a parked car monitoring the block when we pulled into the driveway. Not even a dog barked. But I didn't feel safe.

Staccato thoughts pounded in my head. This house was surely under surveillance. Neighbors must have noticed how frequently cars stopped after dark and people slipped into her house. Why would this woman who lived alone have such frequent visitors? Neighbors would wonder why people left her house after she went to work and why there was no socializing, no noise, no lights turned on to display a happy gathering after a carload of visitors arrived. Could we be so lucky that there weren't busybodies on the street to notice these things and comment?

I doubted it could be so, but nonetheless I was grateful to this woman. She didn't have to open her door. Like so many Chileans, she courageously chose to do so. From the shadows she offered up a simple act of humanity and a profound gesture of resistance. Yes, this was the deep solidarity among the Chilean people that so moved and challenged me. It resurrected my faith. She was the Good Samaritan who cared for me, and I, the injured, traumatized one wounded on the road. Fears, doubts, gratefulness. Like an excited hamster I chased these thoughts around an endless wheel, wanting to find a resting place, to escape from the gnawing frenzy inside me.

Once inside the bedroom, Rosita lit the small table lamp. We dropped our shoulder bags into the middle of the bed we were to share and sat on opposite sides of the mattress. We spoke in hushed voices for a while, not wanting to disturb our hostess, whose bedroom door had clicked shut. There would be no television nor tea tonight, just the tedium of a restless night and an unknown tomorrow.

The next morning a thin bar of light from beneath the blinds roused me from a heavy sleep. I checked my watch: 8:00 a.m. Rosita shifted on her side of the bed.

"Time to get up!" I said, as I climbed out and checked to see if the bathroom was unoccupied. The house seemed still. Our hostess had apparently already left for work. Nonetheless, I crept across the hallway to wash up. When I came back to the room, Rosita scooted out to do the same.

I peeked into the living area. All the drapes were closed, and the room seemed sad and forlorn. We didn't dare open the drapes. In quick order we packed our things, then tidied up the bedroom and bathroom, trying to erase any signs of our stay. No food had been set out for us, so we didn't venture into the refrigerator or cabinets in search of breakfast. We were ready to leave when Daniel and Ma arrived at ten o'clock.

The Fiat was parked in the owner's space now, mostly hidden by the carport's roof. We quickly followed Daniel and Ma out of the house. As the car backed out from the sheltered, shaded carport the brilliance of the morning dazed me. I felt like an infant peering at light and shapes for the first time. I gazed about with curiosity, my eyes almost hurting from the brightness.

I couldn't make sense of things at first; they seemed so beautiful. Blades of verdant grass covered the lawns, while a cascade of spring flowers blanketed a slope in a nearby field. The heat of the morning, bathed in so much light, felt like the middle of a Midwest summer. Could the chill that chewed at my bones over the past months evaporate so quickly? A nauseous wave of disorientation overcame me, making me feel so faint that I propped my head against the car window, swooning with sensory overload.

Daniel had already driven the car onto a major artery. Traffic zipped around us as we traveled a few miles south toward the center of Santiago. Until now no one had spoken. Shifted into neutral, the car putted to a stop at a downtown crosswalk jammed with women holding on to their children with one hand and grasping their already full *mallas* with the other. Behind them men in business attire waited, unencumbered but equally impatient to cross. I stared at the faces in the crosswalk, feeling like an alien. I described this odd reality to myself: *Oh, this is the everyday world. I am not part of it.*

Peering back toward us, Daniel said, "I think you'd better not look out the window." He paused. I twisted my face toward him, studying his eyes in the rear-view mirror, before he continued: "We want to be as inconspicuous as possible. There is always a chance we are being followed or that someone might be spotted."

His voice was flat, matter-of-fact. He didn't mean to alarm, but my eyes opened wide, fears surging. I turned away from the window and looked at Rosita, seated directly behind Daniel. She already knew better and had positioned her back up against the door, with her hair splayed against the window. Though her eyes were open, she seemed far away. I could see she had been meditating, asking God to get everyone out of this safely.

The car continued downhill, then through the roundabout at Plaza Baquedano and on to the broad Alameda. The Fiat was pressed in on either side by roaring buses, which were frenetically passing us. At some point, Daniel jogged off the Alameda and headed away from the central city, where fewer cars were on the street. Ma appeared relieved that we had maneuvered through the middle of the city without detection.

I hadn't the faintest notion where we were headed. But we were entering a poor, industrial neighborhood with more hulking, cement-colored factories. Single-story, cement-block houses and some shabby *mediaguas* filled in the surrounding streets. Ma whispered something to Daniel, then spoke to us in the back seat.

"We'll be arriving soon at a good place, in the *población* Clara Estrella. It belongs to an international congregation of sisters, but most of those who live here are Chilean. The majority are retired sisters."

Before she could say more my mind rushed ahead. Older Chilean sisters? They might be great women, wonderful teachers or nurses, but what if they're from conservative families who supported the *golpe*? Their brothers might be officers in the military!

Ma continued, "A wonderful sister, Rosario de la Paz, coordinates the convent. Only she knows your situation." Ma said we would likely be here several nights. If there are any concerns, Rosario will contact her. Ma suggested that we present ourselves as religious postulants who wanted a place to be on retreat for a few days. For security purposes, we should use pseudonyms.

Rosita, ever the storyteller, sprang to life. "Yes, that is a good idea. Let's see, from now on I'll be Renée, and Kathy can be Claudia. Does that sound okay to you, Kathy?" I hardly had a moment to absorb what it meant to take on a pseudonym before Daniel drove the car into a large turnabout, the terminal point for one of Santiago's bus routes. Maneuvering around the buses parked in a queue, Daniel swung the car to a stop next to the convent's entryway.

An elderly sister, wearing a short veil and a light gray, below-the-knee habit, answered the door and welcomed us into the convent's powder-blue foyer, saying, "Oh, you want to see Sr. Rosario de la Paz? Of course, I'll go get her."

A few sisters walked by and smiled curiously at us before Sr. Rosario de la Paz arrived. I wondered if they were suspicious. After all, the military's threat, broadcast on Sunday night, to flush out the supposed religious–MIR collaborators surely registered with some of them. We stood stiffly in the foyer, hardly talking, until a lithe, sprightly sister, Rosario de la

Paz, dressed in her community's habit, came bounding down one of the cloister's corridors with a swish of energy. She smiled at all of us, then embraced Ma, pulling her into a nearby room. A happy trail of whispers followed them. Ma shared with her the necessary information and whatever assurances were needed out of earshot.

In short order they returned, with Sr. Rosario de la Paz exclaiming, "Welcome Renée and Claudia! So good that you have come!" Hugging us, she continued, "Please, let me show you to your room."

To the left of the entryway at the end of the corridor was a guest room with two beds. Ma and Daniel accompanied us, as Sr. Rosario de la Paz gently opened the door. After we deposited our satchels on the beds, Ma and Daniel said their goodbyes, promising to visit us in a few days.

As they departed Rosario closed the door to speak with us privately. "I realize these have been some difficult days for both of you. But you are safe here for as long as you need to stay."

Cognizant of our drawn faces, she said, "The sisters will be happy to get to know you, as everyone is friendly here. There won't be any problems." She paused, then suggested, "You must be hungry. Aren't you? It is almost lunchtime. I'll come back for you in a few minutes to show you to the dining room."

The mention of food rallied me. I slipped into the hallway to find the common bathroom. On my way back to the bedroom, I got a better glimpse of the layout of the convent, a cement-block, single-story, square cloister. A fairly large, interior patio garden was surrounded on four sides by window walls, such that anytime a sister stepped out of her room into one of the four hallways, she could view the patio garden and know who was walking around in any other quadrant of the house. Mid corridor there were doorways that opened into the garden. By December there would be lovely flowers in the pots and greenery, but at this moment under the cloudy sky it looked dreary. Doom hit me again as I was observing the cloister's layout. If the DINA ever got past the entry foyer, they'd have a bird's-eye view of every movement, and there would be no place to hide.

Rosario scooted around the corridors to retrieve us, making introductions. I smiled wanly every time I heard my pseudonym, Claudia. Rosita's pseudonym, Renée, seemed to fit her better; it sounded energetic and feisty, a flattering match to her personality. When I tried to utter my pseudo-name in Spanish, Claudia, I sounded awkward and klutzy, drawing unwanted attention to our charade.

Following Rosario into the dining room, we took adjacent seats in the middle of the long table. About a dozen retired sisters joined us. They all seemed quite mobile. After grace, Rosario introduced us, noting that we were postulants visiting Chile and would be staying with them while on retreat. A little bit of small talk ensued as the platters of stewed chicken, rice, and steamed carrots rounded the table.

When everyone was served, the sister across from me asked, "Tell us, Claudia, what is the name of your congregation?"

I dropped a forkful of chicken back onto my plate, stammering as a tableful of eyes landed on me. Rosita and I hadn't thought to anticipate questions. So, in halting Spanish I invented a name for our supposed congregation, trying to avoid the religious orders in the news. "Yes, well, we are the Little Sisters of Mary."

To which the sister responded, "I've never heard of that religious order. Where they from?"

I took a dodge saying, "Oh, I'm from the United States, and Renée is from Peru," hoping we might change the topic. But the questions kept coming.

"Where is your motherhouse?"

Rosita jumped in. "It originated in France, in a small rural village. Initially, the community was cloistered; then it started branching out. I met the community when I was a young student."

"I see . . . ," the sister replied, puzzled, while another pressed on.

"Claudia, what is the charism of your congregation?"

I squirmed inside, not wanting to add fib to fib. I fumbled, "Oh, we are devoted to the education of young children."

But it wasn't enough! Another question came with the same sincerity of interest: "What is the name of your foundress? Can you tell us about her and your history?"

Even Rosita wasn't ready to extend the story: "The truth is, we are new to the congregation and haven't had a class about our foundress yet."

Rosario chided the sisters, "Please, let's allow Claudia and Renée some time to eat their lunch!" With cast-down eyes, we mercifully did.

By the time a custard dessert was served, the conversation had moved on. As the sisters departed to scrape and wash the dishes, we rose to follow them. *"¿Podemos ayudar?"* Can we help? Rosita asked of no one in particular.

But Rosario steered us back to our room, "Go and rest now. Maybe after dinner you can lend a hand." While we went to our room, she popped into the kitchen to check if damage control was needed.

Back in our room Rosita exclaimed, *"¡Eso sí fue horrible! ¡Horrible!"* We burst into laughter, horrified by being their guests, only to lie and give lame responses to all their sincere but "nunny" questions!

"But at least you were once a nun!" I said, trying to defend my ineptness. The laughter felt good, a flicker of normality. Then, something caught my attention, an odor.

"Oh my God! Look at this perspiration! My blouse is drenched!" I jumped off the bed, pulled a shirt from my bag and ran into the washroom to rinse out my top, leaving it to drip-dry.

Tedium filled in the afternoons. Catnaps, the same conversations and worries to review. Not knowing the fate of the sisters or of Isabel's safety gnawed at us. And Sheila? My intuition told me that she had been taken to Villa Grimaldi, but I wondered if the British ambassador had seen her.

22

Reading between the Lies
November 5

Rosita and I were sitting on our beds talking when Rosario knocked. In her hand she held the November 5 edition of *El Mercurio*, saying, "I picked this up while out on an errand. I thought you might want to read it."

I was terrified by the bold headline, "Priests Hid MIR Fugitives." Next to the front-page article was a large photo of our house on Calle Orellana. The caption screamed, "Notre Dame convent was extremist refuge."[1]

When I was taken captive, I had wanted to find a way to warn Gerardo Whelan. Now I knew that any message would have been too late. According to today's lead article, the DINA had executed an early-morning raid on November 2 at Whelan's home in La Ponderosa, where he lived with the seminarians and tended the peacocks.

The details of what happened that morning were later shared with me by Liz Gilmore, a Holy Child sister and member of Santa Rosa's pastoral staff.[2] She told me that somewhere around 8:00 to 9:00 a.m. on Sunday, November 2, DINA agents arrived at Santa Rosa's rectory and pounded on the door. There Liz was confronted by three men, one with a gun in his hand. She blocked them from entering, saying, "I want to see your identification, because Pinochet has warned us about people impersonating the DINA." The agent holding the gun aimed it at her head, saying, "This is the only identification you need." With that, two of the agents rushed past her to search the rectory. The DINA agent with the gun remained in the kitchen with Liz.

Unbeknownst to Liz, during the raid the agents confiscated a wine bottle from Fr. David Farrell's room. Farrell was not there that morning, but hidden in his room was a bottle with $10,000 inside. The bottle had been given to him by a person from "a high-level foundation," who transported it from the United States to be passed on to a contact "working in opposition to the dictatorship."[3]

When the DINA agents departed, Liz ran through the neighborhood to La Ponderosa, having learned from parishioners of an early-morning raid there. Arriving at Gerardo Whelan's house, the neighbors told her that DINA agents had found Martín Humberto Hernández Vásquez, a MIR member, in the house. He had been sheltered by Whelan and the seminarians after the Malloco shoot-out. The neighbors told Liz that Whelan was punched and badly beaten during the raid, as was Hernández Vásquez. Both Whelan and Hernández Vásquez were detained and taken to Villa Grimaldi.

The *El Mercurio* article reported that both Whelan and Fr. Fernando Salas, SJ, were said to be "gravely implicated" in hiding the MIR militants. Though not yet arrested, Salas was now considered a fugitive for his role in hiding MIR leaders Nelson Gutiérrez, Maria Elena Bachman, Andrés Pascal Allende, and Mariana (Mary Ann) Beausire.

My stomach churned as I scanned down the page and saw the names of Peg Lipsio, Helen Nelson, and Paula Armstrong maligned. However, there was no mention of their arrests, so it appeared they were still in hiding. Yet surprisingly the article included an important detail about the sisters' actions, reporting, "As a condition to be hidden in the Notre Dame convent, the extremists had to hand over the two AKA machine guns they carried."

I put down the newspaper I had been reading aloud and looked across the room at Rosita. Her usually bright face was drawn. We were both overwhelmed by this public revelation. Rosita jumped up to get tea and offered to bring me some too. As she left the room, I read on, spying Sheila Cassidy's name a few paragraphs down. Nothing prepared me for what came next.

The newspaper confirmed what I had intuited. Sheila had been detained by the DINA at the Columban Center house on November 1. The article went on to claim that when the security forces arrived, "Dr. Cassidy and a companion sprayed them with machine gun fire, causing the security forces to fire back in kind. In the firefight, the housekeeper was hit by bullets fired by the doctor's companion."

When Rosita returned to the room, I was weeping. I looked up at her and said breathlessly, "The DINA captured Sheila and murdered Enriqueta."

I knew *El Mercurio*'s story was a lie and a cover-up. There had been no firefight. There was no mysterious "companion" with Sheila Cassidy, as the article claimed.[4] The only ones with weapons were the men with machine guns, dressed in Levis, who were running through the shadows as I left the Columban Center.

The memories of that night came flooding back. We were in the foyer chatting. I felt anxious and wanted to leave. Finally, I was able to say my goodbyes to Connie, Sheila, and Fr. Halliden, the Columban superior. Enriqueta accompanied me to the door. We both waved as I closed the front gate and stepped into the dusky night.

Only minutes changed our fates.

I could still hear Enriqueta telling me about her children and her life in Rengo. She had so much love for her family. I thought about how she labored every day, swallowing her pain and loneliness for their betterment. Now her children would never hear her voice again.

A photo of Enriqueta Reyes Valerio from her memorial card. This photo hangs in the Columban Center house in Santiago. Courtesy Fr. Tom Henehan, MM.

I walked away from the Columban Center that night under a waning moon, never suspecting that Enriqueta, the most innocent among us, would be killed. Only the briefest moments had passed before the DINA's machine guns strafed the Columbans' house, mortally wounding her. I learned later that Sheila risked being hit by machine gun fire, while dragging Enriqueta's torn body toward the phone alcove, trying to save her life. Fr. Halliden anointed Enriqueta with a dab of kitchen oil while the two of them prayed over her, as she slipped away.[5]

When the DINA arrived at the SSND convent at dawn on November 2, the puzzle of events from my visit with Sheila the previous afternoon and evening dropped intuitively and wordlessly into place. That morning as I stared into the blue eyes of the American interrogator, I knew his DINA handlers on the other end of the phone were torturing Sheila. Not that I heard any screams; not that I heard Sheila's voice. My knowing was conveyed from the depravity of evil under way. The weaving car, the moon-lit *metralleta*, the footfall stalking me, and the figures running through the shadows were merely its signs.

23

Sheila's Night of Torture
November 1–2

Blindfolded and shoved at gunpoint into Villa Grimaldi before midnight on November 1, Sheila was ordered to strip naked.[1] Sightless, with her body spread-eagle on the metal grid of a bare bunk bed, the DINA strapped her limbs to the bed's frame. They primed her with repeated electric shocks, then interrogated her about Nelson Gutiérrez, whose gun wounds she had treated. She invented answers to keep her interrogators off the trail of the priests and nuns involved, wanting them to reach safety and in some way protect the church.

Any time she hesitated, they pressed the current.

They wanted the address where Gutiérrez was treated. Shock by shock, she invented a fictive location, described a house, its furnishings, saying she'd lead them there. Taken out at gunpoint in a DINA caravan, she led them to a street where she spotted a home resembling the description she'd made up under duress.

Pointing to the house, the DINA threw her from the squad car into a paddy wagon, while they awaited reinforcements for what they hoped to be their capture of MIR's leadership. The house was vacant, except for its elderly caretakers. With Sheila's deception exposed, her captors furiously taunted her. "Back to the *parrilla*, *gringa*."[2]

Back to Villa Grimaldi's "barbeque grill" they took her, binding her again to the bed's grate. This time the electrodes were secured to the most sensitive parts of her body.

Late in the overnight hours they broke her. She could no longer hold out to protect others. She told the truth, that Nelson Gutiérrez had been treated in a convent of an American nun, but she only knew the street's name, not its house number. Once again, Sheila was shoved back into a DINA car and ultimately pointed out the front door of the convent on Padre Orellana.

Sheila was then forcibly returned to Villa Grimaldi, while extra DINA units arrived on Calle Orellana and began to pound on the convent's front door.

Angered a third time by not finding Gutiérrez at the SSND convent as they hoped, they bound her again to the metal grate. Over the open phone line inside the torture cell, she heard the DINA's interrogations under way inside the SSND convent.[3] Meanwhile in Villa Grimaldi, punishing rounds of electric shock followed.

24

Bando 89
November 6

At the retirement home of the sisters in Clara Estrella, I kept being startled awake. In my dreams I imagined Enriqueta's torn body and Sheila's torture. I woke up confused, unaware of my surroundings, my body rigid. I heard the crank of a powerful motor; its purr vibrated the walls. I didn't dare turn on a light and expose my whereabouts to those who were stalking me. Peeking out of one eye, I scanned the room filled with darkness and shadows. Had someone entered the room and left? I felt terrified and longed for the narcotic of sleep, so I could disappear.

When I finally awoke, I counted the days since the DINA pulled up outside our dwelling on Padre Orellana. Five. Now a thick band of tiredness stretched behind my eyes. My mental functions dwindled daily. My speech slowed, and my fluency in Spanish diminished. Even a shower couldn't rinse away the gravel in my skull.

By midday, Rosario slipped us the newspaper. I glanced at the front page, where my eye was drawn to a devastating photo. It was a picture of the diamond-cut windows that had been shattered by automatic gunfire, ending Enriqueta's life. I could only weep.

Then, reading the headlines, I could almost hear the hammer dropping. Overnight the commander of the military garrison, General Garay Cinfuetes, had issued a sweeping post-facto decree, Bando 89, targeting the church and our religious friends.

The first of Pinochet's enumerated Decree Laws, known as Bandos, had been promulgated over the seized radio stations on September 11, 1973. They accompanied the aerial bombing of the Moneda Palace and the death of President Allende.

In today's promulgation Garay warned the citizenry that "persons who shelter, hide, aid in the escape, offer medical service, or in any other manner cooperate with Andrés Pascal Allende, Nelson Gutiérrez, Maria Elena Bachman, and Mary Anne Beausire . . . will be subject to grave penalties . . . no matter their rank, qualifications, or the office they possess."[1] I sucked in my breath. This meant we were now Bando 89's targets.

Cardinal Silva quickly responded to Bando 89's decree, saying, "The position of the church in respect to violence and of those who believe in it as a means and an end for a political gain is well known . . . and there can be no adhesion or direct cooperation with the precepts of violence and hate."

But his next words left me breathless as I read and re-read the pivotal lines: "Distinct is the case of those, inspired by the demands the gospel message created in conscience, that they should offer to whomever requires, the essential aid one needs to preserve life, no matter their political persuasion. It is important to remember that the source of Christian love is rooted precisely in indiscriminate mercy."[2]

Indiscriminate mercy.

The clarity of the words and the demand it placed on every believer's life shook my soul. I knew that in this high-profile clash between the government and the church, many awaited the cardinal's judgment. Unequivocally, he upheld those who risked their lives in witness to the gospel mandates to love, preserve life, and be merciful.

This was the essence of living one's faith. It meant whole-hearted solidarity with the suffering. It formed the core of the *Comité Pro Paz's* work in the *poblaciones* and the commitment to accompany the families of those detained or disappeared. To reduce such a witness to mere partisanship distorted the truth of the gospel.

The cardinal added, "Those who have acted in such a manner have a right to be heard, understood, and respected by public opinion." I could see that Cardinal Silva would not be penned in by the government. To me he was serene and willing to challenge the dictatorship. He ended with a request that the dictatorship "fully investigate the death of an innocent victim," a clear reference to the life of Enriqueta.[3]

Six days ago, when Sheila and I met, enjoying the tea and sandwiches Mercedes had prepared for us, I sensed something momentous occurring in our conversation. I remembered the visceral anguish with which Sheila described letting go of the life she had built. I didn't understand it then, but at that moment she was emptying herself to live as a witness to a deeper truth. The depth of what she would face was beyond my imagination.

I felt sick with worry about Sheila. Somehow, I imagined that the British consul had already seen her and was able to blunt the retaliation on her for treating Nelson Gutiérrez. She'd been held incommunicado by the DINA for six full days. I wondered if she was even alive. I read that Chile's foreign minister, Patricio Carvajal, again denied the British ambassador, Reginald Louis Seconde, his right to visit Sheila.

Seconde protested Carvajal's decision vigorously. Then in a sharp response, Carvajal declared that Sheila had been found guilty of providing medical attention to a fugitive with bullet wounds and failed to inform the authorities.[4] With this statement, Carvajal subjected Sheila to a military prosecution under the just-formulated Bando 89.

Reading this, my fears deepened. I didn't doubt the military regime's resolve to enforce Bando 89, nor its plan to scour Santiago's religious institutions.

I stepped out of our guest bedroom and walked down the cloister's corridor for a stretch. I turned a corner and saw one of the retired sisters talking animatedly on the house phone in the convent's telephone nook. As I approached, she turned and peered at me coldly, cutting off her conversation.

Had she been chatting on the phone about the headlines of the week? Might she have mentioned us, the young, foreign postulants visiting her convent? If so, might her telephone partner inquire further and pass the tip along?

I raced back to our room and laid on the bed, telling myself my plight pales before those being tortured or imprisoned. No matter that I was blindfolded, sequestered, with machine guns pointed at me. They let me go!

While factually true, my words minimized what I faced, allowing guilt and shame to insinuate themselves. Exhausted, I rolled over, warning myself: Concentrate! Stay alert! You are still in danger!

25

Inside the Nunciatura
November 7

I was in the kitchen of the sisters' retirement house when I saw *El Mercurio*'s headline. It landed with the force of a bomb blast: "MIRist Gutiérrez in Vatican Embassy."[1] I wondered if the people of Chile were ready to absorb this fact. Even I paused, trying to fully take in its impact. Of course, I had known for almost two weeks that on October 24, Gerardo Whelan and Patricio Cariola had audaciously ferried Nelson Gutiérrez and Maria Elena Bachman through the embassy's gate in the trunk of the Peugeot.

I couldn't glean much new information from the article, except that the *Nunciatura* did not deny the reports. But the headline itself drew a huge crowd of reporters to the *Nunciatura's* gated entrance. They were quickly joined by a crowd of Catholic protesters, hailing from the wealthy neighborhoods of Ñuñoa, Providencia, and Las Condes. These protesters were allowed to stay outside the *Nunciatura* until 11:00 p.m., singing the national anthem, shouting patriotic slogans and anti-church invectives, with additional police called in to control the crowd.

Much later I learned that the dictatorship had kept up the pretense of a frenzied search for Gutiérrez and Backman for the past seven days, while, in fact, the DINA had learned of their whereabouts Sunday, November 2. When the DINA forced Sheila to point out the SSND convent, the DINA fully expected to find Gutiérrez and Bachman inside. In retaliation for not finding them there, Sheila was dragged back to Villa Grimaldi, where they amped up her torture until she broke. She told the DINA that Gutiérrez and Bachman were inside the *Nunciatura*.

Sheila's stark confession and its truth "enraged her torturers."[2]

26

Pudahuel
November 7

After dinner, Rosario de la Paz came by to ask us if we would like to join the sisters in the parlor to watch television. Anxious for any break, we walked with her into their large community room, where a number of sisters were gathered in a semicircle around a smallish television set. It seemed each sister had their special chair, some a rocker, some a straight back, others upholstered, with the preferred spot marked by its knitted blanket or a frayed pillow.

Rosita and I came in quietly, pulling dining chairs up behind the sisters. The audio buzzer blared, announcing the evening news, followed by a stern and breathless television reporter who was at Pudahuel airport. The camera panned to a Braniff Airways plane, glowing on the vacant tarmac as darkness quickly descended. There, through its strand of windows, amber interior lights revealed spiffily dressed airline hostesses checking on the passengers.

I watched the television screen in amazement. Swarming around the reporter on the tarmac were hundreds of angry Chilean men and some women carrying protest signs and chanting. The protesters were standing on the tarmac outside the airport building. Above them on the airport's roof was an open sky deck, where family and friends typically waited to wave goodbye to loved ones boarding their flights. The television images felt surreal, as the *carabineros* and some Air Force guards sauntered around and paid the protesters no mind.

Several other guards stood near the protesters by the exit door. The camera filmed the passengers inside the building who were handing over their *cédulas*, passports, and *salvoconductos,* safe-passage documents, for scrutiny by the police.[1] Typically, travelers boarding flights exited on foot out the doorway at ground level, walked across the tarmac with their hand luggage, then climbed the stairway ramp up to the awaiting plane. Before entering the plane's doorway, travelers would twist and blow kisses to their family and friends, who waved and shouted their goodbyes.

Not tonight. By now, darkness encompassed the airport, and the television lights only partially illuminated the scene. The crowd's vehement shouts grew louder as the television lights and cameras focused in on a caravan of vans driving up the tarmac.

How weird, I thought as I watched the news. *A protest under this dictatorship? Why aren't the police shutting it down?*

Then the reporter's voice grew louder, booming over the rambunctious crowd, panting as he tried to run down the tarmac with the cameraman to get closer to the approaching vehicles.

"They are arriving now! They are driving up in the U.S. embassy vans. Here they come, the three North American religious who were involved in the cover-up of the MIR fugitives! They are getting out of the car! Look, there is the U.S. consul!"

The passenger doors of the embassy van opened. Their figures were unmistakable. First, diminutive Helen, then the tall, lithe Peg, and finally Paula emerged, identifiable by her ambling gait. The television camera caught the look in their eyes. Determined. Bewildered. Distraught.

But they were alive! Then a sense of doom overtook me as I realized they were being ushered into exile, like thousands of Chileans before them.

On cue, the crowd of protestors began to approach them, cursing and tossing handfuls of small coins, called Judas coins, toward their backs while shouting vociferously: "*¡Fuera Comunistas! ¡Fuera traidores!*" I didn't see traitors and Communists on the screen. Instead, I saw the three of them, dedicated educators and unassuming missionary women in rumpled clothes, with vengeance raging around them. This was the finale after their years of committed labor and *entrega*.

The staged vitriol continued with increasing ferocity as they climbed the portable stairwell up toward the plane's doorway. They disappeared into the plane as the hostess pulled the heavy door inward, then bolted it shut. The camera zoomed in to catch a last glance of them through the portal windows as they took their seats. I wondered if they would arrive safely or ever return.

While the plane revved up and began its move toward the runway, its power drowned out the shouting as the crowd drifted back toward its staging area. The television camera swept away from the protesters, illuminating the U.S. embassy vans driving cautiously down the runway's service lane. The vans lingered long enough to assure the consul that the plane had reached its take-off position.

Watching the plane become airborne, the television reporter repeated the same allegations and condemnations, in the second spin of the news. Rosario de la Paz glanced over and saw Rosita, ashen and drawn, and me with a stream of tears dripping down my cheeks. She signaled with a toss of her head that we should depart quickly, before our tell-tale emotions were detected.

We were already out the doorway when Rosario politely said to the sisters transfixed by the news, "Excuse us. We're tired and will retire now."

Momentarily the puzzled faces of the nuns turned away from the television set and toward her, perhaps ready to ask her what she made of the situation. She had clearly aroused the stunned hive. Suddenly, I could hear the buzz of the elderly nuns' voices chasing us down the hallway with their thoughts on the matter.

Rosario de la Paz slipped into the bedroom behind us. She pulled up the desk chair. I flopped on the bed, wiping my tears on the pillowcase. I didn't know the term for it then, but I was decompensating, experiencing myself unravelling psychologically. Days of fitful sleep, terrifying dreams, and paranoid thoughts had hollowed out any coping reserve I had.

Rosita, certainly the sturdier of the two of us, sat upright on the bed and met Rosario's gaze. Rosario had a more intuitive grasp of what we needed to focus on. With the sisters' exile, everything had changed. She urged us to be ready to move forward and consider new options. Her hopeful spirit was comforting. Somehow, she reminded me of my mother. I drifted from the conversation and made a pledge to myself: If I ever have a daughter, she will be named Alicia de la Paz, after my mother and Rosario.

The airport scene barely disguised the power play between the Chilean and U.S. authorities. If it had been otherwise, the three nuns might have been sent out of the country quietly, without a diplomatic escort, blending in with the other passengers. Watching the U.S. consul on the tarmac, I clearly understood that the guarantees made to safeguard the sisters' passage were violated. In front of the indifferent police and military agents, they were ambushed by the crowd. I wondered, what kind of eruption might these fissures between the junta and their U.S. sponsors foretell? Just as notable was the absence of any religious authority. Begging the question, what confrontations awaited the Chilean Catholic Church and the ecumenical *Comité Pro Paz*?

27

Pascal Allende, Phil Devlin, and Diplomats
November 8

When I woke the next morning, Rosita was already up and getting dressed. She suggested we not go to breakfast right away to avoid seeing the sisters and talking about last night's news. It sounded perfect to me. I got up, gathered my clothes, and headed toward the shower room, pausing first to scan the hallway. Fortunately, no one was around. We took our time, then slipped into the kitchen for coffee and toast. The convent was surprisingly quiet. Rosario de la Paz poked her head into the kitchen to see how we were doing and told us that many of the sisters had left earlier on an excursion.

When we were finished eating, we took the newspapers from the common area and headed back to our room. Another blockbuster headline sailed across the front-page: "Pascal Allende takes asylum in the Costa Rican embassy."[1]

We read that just before the curfew lifted yesterday morning, Andrés Pascal Allende and Mary Ann (Mariana) Beausire entered the grounds of the Costa Rican embassy without identity documents. When Ambassador Tomás Soley was alerted to their presence, he asked to see proof of who they were. They told him their names and that they feared for their lives, asking him to provide refuge. Citing "humanitarian" concerns, Soley granted them temporary asylum, then informed Patricio Carvajal of his decision.

Carvajal reacted swiftly, rejecting any notion that Chile would now, or in the future, grant Costa Rica the necessary *salvoconductos* for Pascal Allende and Beausire to leave the country.

I was amazed at Mariana Beausire's fortune, to finally be inside the embassy of a sympathetic country. From one of the whispered *confianzas* during the nights we spent in Buzeta, I learned that Mariana had been moved to another safe house a day or two after her arrival on Padre Orellana. Even so, I wondered how she and Pascal Allende had managed to enter the embassy with all the surveillance. Was the cat-and-mouse hunt for them finally over? If so, I could only imagine the DINA's fury.

I stared at a large photo of the mayhem at Pudahuel last night. I was sure Helen, Paula, and Peg were shaken to the core, but they no longer had to live with fear of the DINA. I guessed that by this time they'd left Miami and were en route to New York City.

In the same article about Pascal Allende, I was shocked to see *El Mercurio* report that the U.S. ambassador, David H. Popper, was requesting a *salvoconducto* for Fr. John [Philip] Devlin to leave Chile. I hadn't seen Phil or any of the Notre Dame students since mid-October and wondered what involvement he had in these events.[2]

Finally, there was some news about Sheila Cassidy. British consul Derek Fernyhoug had been allowed to visit her. I felt uneasy reading her consul's remarks; they seemed too upbeat. He claimed Sheila was "in good health." Could that be possible after being held for seven days, incommunicado in the atrocious Villa Grimaldi? Obviously, Sheila was under duress when she spoke with Fernyhoug, given that "two prison officials" monitored their conversation.[3] Still, I felt elated that Sheila was alive and had an advocate.

Carvajal made it clear "that her actions were utterly distinct from the North American religious," and she would not be eligible for asylum due to her involvement with the MIR fugitives. But to my mind Carvajal was making a face-saving statement for the humiliated dictatorship. There was no difference between the motivation and actions of the women. They had risked their lives to live out their vocations, Sheila as a doctor and the sisters as committed religious. The only difference was Sheila had been captured.

Still, it was all too much to take in. Rosita and I were sad, thinking about the loss of Helen and Paula in our lives. We silently bid them farewell, watching their vulnerability in front of the protesting mob. We understood the depths of their faith and courage, and the relinquishment of their own safety to protect the Chileans caught in the dictatorship's wrath.

They were irreplaceable leaders and teachers at Buzeta, and much like their expulsion from St. George in 1973, it would be their students who would suffer the most. Rosita and I knew it might be years before we would speak to them again.

Bernadette, the only SSND sister left in Santiago, was presumably hiding like we were. I wondered if she was at greater risk now that the others had departed. Or in the public exile of Helen and Paula, had we, the remaining household members, been somehow exonerated? Would it be safe for Bernadette, Rosita, Isabel, and me to return to Padre Orellana?

In a mere week so much had shifted. Inside the cloistered patio, flower shoots and sprigs of green poked through the garden beds and popped out of last year's ceramic pots. With the sun's rays pouring into the hallways, I felt the winter chill finally melt away.

We spent the next few hours in our room in pensive boredom, broken suddenly by incessant knocking on the front door. Rosita sat bolt upright, hearing voices at the door. First, they were low, then louder. My heart pounded, fearing the DINA's pursuit.

Rosita crept closer to the door, whispering nervously, "Kathy, can you hear them? They know our names. They are asking for Rosita and Kathy."

"Who here knows our names? It has to be the police!" I whispered back.

Rosita opened the door a crack, saying, "I think I recognize their voices."

The sister who answered the door denied knowing anyone named Rosita or Kathy, repeating all the louder, *"¡No! ¡No! No hay nadie aquí con los nombres, ¡Kathy y Rosita!"*

Then Rosita turned back to me, saying excitedly, "Kathy, it's Helen Carpenter and Gerry Doiron from Buzeta. They're at the door!"

Hearing the commotion, Rosario de la Paz hurried toward the door, thanked the sister for her help, and tried to usher her away. By then Rosita was already out in the hallway, embracing Helen and Gerry as I scrambled out behind her. The elderly sister who answered the door looked at me squarely in the eye, saying accusingly, "But you told me your names were Claudia and Renée!"

I looked at her sheepishly and felt remorse for our deception that made her look like a fool. Her pique was justified. But I barely offered an apology, then stepped around her utterly relieved to see our friends.

Before I could even say hello, I heard Gerry say to Rosita, "Go get your things and come with us," as a broad smile broke across her face. I stood frozen.

"Don't look so worried, Kathy!" Helen Carpenter said. "We're heading to Buzeta. Get your gear!" Rosita and I rushed down the hallway and threw our belongings into our satchels. At the door, we gushed our gratitude to Rosario de la Paz and gave her a farewell embrace.

Outside the convent door I surveyed the neighborhood, seeing a row of modest block houses with clothes flapping on outdoor clotheslines. I couldn't piece it together. Everything looked so plain and unthreatening. Yet, for the past few nights, the rumble of the buses and the pulse of their motors had stirred the most fearsome thoughts in me.

Hoping to dispel my fears. I climbed into the Maryknoll car. Helen gripped the steering wheel, shifted into gear, and with a rumble that rivaled the buses across the way, we headed off to Buzeta.

The car doors barely slammed shut before questions poured out. "How did you know where we were?" "Did you see Helen, Paula, or Peg before they left?" "Have you seen Isabel or Bernadette? Are they okay?" While Helen Carpenter drove us through a stretch of neglected neighborhoods, a few fragments of our collective story fell into place. But there was no answer to the key question: Dare we resume our lives?

Just like so many other long, cross-town trips through Santiago, our route converged on the Alameda, the cacophonous throat of the city. The street seemed to surge, alive with the onset of spring. Children bustled along the sidewalks, with their mothers trying to finish errands. Street vendors narrowed the pathway with wares. Streams of high-school students walked arm in arm, ducking into cafes for sodas and sweets, stretching their time to chat and dream.

Upon docking the car inside the school compound, Helen and Gerry urged us to settle into the rooms they had prepared for us. In spite of their welcome, I felt drained climbing up the cement stairwell.

By the time I went down to the kitchen, there was Gerry, who always had two pots cooking on the stove, one filled with healthy ingredients for our meal and the other with vegetable peelings and portions of leftover rice to feed the dogs and chickens she tended. As the food was cooking the doorbell rang. Suddenly we heard happy noises coming toward the kitchen. Isabel and Bernadette had arrived. We quickly gathered around the dining room table while Helen poured a glass of red wine for each of us. Soon enough, Gerry's chicken stew was served. We couldn't wait to catch up. But excited as we were to be together, we knew our safety was still in question.

28

No Need to Say Anything
November 2–8

We talked well into the night. Isabel, Rosita, and I described the DINA's raid and the places where we were hidden. Bernadette filled in with her days on the run. Unbeknownst to me, Isabel had faced a great deal of peril as she crisscrossed Santiago, trying to ensure the safety of all of us, while many showed us their solidarity. It would be years before I learned all the details.

Bernadette's Experiences, November 2–7, 1975
On the morning of November 2, Bernadette was in El Tabo, relaxing in the coastal home of a colleague when she heard a knock at the door. On the doorstep a young man from the general store handed her a slip of paper that read, "Call me at this number, Isabel." Bernadette reached for some change, tipped the messenger, then rushed down to the store, which boasted having one of only three phones in town. Bernadette anxiously dialed Isabel, who alerted her to the dawn raid at Orellana. Isabel urged Bernadette to take a bus to the Maryknoll Sisters' retreat house in nearby El Quisco. Upon arrival Bernadette moved swiftly through the dining room looking for Srs. Gerry Doiron and Helen Carpenter. She joined them as they spoke privately with Sr. Cecilia Vandal, the Maryknoll superior. They informed Cecilia that they and Sr. Peg Lipsio aided the SSND sisters while the MIR leaders were hidden at Orellana, and told them of Peg's discovery of weapons.

Cecilia hurried into town to call Sr. Katherine Gilfeather, who told Cecilia that the DINA had brought me as their captive to the Maryknoll Sisters Center that morning.

A few hours later Fr. Fernando Salas, SJ, who had been informed about the raid by Isabel, showed up at the Maryknoll retreat house, hoping Bernadette had more information. Grasping the severity of the situation, Salas blurted out in English, "The shit has hit the fan!" Their nervous laughter over the expletive belied their fears for what lay ahead. Cecilia urged Bernadette to remain in El Quisco, fearing the dangers a return to Calle Orellana might bring. Likewise, Salas's superior advised him to lie low until more was known.

On Monday, November 3, Daniel Panchot and Ma arrived at the Maryknoll retreat house in El Quisco and drove Bernadette into Santiago. At the home of her friend Liliana, she poured out her fears. The next morning, Bernadette went to the U.S. consulate to speak with Vice Consul Nancy Hudson. As she departed Hudson's office, Josiah Brownell, the consul, came up to her and quietly said: "We are taking care of your friends. They are safe." Comforting words, but in reality, Bernadette had no idea of anybody's whereabouts. She returned to Liliana's house, just as Liliana was called into her father's bedroom, where due to cancer he was resting. The news was on, broadcasting the search for the "MIR accomplices, Helen Nelson and Paula Armstrong." From his sick bed he looked at his daughter, asking, "Doesn't Bernadette live with them?" That night friends took Bernadette to three houses, until they found a safe place for her to stay.

On Wednesday, November 4, Bernadette returned to Liliana's house for lunch. Within minutes the doorbell rang. Looking out the window, Liliana exclaimed, "It's Paula! Oh my God, she is so tall, and the police headquarters are right across the street! What if they recognize her?"

Paula's Experiences, November 2–8, 1975
Paula didn't expect to encounter Bernadette, but she was eager to have Bernadette accompany her to a meeting with Bishop Sergio Valech, a strong defender of human rights, who was Cardinal Silva's designee to interact with the Chilean government. In the little time they had before the meeting, Paula told Bernadette about the DINA's dawn raid and her call to Consul Brownell from the San Andrés rectory.

On the morning of the raid, Paula fled to the house of her colleague Ciral. He wanted to help her, but the DINA had surveilled parishioners leaving Santa Rosa's Masses that morning and observed him speaking with Fr. Fermín Donoso. He drove Paula to the home of a couple with two little girls. After dinner the couple invited Paula to watch the news, only to see Paula's photo appear on television. Paula told the couple, "Please, you are free to reconsider your decision. But they immediately said, "Oh, no, you are most welcome to stay here."

Having exchanged a few stories, Paula and Bernadette hurriedly left for the meeting with Bishop Valech. Isabel drove them to the meeting. Bernadette rode in the front seat, while Paula pushed herself onto the car's floor, hiding under a blanket. At the vicariate office, Bishop Valech and Vicar Juan de Castro greeted the women warmly. Valech told Paula that the security forces were actively searching for her. He urged her to seek refuge through the U.S. embassy. She agreed to do so. Valech and Juan de Castro then met with U.S. embassy officials and were given guarantees that the United States would not turn Paula over to the Chilean authorities.

With this agreement, they returned to the vicariate office, where Valech addressed Bernadette's situation. In his estimation, Bernadette's name had not surfaced in regards to sheltering MIR. He believed she could return to her work and life could go on. As Bernadette waited with Paula for the embassy car to arrive, the profundity of Paula's decision sank in. After nine years of ministry, teaching at St. George's, Buzeta, and CIDE, Paula was leaving without even a goodbye to her students and friends. When the U.S. embassy car pulled up, they hugged each other, stoically avoiding eye contact.

Paula departed in the car of U.S. consul Josiah Brownell, but didn't know where they were headed. She wondered: Will the DINA intercept me on their own? She had seen so much since the coup, the disappearances of people she knew, and the U.S. government's involvement in it all. When the car pulled to a stop, she was shocked to be outside the consul's home. Over dinner Paula learned that the consul's wife, María, was from Mexico and was moved by her kindness and hospitality.

After supper, Charles Stout, one of the U.S. embassy's political officers, arrived to speak with her. Stout led the conversation, dropping details Paula thought could only come from contacts within the DINA.

Stout's manner was cold and annoying. He discussed the possibility of her leaving Chile under U.S. embassy protection, on the condition that she write a confession.

Just then, Brownell entered and cut short further conversation. Brownell reminded Stout of a reception commencing within minutes in the consul's living room. To Paula he said, "Let me show you to your room."

Brownell then escorted Paula up the stairs and knocked on a door, saying, "I want to show you something." The door opened, and standing inside the room were Helen and Peg! Seeing their excitement and relief, Brownell excused himself to greet his guests.

Helen, Peg, and Paula's Experiences, November 4–8, 1975
Isabel had been the one to reach Buzeta the morning of November 2 to warn Helen and Peg that the DINA was looking for them. Sr. Maria Visse, a Loretto sister, had also spent that night at Buzeta. Maria called a Quaker couple, who then picked up Helen and Peg at the Estación Central and drove them to their home. But when Helen and Peg saw their two small children, they felt the risk to the family was too great. They contacted a woman who worked at the U.S. consulate. She took them into her home. That same night Brownell picked them up at the staff member's house, instructing them to "keep their heads down," as he drove them to his home in the upper-class neighborhood of El Golf.

Shortly after Helen and Peg arrived, Charles Stout arrived at Brownell's home to interview them. Stout sat across the table from Helen and Peg and asked, "Tell me, what is going on?" Helen offered that the DINA was looking for them because she had lent her car to Gerardo Whelan, later learning the police had taken custody of it.

Stout punched through her cloaked remarks, asking, "Do you know where the MIR leaders are now?"

Helen replied, "I don't."

He then pressed her, "Did you answer that honestly?"

"Yes," she said, aware she answered honestly but not fully. With that their conversation ended.

Back upstairs in the bedroom, Peg asked Helen, "Why didn't you tell them that Gutiérrez was in the *Nunciatura*?" Flustered, Helen went back downstairs and told Stout that Gutiérrez and Bachman were in the *Nunciatura*, obviously confirming what he already knew.

Helen and Paula were resolute in their agreement that they would not sign a confession. They knew that compassion, mercy, and love were the soul force of faith. What was there to confess if your motivation was living as Christians in the world?

They thought about the people they had sheltered, remembering the first person who arrived at Orellana. He was a university student picked up by the police for an incident with a girl about which he knew nothing. The authorities had taken him to the Mapocho River, told him to get out of the pick-up truck and run. As he ran, four bullets struck him. He fell into the river. The cold water shocked him awake, and he pulled himself out. He sought help in a nearby *población,* and they took him to the *Comité Pro Paz*. While living at the SSND convent he was so filled with fear and anxiety, he couldn't keep track of his assumed name. After two weeks he left for asylum in Switzerland.

They remembered Marcelino, his kindness and helpfulness in the house. They brought him hair dye to disguise himself before he left for an embassy. They recalled Sergio, a political activist and intellectual, who kept them up talking past midnight. Soon Sergio's wife was in the house; then their baby was snuck in. Helen was driving Sergio and his family to the French embassy when an earthquake hit. Unable to transfer them to the embassy car as planned, Helen nervously trailed the diplomatic car out to Pudahuel. They remembered the nights they prayed over each case along with Bernadette, Isabel, and Rosita. Since 1974 they had sheltered fourteen.

The women held steadfast, refusing to confess any allegiance or collusion with MIR, because they held no such allegiance. Instead of a confession, they each wrote a sparse statement, noting the names of the MIR members who stayed in the house and the need to provide care to a wounded man, who otherwise would die.

Their signed statements signaled their motivation and belief.

Helen wrote, "It was preserving a human life." Paula called her actions "a humane response." Peg wrote, "It was Humanitarian and Christian."[1] Unbeknownst to the sisters, their very thoughts were echoed in Cardinal Silva's words. They had offered "indiscriminate mercy" to those who might otherwise be killed outright.

The Chilean government abhorred their statements. The government wanted something that would pit the public against the Catholic Church, delegitimizing it. The government of Chile refused to grant the religious women their *salvoconductos*, the safe-passage documents every person leaving the country was required to obtain. Discussion over the impasse kept U.S. Ambassador Popper and Foreign Minister Carvajal negotiating for days as the Chilean media intensely tracked the story.

The morning of Friday, November 7, the sisters were told they *might* leave that evening. At the U.S. consul's residence, more preparedness measures were under way. A doctor was called to screen each of them. Odd questions were asked: Do you have any scars? Previous bone breaks? Missing or chipped teeth?

That clinched it for Paula. She understood the authorities were documenting their physical condition and markers, anticipating something might happen on their way to the airport or during the flight. Instructions were given to the women that they should not deplane at any stopover. Still, there was no firm word about their departure. What was the hold up? "Money," Paula surmised, having overheard some remarks. If the United States wanted the women to leave the country, it would have to pay something to the government of Chile. How much, or what kind of "chit" was under negotiation, she didn't know.

Days earlier, when the U.S. media first reported that the religious were being sought by the Pinochet dictatorship, the shocking news spread rapidly. The SSND and Maryknoll religious mobilized their networks across forty-eight states. Telephone-tree communiques were relayed to convents, schools, parishes, and supporters, asking that calls and telegrams be immediately sent to their senators and congressional representatives. Hundreds of telegrams and phone calls poured into a stunned State Department over those same days.[2]

Bernadette's Experiences, November 5–7, 1975

As Bernadette watched Paula depart, she felt overwhelming loneliness. She returned to Liliana's house. There, Liliana was on the phone securing yet another place for Bernadette to spend the night.

Liliana had a code to use with this contact. "I'd like to bring the book I borrowed by your house tonight. Will you be home?"

To which her friend replied, "Tell her to bring a sleeping bag."

Liliana slammed down the phone. Angry about the miscue, she said aloud, "What are you bringing a sleeping bag for if you are returning a book?"

Nonetheless, Bernadette was grateful for a place to sleep that night. The next morning, she awoke only to wander the streets. She decided to visit the SSND sisters who worked in San Felipe, a town northeast of Santiago. She had avoided going there until now, uncertain if it would be safe to visit Srs. Ruth and Mary, given the prominence of the SSND name in the news. Bernadette was met with comfort and tears, a balm she sorely needed.

On Friday, November 7, Bernadette rose early to return to Santiago for an appointment with Brownell. Isabel happened to phone the sisters in San Felipe, and arranged to meet Bernadette at the Estación Central. Upon her arrival they huddled in an empty restaurant. Isabel urged Bernadette *not* to go back to San Felipe, wary of the government's continuing threats. Isabel reminded her that even though her name had not surfaced, no one was out of danger.

At the consulate Brownell reassured Bernadette about "her friends," Helen, Paula, and Peg: "They are safe. I'll tell you about their departure when we know. I'll be staying in touch with Sr. Cecilia from Maryknoll. Please remain in touch with her as well."

That would be easy for Bernadette to do, as both she and Cecilia had already arranged to "casually" bump into each other at five that afternoon at an upscale grocery store in Providencia. Bernadette avoided arriving early. Hungry, she went into a nearby restaurant and ordered something to eat. When her food arrived, she took a few bites and paged through the afternoon paper, *La Segunda*, only to see a headline announcing Helen and Paula were being *expelled* from the country.

Why hadn't the consul told her this hours ago? she asked herself furiously.

Keeping her anger in check, she trudged over to the grocery store for her rendezvous with Cecilia. There instead of Cecilia was Sr. Ita Ford, a young Maryknoll sister entrusted with Cecilia's message.[3] At the grapefruit stand, Ita approached Bernadette tentatively, giving Cecilia's apologies for not coming in person.

"Bernadette, this is what I am supposed to tell you," she said, pausing, "you have a meeting with Vicar Juan de Castro tonight. Afterwards you are going to spend the night in Lo Curro." She handed Bernadette a slip of paper with a property lot number scrawled on it, without a hint of the homeowner's name.

The meeting at the vicariate ran late. Bernadette felt depleted. She had been on the move all day. Now in the hovering darkness, she took a cab to Lo Curro, but the cab driver couldn't locate the house. Trying not to be obvious Bernadette got out of the cab and knocked on a door, asking for help. She was directed to walk down the hill toward a cluster of homes.

"*¡Hola! Hola!*" she called out as she stumbled through the darkness, until she saw a man standing outside his home. He spoke to her softly, "No need to say anything, just come in." Then added, "We thought you were coming earlier and were waiting for you."

It was the home of a young couple with three children, who had been sent to their grandmother's house for the night. They fixed Bernadette a plate of food, brought her tea, then asked if she would like to watch the news. She was invited to sit on their couch as they took their places on either side of her. The newscast started with the breathless voice of a TV journalist, positioned on the tarmac of Pudahuel airport, pointing out the arrival of two U.S. embassy vans ferrying the "MIRist nuns." Bernadette sat mutely between the couple, trying to hold back her tears, seeing her life companions pelted with Judas coins.

When the news finished, the husband said to his wife, "You remember when our kids were at St. George's school? I think there was another sister; wasn't her name Sr. Bernadette?

Bernadette sighed, "I am that sister."

The husband turned to her, saying, "Please don't worry. You can stay here as long as you need." Turning off the television they spoke about the terrifying days surrounding the *golpe* and the military intervention of St. George. Before saying good night, they told Bernadette, "We want you to know, when the military confiscated St. George, we withdrew our children in protest."

Part VIII
Take Cover
November 9–19, 1975

∽

29

Isabel

After reconnecting over dinner on November 8, Isabel, Bernadette, Rosita, and I spent the next several days in Buzeta with Gerry and Helen Carpenter. In one of our conversations, I naively asked if anyone thought a pause button had been pushed. Was the expulsion of Helen, Paula, and Peg enough to pierce the wound? Were the church and the government ready to pull back, possibly seek a temporary détente?

"A pause? Détente? No way!" Isabel exclaimed. "The DINA has been on this day and night! For the DINA *not* to have captured their MIR targets was an atrocious defeat. Don't think the DINA will just walk away with their targets safely inside the *Nunciatura* and Costa Rican embassy. *¡Ni lo pienses!* Somebody will pay for this!"

The only question was who.

I worried most about Isabel, because she worked at the *Comité Pro Paz* and was Chilean. There would be no government backstop for her. She had been a strong supporter of Allende and belonged to a political party that backed Unidad Popular. Post-*golpe* she joined MAPU.[1] It aimed to mobilize the populace in defense of the poor and unite with other movements to create a political path to end the dictatorship.[2]

180

Her political tasks, undertaken in her "off hours," were serious and dangerous. They involved aiding leaders of the party who were working clandestinely, with food, money, safe houses, and places to meet. Needless to say, MAPU members were in the DINA's crosshairs.

Although she was a leftist activist, Isabel was vehement in her dislike of MIR. She told me, "I distrusted them! I didn't believe in their way of resisting the dictatorship. I was in a political party that opposed armed insurrection, but MIR relied on armed struggle to end the dictatorship."

Yet on October 20, the night of Helen's birthday party, Isabel centered herself around one belief. She told me, "There wasn't much time that night, so Bernadette, Helen, Paula, and I discussed it quickly. We did a discernment and agreed that if we didn't give the MIR members shelter, there was a strong possibility that they'd be killed. That moral issue came up very strongly. It was saving lives. We prayed and put the decision in God's hands."

But before the decision was finalized, Isabel insisted on two conditions: "No arms in the house!" She told the sisters: "Beware. We could be used. They are *not* going to follow our guidelines, criteria, or requests. They can have *no connection* with MIR while in the house. *No connection!* They will need to be *watched* and *stopped*. There can be no *enlace*, no linkage between them and the outside."

A night or two after Helen's birthday party, when Isabel learned MIR had entered the house with hidden weapons, she snapped her fingers and sucked in her breath, saying, "I knew it! They can't be trusted."

Perhaps because of MIR's indiscretions, the weapons they brought in and their attempts at outside contacts, Isabel was now the household member whose life was most in danger.

Something else still gnawed at Isabel. She told me it occurred on Sunday, November 2, when the DINA squad leader corralled us in the bedroom, reviewing *cédulas*. Her gaze was focused on the squad leader, who asked her, "Are you German?"; to which she said, "Yes, I am German."

She told me that her head was spinning at that moment, thinking: I know this person . . . I've seen him many times in my life. It wasn't through MAPU, but he might have been part of meetings at the *Comité Pro Paz*. If her intuition was correct, he was likely a DINA infiltrator inside the *Comité Pro Paz*. If she recognized him, surely he recognized her. Was Donoso Ureta a plausible German surname? Did he ask the diversionary question to protect his own cover, or so that Isabel could continue to be tracked?

After the DINA raid at our house on November 2, Isabel went into constant motion, keeping up with her work at the *Comité Pro Paz,* while discreetly monitoring the well-being of all of us. She too was on the run. Each night, friends and unknown people willingly extended their hands in solidarity to give her a place to sleep. She was touched by a young couple with an infant, who were "so open and brave." They took her into their humble home, no names exchanged. During the day, she walked through the streets of Santiago giving thanks to God, saying: "I'm alive at this minute, I'm alive!" But pulsing through her gratitude came the incessant thought: "I don't know what will happen next."

Now she was facing another profound decision, similar to the moment she faced in 1973 after the coup, when many of her friends went into exile.

During the nights we spent in Buzeta, I often saw her in the chapel weeping and praying. For the past two years, the atrocities of the dictatorship had rained down on her and the families served by *Comité Pro Paz*. It was her faith and belief in justice that kept her pressing through each day, always a hopeful spirit in the midst of so much suffering and inhumanity. She told us rumors were afoot that Pinochet had demanded that Cardinal Silva shut down the *Comité Pro Paz*. She began to grapple with the inevitable but was tormented by how to tell her parents she was leaving the country.

She told me, "My father believes every one of the government's pronouncements: there is no torture, no one has been disappeared, the country is doing great, and Pinochet has saved us from Communism."

A day or two later, she discreetly went to say goodbye to her parents, letting them know she was seeking her *salvoconducto* and would leave Chile soon. Her father said, "Isabel, if there is some trouble you are running from, all you have to do is present yourself to the authorities. If you do so, everything will be fine, and nothing will happen to you."

She grimaced, wishing there was a way to bridge their two realities. Instead, she hugged and kissed her mother and father goodbye. Stepping outside her parents' house, she exclaimed under her breath, "Trust these authorities? *¡Nada que ver!* Never!"

Having made her decision, she had to face her co-workers at the *Comité Pro Paz*. She felt guilty leaving them in this moment of crisis. If the *Comité* were to close as rumored, all of them would soon be without jobs, *fichados*, and in danger. She was the lucky one who could take a plane to the "land of freedom."

30

Conflict in the Pews
November 9–10

On Monday, November 10, I was drinking some coffee and reading *El Mercurio* before I returned to my classroom to teach. The paper reported on yesterday's Mass at Nuestra Sra. del Carmen in Ñuñoa. Cardinal Silva's call for "serenity and moderation" earlier in the week had set off a firestorm in the pews and press. Angry protesters gathered on the church steps before the Mass started. During the Prayers of the Faithful, one shouted out: "Pray for the Catholic Church in its struggle against atheist-materialistic communism!" At which point the youth choir launched into song to overpower the shouts. As the parishioners processed out of Mass, a wall of protesters with signs met them, expressing their disgust for MIR and their alleged priests and religious partisans.[1]

Meanwhile, more debates broke out. *El Mercurio* ran an interview with Archbishop Emilio Tagle Corraubias of Valparaiso and Bishop Salinas of Linares. Archbishop Tagle said it was "unacceptable to cooperate" in saving the MIR members' lives above "the love of one's homeland." Bishop Salinas stated that the priests involved "have failed in their duties and deserve censure; and in this case, though it is difficult to say so, they merit its punishment."[2]

Attacks aimed at the cardinal's leadership kept coming. A prominent attorney and arch-conservative commentator, Jaime Guzmán, severely criticized Cardinal Silva on TV Nacional. In response, Cardinal Silva pressed the television station for equal time.

El Mercurio had been full-throated in its support for the overthrow of the Allende government, readily embracing the military junta. Today was no exception to the journal's viewpoint. The paper included a special pull-out section alleging "extremism" among the Holy Cross priests and the "Marxist penetration at Colegio St. George." Specifically profiled in the multipage article were SSND sisters Helen Nelson and Paula Armstrong, and Holy Cross priests Phil Devlin, Gerardo Whelan, Fermín Donoso, and Robert Plasker.[3]

While the sparring between prominent officials, high-profile organizations, and the press could be expected, the other morning's news would rock the moorings of the *Comité Pro Paz*. The Orthodox Church, one of the ecumenical founders of the *Comité Pro Paz* in 1973, withdrew from the *Comité* over the assistance given to the MIR fugitives.[4]

31

Testing the Waters
November 10–16

Gerry and Helen Carpenter had covered Helen's and Paula's classrooms in their absence. But when their photos appeared in the news, they worried the school might be impacted. A member of the military came to the school and questioned Sra. Grumilda, the principal, wanting to know where Helen and Paula lived. She chatted with him, giving vague answers until he walked out the gate. A number of the students' fathers were police and lower-level soldiers. Upon seeing Helen's and Paula's photos on television, the kids got upset, telling their parents, "*No, no, no, Hermanas* Helen and Paula wouldn't do anything wrong!"

As a new week rolled into view, Rosita and I returned to our classrooms and pitched in to help Gerry and Helen Carpenter in the seventh and eighth grade classrooms. It was exhausting.

Bernadette dreaded going back to her school in Borja de Echevarría. She knew the teachers were conservative, referred to in Chilean slang as *momios*, or mummies, for backing the military take-over and unwilling to speak out against its atrocities. Helen's and Paula's faces were well known to the school's faculty, as SSND sisters had taught at the school since 1964. Bernadette was fearful of her colleagues' reactions, expecting that they'd seen the television coverage over the past week. Nevertheless, they welcomed her back, communicating through their eyes and hugs their *apoyo*—support.

During the morning recess Bernadette met the principal in her office, taking care not to "enlighten her" about her absence. The substitute teacher in Bernadette's classroom entered the office, saying, "The kids are refusing to go back to class because they saw Sr. Bernadette. Bernadette left and greeted the kids in the schoolyard with a big smile, saying, "Don't worry, I'll be back tomorrow!"

Isabel, Bernadette, Rosita, and I finally returned to our home on Padre Orellana mid-week. Rounding the hallway toward my bedroom, I glanced into Helen's room. Usually tidy, it was now a tumult of strewn belongings ransacked by the DINA. Bernadette hesitated as she walked toward Paula's room, imagining how on November 2, Paula had dressed, then fled. With tears she began to tuck away Paula's clothes, smoothing the bedspread as if it could cover up the reality of Helen's and Paula's expulsions from Chile.

We didn't really settle back into the house. Perhaps over those three to five days someone cleared the refrigerator of any spoiled food, and maybe a few groceries were purchased. The laundry from eleven days before was plucked off the patio clothesline. We shoved the upturned furniture back into place and put the phone handle back on its base, a useless exercise, given that the DINA had pocketed the mouthpiece. Isabel believed the house might be under surveillance, but reasoned that life was dangerous all around, and this was just another factor.

With the phone not working and the need to prep lesson plans for the many classroom segments I was teaching, there wasn't much time to think. I wanted to connect with Bernard, but I didn't dare take the long bus ride alone up to Lo Baranecha to meet him. I feared that my presence might endanger anyone I visited. Bernard was now living with the Barranechea family near Santa Rosa Parish, where Fr. Fermín Donoso had also been detained. I had no idea how Bernard and the other Notre Dame students were doing, given that several of the Holy Cross priests who interacted with the LAPEL program were in prison.

In today's news, Foreign Minister Carvajal announced that he would "graciously" provide a *salvoconducto* for Fr. Phil Devlin, who was sought by security forces. He would do so as soon as Devlin provided a statement "confessing he hid Marxist elements."[1] I wondered who Phil might have aided, as Carvajal did not reveal whom Devlin was accused of hiding.

The next day, Phil Devlin's "confession" was printed in the newspaper: "Members of my congregation were not aware of the aid I provided to those being sought by the security forces. My motivation was not political. My decision was made solely for humanitarian and Christian reasons. As a priest, I felt it was my duty to do so."[2]

32

A Photo of Sheila
November 12

I remained deeply concerned about Sheila, so little appeared about her in the news. On Monday, November 10, she was taken by guards to face Joaquím Erlbaum Thomas, the military prosecutor assigned to investigate and charge her. He questioned her repeatedly about those who were present in the Columban Center house the night of November 1. She named the four of them: herself, Enriqueta, Sr. Connie, and Fr. Halliden. He challenged her, asking about an accomplice and weapons being fired from inside the building. Unsettled by Sheila's insistent refutation of his line of questioning, Erlbaum ended the session.[1]

On Tuesday, November 11, Sheila again entered the Second Military Court. She was paraded past waiting photographers, next to Fr. Rafael Maroto, a worker-priest, who had been similarly accused of aiding the militants. The prosecutor's assistants led her through an all-day interrogation, each answer typed into the carbon-copied record. She was given a cup of coffee, which she held in her trembling hands. By mid-morning she was faint with hunger. Upon seeing her distress, the prosecutor exclaimed, "Good God! Have they not fed you?"[2]

At 6:00 p.m. Erlbaum Thomas charged her under the State of Siege laws in effect when events occurred in Malloco on October 15–16. His ruling meant she would be sent to the *Casa Correccional*, Santiago's prison for women, and would no longer be under the DINA's control.[3] *El Mercurio's* coverage of her first visit to the prosecutor's office ran on Tuesday, November 11, without any photo, making it hard for me to imagine Sheila's true condition.

Gerry caught me at the end of classes, to tell me that Cecilia Vandal, the superior of the Maryknoll sisters, wanted to meet with Bernadette,

Isabel, Rosita, and me that evening at our house to discuss precautions. On the bus ride home to Padre Orellana, I found a window seat, pulled open the newspaper, and almost vomited.

On the front page was Sheila's photo as she entered the military court building the day before.[4] Her eyes were dead orbs. Her jeans bagged out and seemed to slide off her hips. Her sweater drooped over emaciated shoulders. Her arms hung lifeless against her body. She had lost so much weight. Her hair was matted against her forehead and greasy. Eleven days had passed, and she was wearing the same clothes from the day we had lunch together at her house!

I felt Sheila's deadness inhabit me. I limped off the bus at Portugal, the same stop where I had shaken off the man tailing me on November 1. This time, instead of running I dragged myself across the street and numbly entered our house.

Within an hour or two, Sr. Cecilia was at the door. She was a middle-aged woman, short in stature, with a serious demeanor. We met in the living room, pulling a few chairs closer to the couch to form a circle. The tension, strain, and mental exhaustion showed on all our faces. Cecilia set forth her concerns. She thought we should move out of the house immediately, given that a photo and the address of the house had appeared in last week's paper. She warned, "Just because the government let Paula, Helen, and Peg leave the country, it doesn't mean that more retaliation couldn't happen. Politically, everything remains very unstable." Then she asked for our thoughts.

Bernadette spoke first, telling us that today she met with Fr. Guillermo Marshall, the Jesuit superior, who said, "I've visited the jail where Fr. Patricio Cariola is being held, and he is quite concerned for you. He asked me to share his fears that the DINA may be allowing you to remain free, so they can follow you in order to grab or arrest other people."

Bernadette tried to reassure him that she had been taking extra precautions and planned to see her family when classes ended in December. Unconvinced, he replied, "I think you should make a visit to the United States as soon as possible."

Rosita also had plans to visit her family in Peru when school ended. With great anguish, Isabel had resolved to leave the country for several months. She had seen a travel agent to inquire about flights to New York, where she would stay with Paula and Helen and make other plans from there. But she had not yet obtained her *salvoconducto.*

I, for one, couldn't think. I was hanging on to a weak game plan of testing out a return to normal. I wanted the terror of being in the DINA's hands, living on the run, using pseudonyms, and hiding while in the national spotlight to just go away.

Cecilia rose to leave, saying, "Please consider what I've said. Remember, Sheila is still detained."

The next morning, as we grabbed some breakfast, Isabel said, "Maybe we should just get away this weekend and go to the coast. I'll ask my friend Charo if we can stay at her house in Quintero. We can go there after work on Friday."

I couldn't think of a better plan.

33

Quintero
November 14–16

Isabel's friend Charo Downey generously opened her port-side home in Quintero to us for the weekend. Isabel, Rosita, and Rosario's friendship dated to the years they were members of the IHM religious community.

After classes ended on Friday, Rosita and I met up with Isabel for the two-hour bus ride to the coastal town, immediately north of Valparaiso and Viña del Mar. Once we were on the highway outside of Santiago, the bus veered through the countryside as we headed northwest toward the coast. For a few hours the sun shone warmly on the earth, already exploding with its springtime flowers alongside plots of tilled land. I knew we were nearing Quintero, a town known for its natural harbor, when the sea-salt smell coursed through the air.

The bus dropped us off on the main road, and we popped into a few stores to buy wine, empanadas, cheese, bread, and a few sweets. We walked up the road to Charo's house with our satchels hanging heavy on our shoulders. Rosario was already in the kitchen, prepping some fish for dinner. The fireplace crackled, warming the air to fend off a slightly chilly ocean breeze.

The home was ample, with enough bedrooms to house a multi-generational family for weekend visits or summer holidays. Chilean art, pottery, and Mapuche artifacts filled the walls and bookcases. Intricate woolen weavings with deep colors were everywhere. Out the window I could see a stand of eucalyptus and pine trees, and just beyond, the frothy sea. Charo eagerly welcomed us into the kitchen, where she had begun dinner preparations. She was a vibrant, tall woman with chestnut hair. After several rounds of hugs and some light-hearted teasing, we pulled out the warm empanadas, opened the bottles of wine, and gathered near the fire for appetizers. For the first time in weeks, I felt safe.

After a delicious dinner and more conversation, I headed for bed. I knew Isabel and Rosita wanted some time alone to talk with Charo. I woke up the next morning to the smoky smell of last night's embers. The day was clear and light as the sun crested into sight. Soon we were drinking coffee with warmed milk and eating the buttered bread rolls with jam and scrambled eggs.

By noon, Rosita, Isabel, and I headed to the beach. Isabel led the way down a path that traversed through a small grove of trees and then opened to huge stretches of flat, weathered boulders. We traipsed across the worn face of boulders as the sea spray fanned the atmosphere with its moisture. The air was exhilarating, and the sound of the ocean's pulse seemed to reach my heart. Even though the newspapers were advertising mini bikinis, this was still a day for slacks and jackets.

It was also a time to start saying goodbye. Isabel told us she hoped to pick up her *salvoconducto* on Monday. If so, she might leave as early as Tuesday night.

I didn't want to think about Isabel leaving. She probably didn't know how much I had come to rely on her hopefulness in dire moments or her concise analysis of complex realities. I'm pretty sure that after she accused me of being a CIA plant, she had believed my sincere desire to understand the realities of Chile. Maybe she saw me as unfocused, too young or too American, but she had befriended me and continued to teach me about Chile.

Isabel embodied something few people have—a deep spiritual commitment to bring both joy and justice into her personal encounters and a drive to transform the societal structures that keep joy and justice locked away from the poor and outcast. Her life was an *entrega*—a prophetic, lived witness with all its risks to body and soul—to bring the vision of Medellín alive and to answer with her life "the cry that pours from the throats of millions."[1]

She shouldn't have to leave Chile, especially with no guarantees that she could return. That afternoon, we sat on the rocks as she told us how she came to the decision to leave. "The strength, the thing that kept me going was faith. By all means it was faith! I did a lot of reflection during those nights I was hiding in other people's houses. I kept experiencing myself as a mere creature. Then suddenly the image of the Creator came into my mind. Being a creature means your life is so limited. Sometimes you think you have the whole of life, the power of life, within your grasp, but that is baloney! I was nothing more than a *pulga*, a flea, and anybody with big feet could crush me. I realized then that the only one who had the power in terms of life was God. I cried my thanks to God for being alive. I came to the decision. Now, I am alive, I have to continue!"

As the waves crashed around us, my mind began to clear. We were quiet for a long time, covered by the immense blue sky with the warm sun sparkling on the waves below. I thought about my next steps. How feasible was it for me to remain in Chile? I could probably live with Gerry and Helen and help out in Buzeta's summer program. But when would I know if I was safe?

A quiet moment in Quintero. Kathy Osberger and Rosita Arroyo.

I knew I didn't want to go home. It would be wonderful to see my family, but after a few weeks in South Bend, what would I do next? Just the thought of it made my heart sink. All my college friends had moved to new jobs or graduate school. I'd be floundering if I went home, with months of winter snows ahead and slim job openings until the spring. All my hopes had been pinned on spending two years in Latin America. I didn't want to leave. I had only been in Chile for four months and felt I needed to process my experience and gain a deeper understanding of this reality, especially by moving closer to the poor.

We had been sitting quietly when Rosita piped up, *"Oye, Kathy, ¿por qué no vienes a Perú conmigo? ¡Puedes quedarte con nosotros en la casa de mis padres! ¡Ven! ¡Sería regio!"*

Rosita asked me, "Kathy, why don't you come to Peru with me? We can stay in my parents' house. Come!" I was overwhelmed by Rosita's kindness and generosity. I felt uncertain. But I could envision it as a possibility. I could travel with her to La Punta, Callao, spend the Christmas holidays, and try to connect with the Notre Dame students and Holy Cross priests in Chimbote. If I couldn't return to Chile, maybe I could find some other volunteer opportunity in Peru.

34

A Bait and Switch
November 15–17

While Isabel, Rosita, and I were at the coast, unbeknownst to us, Sheila Cassidy entered into an even deeper nightmare. On Friday, November 14, Sheila was transported for her third visit to the military court. As Sheila descended the stairwell to Prosecutor Erlbaum Thomas's office, three bound men tramped down the steps behind her. She looked backwards in amazement to see Frs. Gerardo Whelan, Patricio Cariola, and Fernando Salas. They hugged, grateful to see each other alive, but were under orders to remain silent.[1] Since his arrest on November 2, Gerardo Whelan had been under the DINA's control, where he suffered greatly, then was transferred to Tres Álamos. But now Whelan was in the Cárcel Capuchinos, a lower-security jail, with both Salas and Cariola.

With great emotion Cardinal Silva described the reception Frs. Salas and Cariola received when they arrived at the jail. "The prisoners formed an extensive human corridor from the jail yard to the stairs, right up to their cell door; as they advanced, spontaneous applause began to grow among the prisoners, becoming a thunderous reception. . . . This was their crazed blessing!"[2]

Among the four, Sheila was the first one interviewed by Erlbaum, who lifted the incommunicado ban. She instantly contacted her consul, Derek Fernyhoug. Upon telling him of her torture, he left to cable this information to London. Later that day Erlbaum dropped Sheila's charges under Bando 89, lowering them to a lesser charge of not reporting the treatment of a man with a bullet wound. Erlbaum said she was now free. Shocked by his ruling, Sheila returned to the anteroom to share her joy

An arpillera *made by women artisans and sold by the* Comité Pro Paz *that depicts the struggle for human rights in Chile.*

with the priests. They immediately sensed danger. She should *not* be without embassy protection for a single moment, in case the DINA tried to re-arrest her.

By 6:00 p.m. the court closed for the weekend. Hernán Montalegre, an attorney from the *Comité Pro Paz*, accompanied Sheila to the women's jail to await her release papers, while Fernyhoug made calls into the night to Prosecutor Erlbaum to obtain her release. Sheila's intuition told her the DINA wasn't going to allow her freedom so easily. The next morning, a cruel bait and switch played out. With Fernyhoug at her side, she was told she'd be moved to a prison under police control. Then suddenly, a guard approached and forced her to follow him. Minutes later she was back under the DINA's control.[3]

While Sheila's advocates could not reach Prosecutor Erlbaum the evening of November 14, apparently many powerful people in the government had reached him. Unbeknownst to Sheila's advocates, overnight, Patricio Carvajal had contravened Erlbaum's order to free her, effectively reinstating Bando 89's charges against her.

Yet, at 1:30 a.m., Saturday, November 15, Erlbaum was obviously awake and reachable. At that dim hour he issued a media gag order, prohibiting any reports related to the matters of the MIR case.[4] One had to wonder, after weeks of intense coverage, what was this order intended to hide?

35

The United Nations Condemns Chile November 12

The bait and switch Sheila Cassidy faced on November 15 occurred just after the United Nations voted to condemn Chile for its human rights abuses. Clearly, no gag order would keep the world from repudiating the dictatorship. For over a year the "Ad-Hoc Working Group on Human Rights in Chile" documented the disappeared, extrajudicial deaths, and torture of civilians.[1]

Chile's ambassador to the United Nations, Sergio Diaz, disparaged the report as biased, but the chair of the Ad-Hoc Committee, Ali Allana, representing Pakistan, said the report was "impartial and based on direct testimonies." He cited the case of Luis Alberto Corvalán, who was found "physically and emotionally destroyed . . . experiencing frequent loss of memory brought on by the tortures he suffered." Another prisoner was severely beaten and was forced to rape a young leftist woman. Holland's representative confirmed that electric shock torture was systematically applied by the DINA. Ninety countries voted in favor of the condemnation; eleven countries—all from Latin America—voted against the resolution, and twenty countries abstained.[2]

Ultimately the United States joined the vote to condemn Chile's human rights record. Yet prior to the vote, when Secretary of State Henry Kissinger and Foreign Minister Patricio Carvajal discussed the matter, Kissinger openly disparaged the State Department staff who briefed him on Chile's record, saying sarcastically, they "have a vocation for the ministry."[3]

To protest the U.S. vote, Carvajal immediately called U.S. Ambassador Popper into his office. Afterwards Popper told the press he met with Carvajal "to make a general analysis of our bilateral concerns," and to that end he would be traveling to Washington, DC, for meetings.[4] After Popper's meeting, diplomats from all the embassies in Santiago filed in to face Carvajal, who reproached their votes.

36

Cardinal Silva in Rome
November 16–28

Cardinal Silva flew to Rome to discuss with Pope Paul VI the increasing attacks on the church. While he arrived in Rome buoyed by the messages of solidarity sent to him from prelates around the world, he hoped to have time for reflection amid the bitter public disputes. Meeting the press upon arrival, they questioned him about tensions with the government. He responded, saying, "The Chilean church is experiencing a difficult situation, but it has its own conduct, which is the gospel, that is neither to the left or the right, but of truth."[1]

In Rome, Cardinal Silva made it a point to seek out Sr. Georgina Segner, the general superior of the School Sisters of Notre Dame, to tell her that "Your two sisters, Helen Nelson and Paula Armstrong, were good sisters."[2]

On November 28, Cardinal Silva met with the pope at the Vatican for an extended conversation, including Pinochet's demand to shut down the *Comité Pro Paz*. While the pope lamented the loss of the ecumenical character of the *Comité*, he nonetheless "realized it would allow the Catholic Church to fully assume the prophetic task of defending the gospel in a climate of severe misunderstanding." Prior to ending the meeting with Cardinal Silva, the pope inquired about the priests who were imprisoned. He then told Silva to tell Chile "that for him the imprisoned priests were martyrs of Christian charity."[3]

After meeting with the pope, Cardinal Silva held multiple rounds of meetings with Vatican officials, including French cardinal Roger Etchegaray, the president of the Synod of European Bishops. With the confidence of support from many European dioceses, Cardinal Silva traveled on to Germany to solidify the critical financial resources needed to continue the church's human rights and solidarity work.

37

Rattled
November 17

We arrived back from Quintero on Sunday night with just enough time to grab a bite to eat and pick out clean clothes for work the next day. Monday morning at Buzeta, Gerry and Helen told me there was a rumor that Sheila had been released to her consul on Friday night, and then was re-captured by the DINA. I felt sick with fear.

Still, nothing about the rumor made sense. Did the DINA dare to grab her from the British consul, violating all governmental protocols? I thought, this is a government going off the rails, heedless of world opinion. They were going to show who ruled, no matter the costs. It also meant they might double back for us.

Isabel hadn't heard the rumors about Sheila. She had taken the day off to reconfirm her flight at the travel agency, then packed her bag. Feeling unnerved, Isabel had asked friends from the *Comité* to accompany her to pick up her *salvoconducto*. In other words, she wanted witnesses in case something happened.

Bernadette also looked drawn. She had a plane reservation to leave in a week, but that afternoon a second message from jail had been sent her way. This time it was from Gerardo Whelan, who urged his visitor to locate Bernadette with the message: "Tell them to take cover."

While we were piecing together the news about Sheila and the message sent by Gerardo Whelan, the overnight press wires from London were heating up. The British government demanded clarification about Sheila's continued detention, going so far as to say, "Either free Dr. Cassidy or press charges without delay."[1]

38

Elfriede and Edelweiss
November 18

I couldn't sleep last night. I showered in cold water, hoping to stir my brain enough to face the full day of classes ahead. I stuffed the warning signs from last night's conversations into some mental chute. I couldn't allow those thoughts to come to consciousness, or I'd collapse. I had to keep going, at least until the end of the school year, when Rosita planned to leave.

Now back from Quintero, I made up my mind to take the bus to Lo Barnechea. I needed to connect with Bernard and the Notre Dame students. I hoped to talk with Fr. Fermín Donoso at Santa Rosa, but I wasn't sure if Fermín was out of jail yet. I took a deep breath, bit into the last corner of my toast, and exited the front door with Rosita to catch the bus to Buzeta.

I stayed at school several hours after the children left, fleshing out lesson plans and catching up on grading math homework. Rosita was still wrapping up her work when I left school and headed downtown by bus. I was only a block away from the main post office. I walked into its elegant, but crowded, lobby toward our post-office box.

Idiotic terror gripped me as I approached the wall of boxes. I was afraid that a DINA agent had been posted nearby to grab one of us. My heart started racing. I turned the key, slipped my arm into the slot, and pulled out the mail, dropping it quickly into my satchel, then hightailing it out of there.

I felt safer being out in the open. There were lots of people crisscrossing the plaza, completing their workday and errands. I jumped on the bus and arrived back at Matta and Portugal. Then, just as I was about to put my house key in the front lock a huge car careened around the corner behind me, jamming itself up to the curb. Frightened, I turned my head to see Helen Carpenter in the driver's seat anxiously calling my name and telling me, "Get in!" I glanced up and saw that Gerry and Bernadette were in the back seat of this tank of a car.

"What's going on?" I asked as I climbed into the front seat next to a Maryknoll sister whom I had met once. No one answered for a minute. Bernadette's face was ashen, and Gerry's was grim.

Helen replied, "We got a call from Cecelia Vandal; she wants to speak with you and Bernadette. We are headed over to the Maryknoll Center house."

Then Bernadette said from the back seat, "Kathy, someone from the U.S. embassy will be at the meeting."

I knew this was about Sheila's re-capture. She had become a pawn for the Pinochet regime to dangle, a means to portray indifference to a world that had just humiliated their rule. No doubt every embassy in Santiago understood the message quite clearly. I crumpled in my seat as Helen Carpenter sped toward Los Leones.

After a long silence, Elfriede, the sister next to me, said, "I'm glad to see you, Kathy.[1] I've heard you've been through some difficult weeks. I just arrived a few hours ago from Austria. Helen and Gerry picked me up at Pudahuel. I was back visiting family. It's been more than ten years since I've seen them."

Obliged to say something, I asked, "Did you have a good trip? Is your family well?"

"The country is so changed since the war," she said, continuing, "most of my family are now gone; the few that are left are nieces and nephews I hardly know."

Helen chimed in, "Elfriede, tell Kathy about what you did during the war."

Elfriede didn't hesitate. "I was in the refugee camps. As a child I helped to run messages for the resistance, who were fighting the Nazis. When the war ended, things were so destroyed. I prayed and found my vocation with the Maryknoll Sisters and was sent as a missionary to Chile. I've been here twelve years now." I barely had the ability to comprehend what she was saying, but it was a version of the story we were living. She had risked her young life to defy a fascist regime.

We were almost at the gate of the Maryknoll Center house. I saw the semicircular drive paved with the upturned river stones. I felt woozy. Elfreide then opened a book on her lap and pulled out some pressed flowers wrapped in wax paper, saying, "I'd like to give you this. It is edelweiss, the delicate white blossoms that bloom in the Alps. They represent purity and friendship. Please take it." I extended my hand as tears started to roll down my cheeks. When the car stopped, Elfriede looked at me and said, "Don't worry, worse things can happen."

When I stepped out of the car, I was standing exactly where the DINA had taken me back blindfolded into their Fiat, seventeen days before.

PART IX
INSIDE THE CONSULATE
NOVEMBER 18–DECEMBER 5, 1975

39

Charles Stout
November 18

I was the last to enter the Maryknoll Center house. We were all bunched up in the screened entry foyer, with happy sounds emanating from the sisters as they welcomed Elfreide. Gerry and Helen handed off her luggage to the other sisters, who escorted Elfreide through the living room and up the stairs to the guest rooms.

As we stepped into the dining room, my mind replayed the scene of the DINA pushing themselves into the foyer, Sr. Katherine Gilfeather trying to hold them back, then seeing the two American men crumpled under the dining room table. I could hear the DINA shouting, "She's coming with us!" I was in a daze. I sat down on a dining chair, but I couldn't feel my body. I became nothing more than a swirl of air hovering over the chair.

For some reason Sr. Cecilia was unavailable, so she asked Sr. Jeanne Sachs to lead the meeting and convey Cecilia's concerns. The doorbell rang, and Charles Stout, the U.S. embassy political officer, entered the room. He scanned the convent layout quickly. Facing the ring of women seated around the dining table, he appeared uncertain about where he should place himself. He was broad-shouldered, stocky, and bald. He had the stiff-backed bearing of military training and was dressed in a black suit, crisp white shirt, and black tie. Large black-rimmed glasses framed his face, a hardened face with dark bullet eyes that telegraphed: Tell me everything... because I already know. Then we'll be done.

Jeanne opened the meeting, stating that Fr. Marshall, the superior of the Jesuit community, called Cecilia after he visited Frs. Fernando Salas and Patricio Cariola, who were still in jail. They asked him to warn us that the security forces were actively seeking us. Already alarmed, Cecilia factored the urgent warning with the news of Sheila's re-capture by the DINA, and immediately contacted the embassy requesting tonight's meeting.

Stout then turned to Bernadette. "Were you in the house with Nelson Gutiérrez and the sisters?"

"I was," she replied.

He pressed her for the exact dates. He didn't bother to ask her motivation.

"And you?" he asked me. "Were you in the house too?"

"Yes, I was there the night of October 20."

I didn't need to brief him further. Because he knew. He knew I lived with the SSND sisters and that the DINA had taken me prisoner on November 2. It had been documented by my telephone conversation with Consul Brownell the same morning.

But I'm sure he and other embassy officials had more than one source for that information as well: the American interrogator, the eyes of the DINA, the ultimate commander of the dawn raid. Stout was stuffed with secrets. Mine were puny by comparison. I certainly didn't trust him enough to share what I knew either.

Jeanne stepped in, saying that she believed it was no longer safe for either of us to remain in Chile, and she'd like Mr. Stout to speak with both of us to ensure our safety.

Stout nodded his agreement and laid out three options. "One scenario would be for the two of you to continue what you are doing, being very careful and making arrangements on your own to leave. A second scenario would be to have a stronger bond with the embassy by residing in a safe house that had diplomatic immunity, where somebody from the U.S. Foreign Service lived. That location would have to remain secret.

You could continue your normal work while residing there until your departure. The third option would be to ask for temporary refuge and reside in a U.S. embassy property until your departure can be arranged."

I asked Stout, "Do you mean political asylum?" He eyed me and acidly replied, "We don't offer U.S. citizens political asylum. You may request temporary refuge."

¡Estúpida! I cursed to myself silently. Of course, the United States couldn't offer political asylum to its own citizens. I wilted back into my chair, awakened again to the fact that my brain wasn't working so well. Bernadette was discussing the first option, envisioning staying a few more nights in Buzeta and following up on her tentative flight reservation.

Stout excused himself from the room to consult with his superiors by phone, allowing us the opportunity to discuss the pros and cons among ourselves.

Jeanne's opinion was clear: "Take cover." But Bernadette was frustrated that she wasn't in command of all the facts that led to this meeting, not to mention she wasn't emotionally ready to leave Chile.

Stout came back into the room, saying, "I've informed my superiors of your desire to reside with friends, make your flight reservations, and seek your *salvoconducto* on your own. This is what they ask me to tell you: Please reconsider."

After a bit more discussion, Bernadette agreed to staying in a safe house with embassy personnel. Somewhat anxiously I followed her lead.

As the meeting concluded, I looked at Gerry's and Helen's crestfallen faces. They were already working so hard at school. Who would cover the classes tomorrow and pay attention to the kids? I would vanish from my classroom once again with no explanation to my students, and weeks still remained until the end of the school year. I could barely come up with words as we hugged each other goodbye and stepped into Mr. Stout's sedan.

Night had fallen, and the heavy overhang of the trees darkened the streets even more. Stout drove without saying a word about where we were headed. We passed through the more exclusive zones of Santiago, winding up the Andes. He pulled into a driveway and motioned that we should get out. We walked up to the house's front step, where Mrs. Stout greeted us.

Under my breath I uttered, *"¡Dios mío!"* It never occurred to me that we might be sleeping in the home of the embassy's political officer.

Mrs. Stout had a genteel manner and showed Bernadette and me to a bedroom decorated with matching fabric of tiny pink rose buds on the bedspread, pillow covers, and curtains. It could have been my grandmother's guest room. It made me think about the choices one makes when living in another country, replicating home or adapting to a new reality. As soon as Mrs. Stout closed the door and said good-night, we each picked a side of the bed and slid to the floor cross-legged, our backs to the mattress, needing a semiprivate space to cry.

The next morning, we were invited downstairs for breakfast prepared by the maid. We arrived dressed in yesterday's clothes. Mr. Stout sat at the head of the table; his wife took her seat to his right. Bernadette was ready to go into downtown Santiago and finalize her plane ticket. She listened to Mr. Stout as he went over last night's instructions.

"Be careful as you travel on the buses. Don't speak with anyone. Don't mention to anyone where you are staying. Use a lot of caution." He said the same thing about three different ways. I started to feel more fearful because Bernadette was going alone.

Then the doorbell rang, and the maid ushered in Josiah Brownell, the U.S. consul. He took his place at the table, greeting Bernadette and introducing himself to me, remarking, "Of course! We've spoken with each other already."

Brownell and Bernadette had already established some rapport from their previous meetings. He got to the point: "I am very concerned for both of you. I've been told, Sr. Bernadette, that you are willing to go on your own to concretize your travel plans and request your *salvoconducto*. I understand your desire, but I think it is unwise and very dangerous. I really recommend that you both take 'temporary refuge' and reside in a U.S. embassy property until we can arrange for your departure."

My head cleared as anger surged. I was sick of these one-way conversations. I wanted to ask, "What is the new information that has made you so concerned? Who is threatening and what specifically are they threatening?" I really wanted to add, "Aren't all your DINA informants on the U.S. payroll along with half of the junta? Is this really about making sure no more citizens spoil the 'special relationship' between U.S. financial and political backers of the Pinochet government, keeping things at a low boil, not a burn?"

Of course, I understood it was the whole package of these arrangements at play. We were trapped in a *pater familias* power relationship with the embassy at that moment, where raised eyebrows and sly smiles would be substituted for straight answers. We both realized that if we were trying to save our lives, temporary refuge was the only viable path. We left with Consul Brownell. Neither of us had any real idea of what was ahead, until the car reached the gates of the U.S. consulate.[1]

40

Inside the Consulate
November 19

Brownell drove the car through the ornate entry gates up to the consulate's massive doors. He put the car in park as the Marine guards approached to open our doors. Brownell motioned that we should follow him inside. We stepped into the busy office lobby, where many people were in lines to transact business and obtain passports and visas. We swiftly passed them, maneuvering through the warren of desks staffed by U.S. and Chilean employees.

In his office Brownell pulled up chairs and offered us some local newspapers to read. He stepped away briefly, then returned to his desk, saying we needed to provide a statement to the Chilean authorities regarding our involvement in aiding the MIR fugitives. He then handed us copies of the statements made by Helen, Paula, and Peg.

Touching Helen's statement, I trembled with the overwhelming memory of the DINA shoving the filthy warrant for her arrest into my hands on November 2. It took some time to calm the hum racing through my body. Then I penned a few lines, stating I was at the convent on the night of October 20 when the MIR members arrived and were given humanitarian aid. Bernadette's statement was longer, emphasizing her acts of compassion undertaken congruent with her Christian faith.

A few hours had passed when a contingent of Marine guards entered the consul's office to politely serve us lunch. They seemed to be about seventeen to twenty-two years of age. They addressed both of us as "Ma'am," which I thought was a hoot, since I was their age. They told us they secured the consulate, wielding machine guns at the facility's entrance; but when on duty inside, they were usually unarmed. We asked where they were from and learned that they grew up in Indiana, Kentucky, and Tennessee. Their boyish faces reminded me of guys who had been my high school classmates, the faces of those who signed up for Vietnam or were drafted. Studying their faces gave me pause.

What guiding star landed each of us here? I felt an affinity with them. We were all Midwest kids from smallish communities with struggling industries or from farm country. Perhaps we had in common being seekers, anxious to see a bigger world and trying to chart our paths. I'm sure that being part of the Marine Corps and serving at an embassy was an honor for them. But I wondered if they knew the depth of the U.S. government's role in destabilizing Chile's long-standing democracy or that the stripping of U.S. aid after Allende's legitimate election led to an accelerated economic collapse and the pervasive poverty they saw around them. Were they told, or did they believe, that the DINA "security forces" were legitimate and necessary, in spite of the atrocities they committed?

After lunch we spent the afternoon making a list of items to retrieve from Orellana. Mr. Brownell promised to be in touch with Maryknoll sisters Gerry and Helen to ask their help in packing up our belongings. Obviously, the house remained a place of danger, and we greatly appreciated their efforts.

Sitting in Brownell's office, we spoke quietly. We were afraid of inadvertently endangering someone by mentioning them, especially Isabel. Had she made it safely through the National Police's checkpoint at Pudahuel and onto last night's flight to New York? And Rosita? Did she get word that we *weren't* coming back to Orellana? Was she safe and staying at Buzeta for the time being?

At some point that afternoon we heard loud sounds overhead. Brownell returned to his office, and Bernadette asked, "What's going on up there?"

He broke into a smile saying, "Oh, I just came to tell you that we have prepared a room for you upstairs. I hope that it will be adequate for your needs." He then escorted us to a large, nearly empty room on the second floor with no windows, but two glass doors that opened to reveal a small balcony ledge. The room had a worn area carpet, twin beds with a nightstand and lamp between them, and a chair or two. In my head, I tagged it as our garret room. We expressed our appreciation for the trouble he and the staff went through to clean and set it up for us.

To which Brownell replied, "This is the first time, and I think it is very important. It was not made for only the two of you, but it may be important for other people also."

When Brownell left to return to his office, we looked at each other, puzzled. Bernadette said, "Did he just indirectly thank us for getting the U.S. government to set up a room in the consulate to safeguard American citizens pursued by the Chilean security forces, which the U.S. supports and funds?" Realizing the absurdity, all we could do was laugh.[1]

41

Daniel Panchot—In the Vortex
November 14–18

Fr. Daniel Panchot, together with Sr. María de los Angeles, known to all as "Ma," had ferried many endangered people, including Rosita and me, to safe houses as part of their work at the *Comité Pro Paz.* The week had been a tense one for the *Comité*, as Pinochet was pressuring Cardinal Silva to shut down the organization. On the morning of Friday, November 14, Daniel and Ma attended the funeral of a longtime leader of the Communist Party, named Castro, at a church in the southern zone of Santiago. That afternoon after finishing work at the *Comité* offices in downtown Santiago, Daniel drove Ma to her convent home in the *población*, where he said Mass with the sisters. After a long day, he returned to San Roque's parish house, where he lived with two other priests. He hoped for a good night's rest. Both he and Ma were scheduled to meet early the next day at 9:00 a.m. at the Hotel Crillón with Fr. David Farrell, the assistant provincial of the Holy Cross order, and with people willing to financially support the *comedores infantiles*, should the *Comité* close. The meeting never took place.[1]

The DINA surrounded the Holy Cross priests' home, located near San Roque's Chapel in Peñalolén at 4:00 a.m., Saturday, November 15. They raided the house with an arrest warrant for Panchot in hand. He was taken to Villa Grimaldi, where he was severely tortured.

Daniel was under the control of the DINA at a moment of extreme personal and diplomatic peril. His detention came on the heels of the United States joining the United Nations' vote to condemn Chile and in the wake of the contravention of Prosecutor Erlbaum's order to free Sheila Cassidy, resulting in her second detention under the DINA.

On the morning of November 15, U.S. Ambassador Popper had a private meeting with an angry Foreign Minister Carvajal to discuss the U.S. vote to condemn Chile. After the meeting, Ambassador Popper promptly traveled to Washington, DC.

Only on November 17 did the U.S. embassy learn of Fr. Panchot's detention and immediately requested the Ministry of Foreign Affairs office to allow consular access. I found out later that on the evening of November 18, the same night Bernadette and I were meeting with Charles Stout, Consul Brownell interviewed Fr. Panchot inside *Cuatro Álamos*, where Panchot was being held incommunicado. Brownell had only a few minutes alone with Daniel before "a detention official" insisted on being present. In those few moments, Daniel disclosed that "he had been struck by Chilean authorities and threatened with electric current to his body if he did not amend a statement he had prepared."[2]

On November 19, the United States sent a note of protest, which read: "The Embassy vigorously protests the action of Chilean Authorities in subjecting Father Panchot to physical mistreatment and the threat of torture as well as their failure to notify him of his right to contact the American Consul. The Embassy requests that the Ministry take steps to assure that citizens of the United States will not, in the future, be subjected to such treatment. The Embassy requests a report from the Ministry indicating measures taken to this end, including disciplinary measures to be applied."[3]

The final section of Brownell's cable weighed the merits of publicly releasing its protest note over the treatment of Fr. Panchot. "Embassy recognizes there may be strong arguments for releasing information about our protest in the Panchot case. Embassy hopes that this can at least be delayed. At the time Charge delivers protest note on Panchot, he also will be seeking Government of Chile (GOC) cooperation with regard to Sister Bernadette Theresa Ballasty and Miss Kathleen Marie Osberger (Ref B) to whom he has granted Temporary Refuge. It would be most unfortunate if our efforts to assist these American Citizens were to be prejudiced by predictable GOC (Government of Chile) resentment at the release of information about our protest."[4]

42

El Pizarrón—The Blackboard
November 20–21

We had a few hours to ourselves in the garret room before the Marines would deliver our dinner. Our meals were the same ones prepared for the Marines, so they were always ample with protein, starches, vegetables, and dessert. The food was mostly prepared American style, with occasional *porotos* or caramelized *flan* on the tray to reassure us we were still in Chile. Around 9:00 p.m., three Marines would arrive, one to remove our meal trays and two others to escort us to the shower room.

Our escorts took us upstairs to the secured area, unlocking the door to a very large space with a conference area with a rectangular cluster of tables. A large blackboard was attached to the back wall. A pile of stuffed manila file folders lay in the middle of the table while others were scattered in front of the numerous chairs. I noticed there were a lot of Chilean first and last names chalked up on the *pizarrón*, some with question marks next to them and a few with check marks.

The young guards moved us past the conference space to show us the large shower area with multiple showerheads, but no partitions or doors. Blushing quite a bit, they explained one could strip down, hang fresh clothes on nearby faucet handles, grab a towel, and dry off. Bernadette took the first shower as I was walked back to the conference area to wait my turn. The guards retreated about twenty steps, to the entry door. To the right of the entrance, along the back wall, was another highly secured door with signage saying "Authorized Personnel Only." I twisted my head and looked at the transom window above the door to see etched in the glass: D.E.A.

The Drug Enforcement Agency? What was its role in Chile? Was there a drug smuggling problem here? If so, I've never heard anyone mention it.

The Marines chatted quietly with each other, keeping their eyes on any movement I made while standing. When Bernadette finished her shower, it was my turn. Then we were led back to our garret for the night.

Once we were back in our room, I asked Bernadette, "What do you think that conference space is used for? What about all those names on the blackboard?"

She was quick to answer. "I recognized quite a few of them. Some are prominent names you see in the newspaper, business types. But some are family names I recognized from St. George's. One was the older brother of one of my St. George's students." She thought they might be seeking visas from the United States to enter the country.

"Did you notice the area toward the back with the super secured door?" I asked.

"No, I didn't see it. What was it?" she answered.

"Etched above the door it says, DEA—the Department of Drug Enforcement. Does Chile have a drug smuggling problem?" I queried.

"Not that I know of . . . ," Bernadette said with a tired voice. "Maybe we can talk about that tomorrow?"

During the daytime we were allowed to walk through the consulate to access a women's washroom next to Vice Consul Nancy Hudson's office. To enter the washroom, we had to walk past a closet with a large open safe, which held documents, passport books, and other official forms.

Brownell always treated us respectfully and asked us to act as if we worked there and to not speak with anyone when moving between floors. This mostly worked until Bernadette ran into two Sisters of Mercy from the United States, who asked, "What are you doing here?"

Bernadette bluffed her way past the question as best she could, vaguely answering, "Oh, just some paperwork."

According to protocol, an embassy or consulate was required to send, within a specified time period, an official communiqué to inform the host government the identities of any persons granted "temporary refuge." Shortly after our arrival, on November 18, Foreign Minister Patricio Carvajal was duly informed that the United States was harboring us and that we "desired" to leave the country. The United States asked Chile whether an arrest warrant had been issued for either of us. In the meantime, Brownell reviewed our passports and potential travel arrangements, in anticipation of the Chilean authorities issuing our *salvoconductos*.

43

Comité Pro Paz Dissolved
November 20–22

Ten days earlier, Isabel had told us the rumors that the *Comité Pro Paz* would be closed. It was still a shock to realize it was actually happening. The announcement was tucked into one of the back pages of today's *El Mercurio*, seemingly denying its importance. Even within the short time I had been in Chile, I could see the phenomenal outreach of its work across Santiago's *poblaciones*. How many families depended on the *comedores infantiles* to feed their little ones at least one nutritious meal a day? Who would support the Families of the Detained and Disappeared searching for their loved ones? What would happen to the *bolsas de trabajo*, one of the few resources to help employ the poor and marginalized? Who would advocate for those imprisoned and traumatized by the human rights abuses inflicted on them? What would happen to all the income-producing artisanal work done by women knitters and the crafters of the impactful *arpilleras*?

I thought about all the ways that men and women who lived in the *poblaciones* had joined in the work of the *Comité* as volunteer leaders, creating networks of friendships and support. For so many abused women, the hours spent volunteering provided a safe space and a break from the isolation of their homes. It was a connection that lifted their self-worth as they helped others in need.

President Pinochet demanded the dissolution of the *Comité Pro Paz* in a letter sent to Cardinal Silva. Silva responded that the *Comité* would cease its work in the near future.[1] But he warned the government that in dissolving *Comité Pro Paz*, it risked further harming Chile in world opinion. The cardinal appealed to the public and government to appreciate those "who served the institution with dedication in all their humanitarian and gospel-based activities, while recognizing that every human effort has its limitations."

I would later read that while accepting the close of the *Comité Pro Paz*, Cardinal Silva told Pinochet privately that "the church would not abandon its duty to preserve human rights." The cardinal's words drew a sharp rebuke from Pinochet, to which the cardinal replied, "Look, Mr. President, we can close the *Pro Paz*, but we cannot renounce our obligation. If you want to impede that, you will have to go and search my house, because I will hide them under my bed if necessary."[2]

44

The Memo Tells All
November 21

I was lying on my bed in the garret room reading an eye-opening piece of news in today's *El Mercurio*, which was only two paragraphs long and tucked away on the inside pages. Yesterday, the U.S. Senate Select Committee on Intelligence issued a detailed report of the U.S. conspiracy to overthrow Allende.[1] The Chileans suspected that the United States had a hidden hand trying to prevent Salvador Allende's assumption into office in 1970; it was now a *fact* that the coup d'état was led by President Richard Nixon, along with the Assistant for National Security Affairs, Henry Kissinger, Attorney General John Mitchell, and the Director of the Central Intelligence Agency Richard Helms.

Covert actions to block Allende's inauguration began on September 4, 1970, immediately after he won a plurality of votes in the three-way presidential race.[2] On September 15, 1970, Agustin Edwards, the publisher of *El Mercurio*, and Donald Kendall, the CEO of PepsiCo, Inc., met over breakfast with Kissinger and Mitchell to discuss Chile's election of a socialist president. A few hours later, Nixon met with Kissinger, Mitchell, and Helms, and he ordered Helms and the CIA to devise a plan to keep Allende out of power. Nixon pledged $10 million, CIA agents, machine guns, and other equipment.[3] Furthermore, Nixon *barred* Helms from sharing any information about these clandestine efforts with the Departments of State and Defense, including the then-U.S. ambassador to Chile, Edward Korry.

Helms's memorandum of Nixon's orders tells it all. This is precisely how it appeared:

One in 10 chance perhaps, but save Chile!
Worth spending
not concerned risks involved
no involvement of Embassy
$10,000,000 available, more if necessary
Full-time job—best men we have
game plan
make the economy scream
48 hours for plan of action[4]

As a result of these orders the United States tried to pressure Army General René Schneider to lead the coup d'état. Schneider refused. He saw it as his constitutional duty, and that of the armed forces, to respect the ascension to office of the country's elected leader. Nonetheless, the American government and powerful multinational corporations in Chile persisted in plotting the coup.

Two attempts on Schneider's life, led by General Roberto Viaux and General Camilo Valenzuela, failed, but on October 22, 1970, with machine guns and ammunition passed along by the CIA to unnamed "Chilean officers," Schneider was seriously wounded in an ambush meant to kidnap him. He died three days later.

Senator Frank Church and the committee wrote, "The Committee believes the truth about the assassination allegations should be told because democracies depend on a well-informed electorate. We reject any contention that the facts disclosed in this report should be kept secret because they are embarrassing to the United States. . . . The Committee believes that foreign people will . . . respect the U.S. more for keeping faith with its democratic ideal than they will condemn us for the misconduct revealed."[5]

45

Consulate Woes

We had been in the consulate for four days when Brownell told us we'd be staying over the weekend. Most mornings I would open the French doors and stand on the narrow balcony ledge and say aloud, *"¡Buenos Días, Chile!"* wishing my words would could reach someone. On the best days the sun would shine through the glass panes for several hours. After breakfast, one or both of us would migrate to the warmed space by the balcony, sitting on the floor to meditate or read. I wanted to write in my journal to help me sort things out, but my head told me, *"No conviene."* It was still too dangerous to record anything.

Strangely, over those days my paranoid thoughts decreased. I started to sleep through the night. I felt less exposed to potential capture and torture. It was a protective façade and an enigma. While I was housed by my government in the fortress-like consulate with Marine guards, it was the clandestine policies of the United States that set the fuse to end democracy in Chile, sanctioning the terror the country was living under.

In our garret room, with my feet on the worn carpet, I stood inside Chile and could see people walking outside in sunshine alongside the Mapocho River. Simultaneously I was in the diplomatically immune quarters, where secret cables wired from the White House to the CIA and military operatives inside Chile targeted the demise of Salvador Allende. Yet on this day, my government was protecting me and several other U.S. citizens from the diabolic rule it inaugurated.

I reflected that morning on the Nixon–Mitchell–Kissinger–Helms coup plot, schemed up with the "Group of Forty," the ultra-connected Chileans and multinational corporate executives who joined forces to thwart Salvador Allende's swearing in as president in 1970. Failing to do so, they worked to destabilize Allende's government by squeezing the economy. All loans and aid were eliminated, followed by staged food shortages and CIA-backed national transportation strikes. Finally, the coup plotters successfully cultivated members of the military command to lead the 1973 coup.

I asked myself, if not for the U.S. intervention and funding, would Allende's democratic socialist agenda have had a chance to carve a new path for Latin American democracies and their people? Of course, it might have failed, and the next six-year cycle of presidential elections would have delivered the people's verdict. If there had been no coup, wouldn't the neo-liberal economic vision of the "Chicago Boys" have had to prove it could work for the poor and middle classes, without a dictatorship enforcing it? How many students and workers who took to the streets to support Allende might still be alive? How many families might still be intact, kept from the unknowable depths and years of suffering over their disappeared loved ones? How might the efforts to model "*educación integral*" at St. George's have offered an academic vision to emulate if the military had not commandeered the school?

On Sunday night we were escorted as usual to the third floor. As Bernadette showered, I found myself staring at the *pizarrón*. More names now had check marks next to them, and quite a few others had been crossed off. I guessed their background checks hadn't sufficiently cleared them for a visa or their sponsors weren't powerful enough. Most of the manila folders we had noticed on the table earlier had been cleared off. A wave of sadness hit me as I realized all of us were in the same situation; the only difference was which government had the last word on our lives.

I turned my attention to the secured DEA doorway. I felt a strange energy when I glanced toward it. It was dark and ominous. It was the same sensation I felt looking into the blue eyes of the DINA commander, somehow knowing he was an American. "Deliver us from evil," we had prayed the morning of the raid. I wondered as the sense of evil enveloped me again, was the DEA some sort of cover for the clandestine work with the DINA? Standing there with no facts in hand, I had the confounding notion that whatever went on behind that door had touched me on November 2 and that it extended beyond Chile.

Years later I would learn that "Pinochet turned over to the U.S. drug administration a plane load of cocaine dealers rounded up after the coup. Their drug dealing could be blamed on Allende's ousted government. Then Pinochet's right-hand man, Contreras, could set up his own men with DINA protection in the same factories and shipping points. . . . The enormous profits went to supplement DINA's clandestine budget."[1]

46

Exile
November 24–26

With the weekend over, I dreaded facing Monday and another week of uncertainty. Even so, the consulate started to buzz with activity. Brownell's spirits seemed good when we bumped into him near his office. We asked if he had any news about our departure, and he said he was hopeful. Hearing that, I felt a bounce of confidence. Then he asked Bernadette if she would come into his office to help with a problem.

"That was unexpected!" she said, as she returned to the garret room. Apparently, the U.S. newspapers had reported on the DINA's search for Helen, Paula, and Peg. A phone-tree campaign quickly reached members of religious communities requesting that they contact their congressional representatives. The response was an avalanche of inquiries to congressional offices, then forwarded to the U.S. embassy in Chile. Consulate staff now had to answer each one.

Brownell asked Bernadette about the various religious communities: "What is the difference among the Holy Child Sisters, the Benedictines, and the Sisters of Loretto? Why were some letters signed by a mother superior, an abbess or superior general or come from both the Denver and Philadelphia Province of the same order?"

By now I was laughing too. All I could say was that Bernadette had quite a tutorial lesson to give. But those letters had a role in saving Helen, Paula, and Peg's lives. They awakened the consciousness of many, reminding official Washington and the State Department of the thousands of eyes upon them.

That afternoon Bernadette's friends from CIDE, Liliana and Cecilia, came to the consulate to visit. They wanted a chance to say goodbye, though Bernadette insisted she'd be returning to Chile soon. As Liliana hugged Bernadette, she handed her a white handkerchief sent by her ailing father and said, "Now when you go up the stairs to get on that plane, you wave this handkerchief, so we can be sure you got on the plane!"

I was worried about my parents. My usual communication with them had been by aerograms, a single sheet of blue paper, folded and sealed, with a preprinted stamp on it. But like all things in Chile, mail was monitored. I had sent a newsy letter to them in late October, telling them about teaching remedial reading and math to a small group of children. After November 2, I sent a couple of aerograms full of coded sentences saying I was "fine" and "on a long retreat" and that the phone in our house "was out of order." My last note was November 15 from Quintero; I had to believe that the Holy Cross priests in Chile were in touch with Fr. Don McNeill and Fr. Claude Pomerleau, the campus sponsors of the LAPEL program, who likely shared any information with my parents. Maybe Helen or Paula had reached out to my family. But, even so, they wouldn't have any current information about me, and I doubted they would want to share the details of my arrest. Brownell never offered either of us the opportunity to call our families, but then again it felt so off limits, we never asked.

What I couldn't have imagined then, but learned later, was that on or shortly after November 2, my father answered the phone when a reporter from the *South Bend Tribune*, who referred to a wire service report, then bluntly asked: "Can you confirm or deny that your daughter, Kathleen Osberger, was picked up by the secret police in Chile this morning?"[1]

Unable to solve the dilemma of reaching my family, I scanned *El Mercurio* hoping to see something about Fr. Daniel Panchot, who had been imprisoned for almost ten days. We had to assume that his case was a top priority for the embassy.

Much later I learned that Fr. David Farrell, the assistant provincial of the Holy Cross priests, was *very* concerned about Panchot. In a meeting with Bishop Enrique Alvear and the U.S. consul, Farrell voiced his frustration over the lack of consular visits to Panchot, saying, "I don't know how much you know about what is going on with Panchot . . . ," when the consul cut in to say, "The DINA got Panchot and believe he has a lot of information, and they are not letting him go. He is being seriously tortured." He added, "Father, we know everything; there isn't anything we don't know. If Panchot were not a North American priest, he would be dead."[2]

Early the next morning, Brownell hinted that our *salvoconductos* might be issued today. I repacked my suitcase as if our departure was imminent. But the day dragged on. Before the Marines delivered our dinner, Brownell stopped by to speak with us. His face looked gray and drawn, his eyebrows almost knit together.

"I was hoping that you could leave tonight on the evening flight," he said, "but I am concerned."

He told us that Fr. Panchot was being expelled from Chile and that he was scheduled to depart the previous night. Brownell had been at Pudahuel to meet him and ensure his departure. But the Chilean authorities never brought Panchot to the airport.

Then he paused, silently acknowledging his concern for Daniel's well-being. He had been working all day on the situation and received assurances that Panchot would be on tonight's flight. He said, "It is the same flight I hoped you would be able to leave on. I do have reservations for you, but I don't recommend that you leave on the same flight."

Tears of disappointment welled up, but I thought of Daniel, remembering his soft eyes reflected in the rearview mirror of his Fiat, glancing backwards, checking on Rosita and me. He had risked his life for us and many others. Brownell continued, "We are afraid something similar might happen with the two of you, and we want to avoid any possible complications."

One could only imagine the possible scenarios for the Pinochet regime to retaliate. Still stashed in the *Nunciatura* were Gutiérrez and Bachman; in the Costa Rican consulate, Allende and Beausire; and at least nine priests and Sheila were detained under the DINA or in other jails. Daniel Panchot had become another pawn for Pinochet, and we were advised not to join the fray.

I felt great relief the next morning when I opened *El Mercurio* and read that Fr. Daniel Panchot had been released from prison.[3]

Years later, Daniel told me about the night of his departure. DINA guards pulled him out of his cell and put him into the back of a pickup truck. He had no idea where he was going and was fearful. They took him to Pudahuel airport. There he learned he was being expelled from Chile. Once inside the airport, he asked several times to be allowed to call the bishop and was refused. He was marched through the security check points, but no one would tell him where he was going.

Daniel said that the U.S. consul was there, but they didn't allow Daniel to speak to him. When Daniel was taken out onto the tarmac, he was told to get back into the pickup truck's bed. Alarmed, the consul immediately jumped into the truck to protect Panchot, thwarting any attempt by DINA to detain him again before boarding.

Daniel made a very poignant comment to me, referring to his exile from Chile. He said, *"Era mucho más difícil el exilio, que la cárcel."* Life in exile was much more difficult than prison.

47

The American Commander
November 25

Isabel was the first person to utter his name to me: Michael Townley. On the weekend we reunited in Buzeta, after hiding out in various homes and convents around Santiago, I had told her about the fear I felt when I was taken by the DINA. I described the features of the DINA commander, who spoke like an American. He was the one who arrived while the squad leader was reviewing our *cédulas* in the front bedroom. He was the take-charge commander who interrogated Paula first, then me. Isabel was never face to face with him, since the DINA kept Rosita and Isabel in the front bedroom at gunpoint. I told Isabel she might have seen him briefly in the hallway when he shouted, "She's leaving with us!"

Mulling it over, Isabel told me, "It could be Michael Townley. At the *Comité* we have had several cases of families seeking missing loved ones who had mentioned the presence of a tall, light-skinned, American-speaking man collaborating with the DINA during their raids." My mind snapped to attention when Isabel mentioned his name. I told myself never to forget it.

This morning the sun warmed me as I sat on the carpet in the garret room. I meditated for a long time, trying to find the precise words to describe the evil sensation I had felt facing the American commander— similar to the feeling emanating from the DEA area inside the consulate. Slowly the words "vaporous, airborne, no boundaries" drifted from a soul space into my awareness. I jotted the words down and stared at them, somehow certain of the depths of truth they contained. Still, I couldn't piece together how they might be connected to the American commander working with the DINA.

From my Chilean friends I learned how much they relished spotting the magnificent condor. With its ten-foot wing span, it soars over the Andes and rides the whipping air currents above the Pacific coastlands. As the world's largest raptor, the condor graces Chile's shield as one of the country's symbols.

It would take years to tease out the truth and a lifetime of work by dedicated scholars, journalists, and experts in human rights to fully piece together the clandestine story of the United States, the CIA, and Latin America's military governments. But on this date, November 25, 1975, while I was sitting in the consulate something momentous was occurring in Santiago.

General Pinochet and the DINA director, Manuel Contreras, were proudly welcoming their counterparts from the military regimes of Argentina, Uruguay, Paraguay, Bolivia, and Brazil. Meeting in strict secrecy, Contreras laid out Chile's vision to unify the six countries' military-intelligence units in order to launch "special forces teams" to seize, torture, and eliminate enemies across Latin America, Europe, and the United States.[1] Their discussions fine-tuned the necessary organizational structure: Chile would serve as headquarters and host the centralized database with the use of CIA-provided computer systems and training. Fully accredited intelligence officials from each nation would be stationed in each of the six countries to carry out covert operations. Its secure communication system, dubbed *Condortel*, would operate by telex and radio transmissions via the U.S. Southern Command's Fort Clayton base in the Panama Canal Zone.[2] This alliance would become known as *Operación Condor*, a world in which Michael Townley's name and his multiple aliases would become notorious.

Sitting in the consulate, I had only my own descriptors to rely on: "the eyes of the DINA," "the American commander," "who dressed in Levi's." He could flip from excellent Spanish to English with an unmistakable midwestern accent. He was "the take-charge guy," "tall and slim," "blue-eyed with light hair, light-skinned." He had ordered my arrest and the movements of the lower-level DINA guards around us.

These descriptors were possible clues to the identity of a man named "Townley." Later, I found similar descriptions used by those I met in Chile. Fr. Halliden's testimony about events at the Columban Center were documented by the *Comité Pro Paz's* legal department. Halliden described the armed men as "dressed in civilian clothes," though they claimed to be the police. Halliden wondered if "they might be MIR" (because they were dressed in Levi jeans). He described the commander as *"alto y delgado,"* tall and slender. Halliden noticed "that the civilian, who acted as the commander . . . continued to order the entire operation."[3]

Another Columban priest, Fr. Aloysius Connaughton, wrote in his memoir that on the morning of November 2, a fellow priest named Vinnie Hughes had just been at the Columban Center. Hughes told Connaughton, "It had been surrounded by armed men last night. Shooting took place and Enriqueta was killed. . . . The attackers were most certainly the secret police, the DINA. Bill (Halliden) thought that one of the group had an American accent."[4]

Sr. Elizabeth Gilmore, who worked at Santa Rosa Parish in Lo Baranechea, was confronted by the DINA at the parish rectory on Sunday morning, November 2, 1975. She told me that the DINA pounded on the rectory door. She answered it. There were three armed men, one with a gun in his hand. They tried to come in. She told them, "I want to see your identification, because Pinochet has warned that there have been some people impersonating the DINA." Then one put a gun to her head, saying, "This is the only identification you need."[5]

As strange as it might seem, the raids on the SSND convent, Columban Center, and Santa Rosa rectory would soon be linked to a bomb maker and international assassin. To tell this part of the story, one needs to know that Augusto Pinochet had a penchant for assassination hits. His targets were prominent Chileans living in exile who spoke out against his regime.

The first assassination occurred on September 10, 1974, in Buenos Aires, where exiled Chilean Army General Carlos Prats and his wife, Sofia Cuthbert, lived in exile. They were incinerated when a bomb, attached to their car, exploded. DINA agent Townley was nearby with his wife seated in a car when he triggered the explosion.[6]

A second such event occurred in Rome. Townley plotted the hit for weeks and hired an Italian assassin to kill Bernardo Leighton. Leighton was a former vice president of Chile and senior leader of Chile's Christian Democratic Party. He hoped to unite the Christian Democratic

The Long Arm of the DINA 1: Assassination in Buenos Aires,
Collection of Isabel Morel de Letelier, Museum of Memory and
Human Rights.

The Long Arm of the DINA 2: Assassination Attempt in Rome,
Collection of Isabel Morel de Letelier, Museum of Memory and
Human Rights.

parties in Italy and Germany in opposition to the Pinochet dictatorship. On October 6, 1975, Leighton and his wife, Ana Fresno, were strolling near the Vatican when an assassin's bullet drove through Leighton's skull. A second bullet nicked his wife's spine. They both survived the brazen attack with serious impairments.[7]

The third hit occurred on September 21, 1976. The target was Orlando Letelier, an economist, diplomat, and government minister during the Allende presidency, who lived in exile with his family in Washington, DC. He was assassinated by a car bomb detonated on Embassy Row. His coworker from the Institute for Policy Studies, Ronni Karpen Moffit, also died in the explosion, while her husband, Michael Moffit, was injured.

The Long Arm of the DINA 3: Assassination in Washington, D.C., Collection Isabel Morel de Letelier, Museum of Memory and Human Rights.

After the Embassy Row bombing, intensive investigations followed. Two years later, on March 3, 1978, the photos of two men with the aliases of "Juan Williams" and "Alejandro Romeral" appeared in the *Washington Star* newspaper.[8] They were believed to be the agents of Orlando Letelier's death. The very next day the same photos were on the front page of *El*

Mercurio. Both men were quickly identified. Williams was actually an American named Michael Townley, and Romeral was Armando Fernández Larios, a Chilean army captain.[9]

When Michael Townley's photo was published in connection to the embassy bombing in both the U.S. and Chilean newspapers, the religious community in Chile took note. Former Columban priest Tom Connelly said to me, "Bill Halliden told us that after Townley's arrest for the Letelier assassination in Washington, DC, he recognized him from the night of November 1, 1975."[10]

Sr. Elizabeth Gilmore said, "I found out about Michael Townley's name from Connie Kelly. She saw his picture in the States. . . . When I saw his picture on the television and in the news, I recognized Townley from the raid at Santa Rosa rectory on November 2, 1975. . . . He was the one who put a gun to my head, telling me: 'This is the only identification you need.'"[11]

I will never forget Townley's face or eyes or demeanor, nor the extent of evil and depravity he and others fomented. Vaporous, airborne, no boundaries.

48

Thanksgiving
November 27–30

Bernadette and I instinctively understood that the intense negotiations around the departure of Fr. Daniel Panchot relegated the two of us to a diplomatic back burner. Over the next few days, reports in *El Mercurio* only highlighted the tensions between the United States and Chile.

From various articles I learned that U.S. President Ford issued an order prohibiting all of his top officials, including Secretary of State Henry Kissinger, Director of the CIA William Colby, and all current and former members of the CIA from testifying before the Senate Intelligence Committee about coup attempts against the government of the deceased Salvador Allende.

President Ford's order drew the immediate ire of Sen. Frank Church. He swiftly countered Ford by announcing the immediate release of all documents and testimonies given during the closed sessions of the committee's investigation into U.S. and CIA operations in Chile.[1]

With his back seemingly against the wall, and wanting to further distract the attention of the public from the deadly deeds of former president Nixon and the CIA, Ford instructed all U.S. intelligence agencies, "Under no circumstances should any agency of this government, while I am President, participate in or plan the assassination of a foreign leader." Adding, "Any government official who does not obey this order will be punished." Ford then tried to reassure the members of the press of his commitment, by stating: "I expect to be fully briefed on all CIA activity."[2]

The press asked Ford if Henry Kissinger should resign because of his involvement in the plot to thwart Allende's presidency by killing Chilean

General René Schneider. Ford responded, "Secretary Kissinger has not spoken to me about resigning. . . . Of course, it is my desire that he continue in his role as long as he wants."[3]

Nothing convinced me of the durability of Ford's commitment to eliminate plots against foreign leaders and, in the case of Chile, its democracy. I had to wonder if any U.S. embassy staff, including CIA assets assigned to Chile, took seriously these new presidential orders. Most likely it was of little immediate consequence, given that today began the four-day Thanksgiving holiday, turning the consulate into a tomb.

Thinking that the long holiday might be difficult for Bernadette and me, Brownell apologized for not inviting us to his house for Thanksgiving dinner. He said he was concerned about our safety should we depart the consulate. Honestly, such an invitation had never even occurred to me. Besides, neither one of us had anything suitable to wear, and what conversation could we engage in with their guests? Instead, he asked if we would like to have some friends visit. That sounded wonderful!

It turned out that my friend Bernard had recently met Vice Consul Nancy Hudson, who arranged for him to visit. Around noon on Thanksgiving, Bernard, Rosita Arroyo, and Srs. Gerry Doiron and Helen Carpenter were escorted by the Marines into the downstairs office area. Once the Marines left, we excitedly embraced one another and plopped down around the coffee table to eat baked chicken with tomatoes, warm rolls, and apple pie. Nothing fancy, but we had a great time catching up.

I hadn't seen Bernard in weeks, nor spoken to Rosita since we had returned from Quintero and learned about Sheila's second imprisonment. Bernard eyed the consulate's surroundings and kicked off the conversation, "Hey, anything been happening with you guys lately?"

We cracked up. Slowly the story of events since Helen Nelson's birthday party spilled out. Each one of us added a piece to the puzzle about sheltering the MIR visitors; Gerardo Whelan's absurdly lucky plan to drive Gutiérrez and Bachman in the trunk of the Peugeot past the *Nunciatura*'s gates; my being tailed when I left the Columban Center house; the DINA's dawn arrival at Orellana; the interrogations and my detention; all followed by being on the run.

"Bernard, what about you?" I asked.

Bernard Nahlen.

He had recently moved from Phil Devlin's house to live with the Barranechea family, who lived near Santa Rosa church.[4] On the morning of November 2, Bernard learned that the DINA had raided Gerardo Whelan's house, where some seminarians also lived. Whelan and MIR member Martin Hernández Vásquez, who was being sheltered in the house, were both beaten and arrested. Several seminarians, including Pepe (José) Ahumada, were locked in the bathroom for several hours. Eventually the door was unlocked, and the DINA told Pepe he was free to go, but he worried it was a trap since DINA agents were still on the property. When unexpectedly one of their cars pulled away, Pepe fled. Moving through the neighborhood on foot he ran into Bernard, who had just learned about the raid at Whelan's house.

Pepe urgently told Bernard about Whelan's arrest and the need to warn Phil Devlin. Bernard said he would warn Phil. They jumped on a bus, and a minute or two later Pepe jumped off, with a plan to quickly visit his parents, then go into hiding.

Bernard stayed on the bus until it neared Av. Américo Vespucio, and from there he climbed the hill toward Phil's house. He worried that the DINA might already be there, but as he got closer, he didn't see any vehicles except Phil's motorcycle. He knocked on the door, calling out Phil's name. Andrés Pascal Allende opened the door in his skivvies, with his *compañera*, Mariana, standing behind him.

"I told Allende I had to speak with Phil," Bernard said. "Allende didn't want to let me in, so I pushed past him and rushed back to Phil's room, telling him, you have to get up and leave, the DINA just arrested Gerardo. The DINA may be coming."

Phil looked confused. So, Bernard told him once more, "I'm leaving, and *you* have to leave now!" Bernard left the house, heading down the hill, along the edge of the school's property. He told us when he glanced back, "I saw Phil, Allende, and his girlfriend come out of the house and climb onto the back of Phil's motorcycle. They took off and made it about halfway down Américo Vespucio on the far side of the road. Just then, I saw the DINA coming up the nearside toward the house."

We all took a deep breath as Bernard paused. Each one of us could picture exactly the scene he described, with the broad tree-scaped parkway that screened the avenues in either direction.

"They got away without a moment to spare," Bernard said quietly. No one spoke. We just pondered the risks and consequences of all of these events.

Fortunately, there was some reassuring news to share that afternoon. Rosita told us Isabel left Chile without incident. Intermediaries got word to Helen and Paula about her flight, and they met her when she landed in New York. Rosita told us Isabel hoped to spend some time in Philadelphia and Phoenix with friends who had been exiled after the coup. If she could not return to Chile within a few months, she would explore graduate studies.

Gerry and Helen Carpenter told us that they were able to say goodbye to Sr. Connie Kelly, who had recuperated enough to fly back to New York. They succeeded in visiting Sheila Cassidy in Tres Álamos, once she was allowed to have visitors. I could tell that these weeks had worn them down, with the loss of so many friends. But at least the end of the school year was only a few weeks away. I hoped they could recuperate over the upcoming summer vacation.

"Next year has to be better than this one!" Helen quipped.

Rosita updated me on her plans to leave for Lima within the week. She had received word that her mother needed an operation, and she was going home earlier to help out. Still, she urged me to come to Peru and stay in her family's home in La Punta, Callao. I felt so grateful for her friendship and kindness. Instead of leaving Latin America I still wanted to at least travel to Chimbote, visit the Notre Dame students, and consult with the Holy Cross priests about possibilities.

Our afternoon ended with teary goodbyes and promises to stay in touch. The Marines escorted our friends out the ornate front doors of the building as Bernadette and I headed back to the garret room. A couple of hours later the Marines knocked on our door, holding a tray of food. A full Thanksgiving dinner had been sent to us from Brownell's home.

49

A Letter to the Editor
December 2

Three weeks ago on November 9, Tomás P. Mac Hale, a conservative journalist, wrote a multipage article in *El Mercurio* in which he labeled the Holy Cross order of priests as "Extremists" and depicted Colegio St. George as "profoundly rooted in Marxism." Mac Hale's critique took particular aim at Holy Cross priests Whelan, Plasker, and Devlin, as well as Srs. Helen Nelson and Paula Armstrong.[1]

While paging through today's newspaper, I read a heartening letter to the editor written by Gustavo Munizaga Vigil in response to Mac Hale's earlier article. Munizaga Vigil was one of the architects of St. George's new school (1967–71) who worked closely with Whelan and praised his leadership. His letter reflected the struggles the school community faced, as it developed its vision for *"educación integral."* Reading his words, I heard the echo of Helen's voice telling me about her personal growth during those years and Paula's excitement seeing older students volunteering to tutor middle schoolers, the kids enjoying the work on the farm, and parents getting to know one another through weekend work days.

Munizaga Vigil acknowledged that the Holy Cross priests, parents, students, and alumni faced difficult moments during those years. Yet he wrote, "There always existed a spirit of willingness to overcome legitimate differences, discussing them within a framework of profound honesty and respect for such differences. This was and remains a part of St. George's patrimony, felt by generations of us and carried with pride."

He ended his letter, saying, "With respect to Fr. Gerald Whelan, I am sure that the hundreds of Georgians that had him as a friend, director, or professor will testify to the true character of this priest and to that of the other members of the Congregation."[2]

Two weeks later, in a new letter to the editor, *hundreds* of St. George alumni expressed their solidarity with Gerardo Whelan. The list of signatories ran more than two columns long. I was shocked to see so many names in print, knowing that expressing their public solidarity for Whelan, who was still jailed, entailed a significant risk to each of them.[3]

50

Neither Yes nor No
November 7–December 2

Alerted that the DINA was seeking him on the morning of November 2, Phil Devlin sped off on his motorcycle with Pascal Allende and Beausire riding behind him. He ferried them up to the Trappist Monastery in Las Condes, where they were sheltered until they entered the Costa Rican embassy five days later.[1]

Phil did not linger at the monastery. He jumped back on his motorcycle and went directly to Cardinal Silva's residence to inform him of what had transpired. The cardinal telephoned the papal nuncio and told him Phil would be coming there on his motorcycle and to keep the *Nunciatura's* gate open.[2]

Almost a month had passed since Andrés Pascal Allende and Mary Ann Beausire entered the grounds of the Costa Rican embassy and requested asylum. The "neither yes nor no" posture of Costa Rica had infuriated Pinochet. Chile provided Costa Rica with a 1,700-page document urging the denial of Pascal Allende's asylum petition. But in today's *El Mercurio*, a Costa Rican cabinet member confirmed that "in light of the Interamerican Treaty covering diplomatic asylum . . . we've concluded that we are looking at a politically persecuted person and not a common delinquent, therefore we will be offering protection."[3] Costa Rica's response did not sit well with Patricio Carvajal, who in a terse reply said the extremists' asylum will be reviewed, but it will be up to Chile whether or not to provide their *salvoconductos*.[4]

51

Balcony Doors
November 28–December 5

After being with our friends for Thanksgiving, misery gripped us. From the sunny spot near the balcony doors, I was glad to read an article in the newspaper that touted Cardinal Silva's successful meetings abroad. It indicated that the archdiocese's human rights work would have the resources to continue, having garnered significant financial pledges from European dioceses and institutions.[1]

Except for this one bright note, the consulate remained tomb-like for the rest of the holiday. The days wore on with little to read or distract us. Gerry Doiron thoughtfully gave us a box of yarn and knitting needles to help us pass time. I had little interest in knitting a scarf or cap. But Bernadette was determined to try by casting-on the requisite number of stitches for an adult-sized sock. The hardest part for beginning knitters to learn is how to maintain just the right amount of tension as the yarn is pulled over the needle to create a new stitch, which can then easily slide off from one needle to the other. A few days later Bernadette showed me her first sock, a squished tube barely large enough to cover the foot of an eight-year-old. Believe me, she put plenty of tension into that sock!

Over those days I tried to rise above my own feelings of dislocation, contemplating the lives of thousands of Chileans who after the *golpe* faced extreme fear and desolation as they hid or catapulted themselves over embassy walls seeking asylum. Many waited inside the walls for months, tormented by the need to leave their families and face a future unknown. I too did not want to leave Chile.

Around mid-afternoon on December 5, Consul Brownell told us the Chilean government had issued our *salvoconductos*, and we would be departing that evening on a 10:00 p.m. flight to New York City, with stopovers in Lima and Miami. Gerry and Helen sent word to Rosita, who had already flown home to be with her mother. She said that either she or one of her sisters would meet me in Lima. Likewise, a call was made to Bernadette's friends, who wanted to be at the airport to see her off.

At dusk we climbed into the embassy van with Consul Brownell and a few armed Marines, then headed to Pudahuel. When we reached the airport, I was filled with trepidation. The van drove up onto the tarmac, riding along the service lane until we reached the exterior doorway of the international passenger lounge. The lounge was almost empty, as most passengers had already boarded. Several armed officials sat at the security table. I presented my passport, then my Chilean *cédula*, which had on it my full name and address in Santiago: 1128 Calle Padre Orellana. The officer looked it over carefully, then raised his head, his eyes meeting mine. He nodded, then stamped my passport, handing it back into my clammy hands. From a distance Brownell scrutinized every move. When we were cleared, he followed us out the door and onto the tarmac, watching to see that everything proceeded without incident.

We were about halfway up the stairwell ramp when we heard our names called out from the faraway visitors' balcony. Bernadette already had in her hand the white handkerchief sent to her from Liliana's father, as she turned and waved to Cecilia and Liliana. In the distance I saw the illuminated shapes of Gerry, Helen, and Bernard waving vigorously from the airport's viewing deck. My eyes filled with tears as I swung my arm into the summer air to say goodbye, knowing I would carry the valor, solidarity, and heartbreak of Chile with me forever.

Epilogue

The Comité Pro Paz—La Vicaría de la Solidaridad
As Christmas 1975 approached, the Chilean Conference of Bishops urged the Pinochet government to offer an amnesty for all political prisoners; only 164 prisoners were freed, among them the imprisoned priests, Gerardo Whelan, Patricio Cariola, Fernando Salas, and Rafael Maroto.

After closing the *Comité Pro Paz*, on January 1, 1976, the Archdiocese of Santiago opened under its sole auspices the *Vicaría de la Solidaridad*. The *Vicaría* continued the work on behalf of political prisoners,

"Our hope will not be broken," a copper engraving, painted with enamel, made by artisans and sold through the Comité Pro Paz.

detainees, and the families of the disappeared. The programs for the unemployed, the *comedores*, and artisanal cooperatives moved forward and expanded to include medical services and educational/job training programs. *Solidaridad*, the *Vicaría's* bi-weekly journal, gained broad readership in and outside of Chile for its focus on human rights. With Chile's transition to democracy in the 1990s, the *Vicaría's* work was turned over to the public sector. Its critical archive of human rights abuses served as the foundation for *The Report of the Chilean National Commission on Truth and Reconciliation*, released in 1991.

It would be no exaggeration to claim that the work of the *Comité Pro Paz* and the *Vicaría de Solidaridad* created a template for the modern human rights movement, which has been replicated across Latin America and the world.

Enriqueta del Carmen Reyes Valerio

Enriqueta was buried in Caracoles, near Rengo. Every year on the anniversary of her death, her family warmly welcomed members of the Columban community to commemorate her life. *The Report of the Chilean National Commission on Truth and Reconciliation* denied any involvement of Enriqueta in the events at the Columban Center on November 1, 1975, stating, "The Commission has come to the conviction that Enriqueta Reyes was killed by government agents in violation of her human rights."[1]

In 2007, I traveled to Santiago for an extended visit. One morning I walked to the Columban Center house. Thirty-two years had passed since I had stepped onto the street. My heart started to race. When I reached the front gate and saw the diamond-cut windows, a powerful darkness came over me. I felt that the sidewalk would shatter and swallow me. Knocking on the door, I introduced myself to the Columban superior, Fr. Mike Cody, who invited me into the dining room, where Enriqueta had served so many meals. There I saw Enriqueta's photograph hanging on the wall. Next to her photo was an empty picture frame marking the multiple bullet holes sprayed into the house on November 1, 1975.

Justice for Enriqueta and her children did not come until January 22, 2015, when General Manuel Contreras Sepúlveda, director of the DINA, was indicted as the "author" of Enriqueta's death.[2] On May 31, 2017, the Supreme Court of Chile upheld the murder charges against DINA agents Juan Morales Salgado and Jorge Escobar Fuentes. Each man was sentenced to five years in prison.[3] According to Radio Chile on January 24, 2018, the government of Chile was ordered to pay 150 million pesos to Enriqueta's children and spouse.

Sheila Cassidy
After fifty-nine days of imprisonment, Sheila was released from Tres Álamos on December 29, 1975, to fly home to England.[4] Sheila became widely known for her denouncement of human rights abuses in Chile. I reconnected with Sheila by letter in 1978. Like her, I carried my own unnamed trauma, while trying to forge ahead with life. In a letter to me she said she overheard the DINA interrogating me from Villa Grimaldi, writing: "I think we must not be ashamed of our fears, but just admit them—fear is outside of our control. God knows I was terrified sick for weeks. What a curious thing to have happened to all of us. I think I am very changed—I am always acutely conscious of the persecution both now and in all time—of the paradox of the strength and perseverance it brings to the persecuted."

In 1979, Sheila was in New York City on tour for her autobiography, *Audacity to Believe*. I, along with Helen Nelson, Paula Armstrong, Bernadette Ballasty, Connie Kelly, Helen Carpenter, Gerry Doiron, and Peg Lipsio, reunited with Sheila after the book launch. It was an unforgettable night full of exuberance, gratitude, tears, and stories. Sheila has dedicated her life to the medical and psychological care for the suffering and dying. Her work and spiritual counsel are documented in her many books and the innovative programs she has developed.

Helen Nelson, SSND, and Paula Armstrong, SSND
Landing in Miami on the morning of November 8, Helen and Paula were startled by the clutch of reporters and photographers surrounding them, unaware of any coverage about them in the U.S. press. Paula ducked away from the cameras, while Helen said, "We are glad to be home and thank you for your concern." Their abrupt departure from Chile led to a period of disorientation and grief. Striving to rebuild their lives, they studied at Pennsylvania State University, each earning a master's degree in education. Helen then became the principal of Most Holy Redeemer School in

Manhattan's Lower East Side, while Paula directed the religious education program at Our Lady of Fatima Parish in Wilton, Connecticut.

In 1979, Fr. Phil Devlin invited Paula and Helen to join the pastoral and educational work of the Holy Cross priests in Canto Grande, an enormous squatters' settlement outside of Lima. They arrived in January 1980, and like all of their neighbors, they lived in primitive housing with trucked-in water and no electricity. Soon the school they worked in, Fe y Alegría No. 25, grew from 1,200 to 2,000 students. While their living conditions improved over time, tuberculosis, typhoid, hepatitis, and pneumonia were rampant, and political turmoil was on the rise. In 1982, a state of emergency was declared to confront the terrorist group Sendero Luminoso. In spite of the myriad hardships, Helen and Paula both described that time of their lives as "wonderful years," due to the close relationships they shared with the families around them.

In 1988, Helen's work pivoted to the religious formation of Latin American religious women, a work she continued until her retirement. That same year Paula was diagnosed with cancer. She returned to Boston for experimental treatment, but reoccurrences and setbacks followed. Through it all, Paula worked in Boston's community-based programs for Latino immigrants. On February 10, 2010, Paula passed away at the SSND motherhouse.

Bernadette Ballasty, SSND

Bernadette had no doubt that she would try to return to Chile. She carried with her the memory of the Chilean families "who risked everything to provide me asylum."[5] While in the United States she cared for her mother and taught in Manhattan's Lower East Side. Returning to Santiago in 1979, she joined an innovative team that trained teenagers from the *poblaciones* to serve as tutors for grade schoolers in their community. Known as the Programa Interdisciplinario de Investigaciones de Educación, P.I.I.E., it was replicated in many parts of Chile. Later ministries included care of the elderly, leading retreats, and developing small Christian communities in Los Andes, Chile. In 2011, she returned to the United States, teaching English as a Second Language to Latino immigrants in Norwalk and Bridgeport, Connecticut, and in Chicago. She retired in 2017.

Isabel Donoso

Isabel left Chile feeling bereft, leaving behind her colleagues at the *Comité Pro Paz* and their vision for a just and humane Chile. Many hands helped in her moment of peril. One covered her plane ticket to the States. The SSND sisters gave her places to stay in New York. She met with the leadership of the National Council of Churches, a major voice promoting solidarity with Chile, and other like-minded institutions. She returned to Chile in March 1976, joining the staff of the newly established *Vicaría de la Solidaridad*. She lived in the *población* of La Bandera and joined the nonviolent direct-action group the Movement Against Torture Sebastián Acevedo, named after a Chilean worker and father who set himself on fire in despair over the torture and disappearances of his son and daughter. Isabel's tenure at the *Vicaría* continued until its closure in 1992, with pauses to pursue two master's degrees, in political science at Notre Dame and in theology at Boston College. In the 1990s, as Chile returned to democracy, Isabel became the coordinator of the International Exchange Program at the Jesuit University Albert Hurtado.

Rosita Arroyo

Rosita loved the profound sense of community she shared living with the SSND sisters and Isabel in 1974–75. Together they forged a bond of trust and unity, which allowed them to risk their lives for others. Rosita returned to Chile in March 1976 and continued teaching at the Maryknoll school in Buzeta until 1978. Later, she spent twenty-six happy years teaching at Colegio Juan Pablo II, in La Granja, Santiago. She retired in 2021 and lives in Santiago.

Bernard Nahlen

Bernard was already fluent in Spanish when he arrived in Santiago, having spent his high school summers in El Capulín, Mexico, working alongside villagers to build their homes. In Santiago he taught English and social studies to boys from poor families who had been previously expelled for disciplinary problems. The work was challenging, but he felt he was learning as much from the boys as they were from him. During the two years he taught at the school, several of his teaching colleagues were disappeared.

In May 1977, he left Chile to enter medical school at the University of Arkansas. His residency training in family practice at the University of California–San Francisco and in preventative medicine at the CDC in Atlanta led to a lifetime of work in epidemiology and global health. Bernard led many studies with community health workers and international medical partners in Kenya and Tanzania, including the use of insecticide-treated nets to prevent malaria; controlling malaria infections during pregnancies; and prevention of HIV transmission from mother to child during birth. He currently directs the Eck Institute for Global Health at the University of Notre Dame.

Geraldine Doiron, MM, and Helen Carpenter, MM

Gerry Doiron and Helen Carpenter continued their teaching and administrative work at San Juan de Dios school in Buzeta until 1978. Like Isabel Donoso, Helen became active in the Movement Against Torture Sebastián Acevedo, a nonviolent movement of "flash protests" against the dictatorship, often met by sprays of toxic chemicals from tank-driven water cannons.

In 1981 Gerry and Helen began a new ministry in the *población* of Lo Prado. After intensive home visits they launched a program focused on the empowerment of women who suffered under the stress of political and domestic violence. Psychologists and social workers provided training to the women from the *población* to serve as facilitators with their peers around the topics of self-esteem, marriage, sexuality, and mental health. I was fortunate to visit Helen and Gerry in 1986 to see the work of Casa Malen in its early years. I visited the women of Casa Malen again on March 8, 2007, as they celebrated both International Women's Day and Chile's first female president, Michelle Bachelet. The work of Casa Malen over its thirty years is documented in *El arcoiris nace al poniente: Casa Malen, su historia.*[6] Gerry passed away at the Maryknoll Sisters Center in Ossining, New York, on May 26, 2008. Helen retired there in 2011.

Peg Lipsio, MM

Sr. Peg Lipsio had been in Chile for ten years, working with poor families in Talca, when she was expelled. While at the Maryknoll Sisters Center in New York, she earned a B.S. in nursing from Pace University in 1981.

She then went to Thailand, where she worked with Cambodian refugees, supervising a maternal–child health program. She returned in 1983 to work with Hispanic women in Monroe County, New York. She later moved to Henderson County, North Carolina, to continue her public health work with women. She is now retired.

Connie Kelly, SC

Connie's health had improved enough for her to leave Chile in the later part of November 1975. She had been a witness to the barbaric assault by the DINA on the Columban Center house on November 1, the murder of Enriqueta Reyes Valerio, and the arrest of her friend Sheila Cassidy.

I reconnected with Connie in 1977, during the years she worked at St. Francis Parish in the South Bronx. Connie left her work in the South Bronx in 1981 to join the New York Sisters of Charities pastoral teams in Sololá and San Marcos provinces in Guatemala, during years of extreme repression against the indigenous population. In 1995 she returned to the Bronx, where she is retired.

Gerardo (Gerald) Whelan, CSC

I had only a few personal encounters with Gerardo from late July to November 2, 1975, when the DINA arrested him. I was forever influenced by the certitude, compassion, and faith by which he lived and acted to save those facing certain death. In 1986, I visited Gerardo, who seemed unchanged, still dressed in his worn poncho and offering his embrace. After Chile's return to democracy in 1990, he served Colegio St. George in various roles until his death on October 31, 2003. Some eight to ten thousand people attended his funeral.[7]

Whelan was the inspiration for the 2004 film *Machuca*, directed by his former student, Andrés Wood. In 2002, Whelan was awarded the prestigious Orden al Mérito Gabriela Mistral by the Chilean government for his contributions to education. A 2008 book dedicated to the life of Gerardo Whelan, *Acto De Fe,* by Patricio Hidalgo Gorostegui, captures Whelan's impact on the lives of his former students and colleagues. Prominent among the thirty-eight testimonials included in the book is that of Andrés Pascal Allende.[8]

David Farrell, CSC

David is a member of the Eastern Province of the Holy Cross Order. He did his theological studies at the Pontificia Universidad Católica de Chile and was active in the student federation. From 1969 to 1974 he lived in Peru, became a citizen of the country, and opened the first Holy Cross parish in the *pueblo jovenes* of Chimbote. He returned to Santiago in 1974 as the assistant provincial, helping several Holy Cross priests leave Chile safely. David's pastoral work focused on laborers, whose unions had been outlawed and members persecuted. A member of the leadership of the *Vicaría Pastoral Obrero*, he taught workers about the social doctrine of the church. In 1982, his life was threatened by the DINA, who informed Cardinal Silva that they planned to kill him. The cardinal replied, "I'd prefer you didn't. I will get him out of the country."

From 1983 to 1987, David worked in El Salvador, during the excruciating war years. After 1987, he was elected to various leadership roles within the congregation. In 2014, he moved into Holy Cross House's retirement community on the Notre Dame campus.

Daniel Panchot, CSC, and Phil Devlin, CSC

Daniel Panchot poignantly told me, "Life in exile was much more difficult than prison." In 1976, both he and Phil Devlin helped to open a community center in Washington, DC, that welcomed Chileans and Latin Americans living in exile. That same year in Chimbote, Peru, Daniel organized *El Comité de Justicia Social* for exiled political prisoners.

In 1977, both Daniel and Phil joined the pastoral effort of the Holy Cross Congregation in the vast *población* of Canto Grande. There Phil led the Fe y Alegría School No. 25, where in 1980, Srs. Helen Nelson and Paula Armstrong joined its educational and pastoral work. In 1985, Daniel became the district superior of the Holy Cross priests in Peru. It was a period of escalating confrontations between the government, civilian population, and Sendero Luminoso. In 1992, he moved to Mexico to initiate a model seminary formation program.

Phil Devlin continued his pastoral and educational work in Peru until 2019. He passed away on November 13, 2019, at the Holy Cross House on the Notre Dame campus.

In 2011, Daniel returned to Santiago permanently and is presently the pastor of San Roque in Peñalólen, the same parish from where, on November 15, 1975, the DINA took him prisoner.

María de los Angeles Marinóm Z., RSC
Everyone knew her as "*la Ma*," for her warm and caring personality. In November 1975, she had to leave Chile under the protection of the Spanish government, due to her work with the *Comité Pro Paz*, but soon returned to Chile to join the *Vicaría de la Solidaridad*. In 1990 she returned to Pamplona, Spain, to care for her mother. She currently lives in Majorca, aiding the elderly and volunteering at a *comedor popular*.

Nelson Gutiérrez, Maria Elena Bachman, and Baby Paula
Nelson Gutiérrez and Maria Elena Bachman remained in the *Nunciatura* for ten months. They spent their years of exile in Cuba and Sweden; returning to Chile in 1990, Gutiérrez taught sociology at the University of Concepción. In a 2014 interview, Gutiérrez was asked, "What did the confrontation and encirclement at Malloco mean?" He replied, "Malloco signified the triumph of life over death: a cry of liberty that has never been silenced, solidarity, cooperation, and affection that surrounded the persecuted." Referring to the help that he and Bachman received, he said, "Unknown *campesinos* sheltered, hid, and protected our daughter, Paula." He added, "In those fateful days, our youngest son, Dagoberto, clung to his mother's womb, expressing his immense desire to live."[9]

The *campesina* woman who took the infant, Paula, into her arms as her parents fled later spoke to a religious sister, who brought the baby to Fr. Cristián Precht, the executive director of the *Comité Pro Paz*. Precht asked his own sister if she would care for the infant—under strict secrecy. Months later, after Bachman and Gutiérrez left Chile, the baby was smuggled out of Chile, hidden inside the ample robes of a religious sister, and reunited with her parents. In the early 1990s, after Gutiérrez and Bachman returned to Chile, a happy reunion was held where Precht, his sister, and her children were able to meet the now-grown-up Paula and her younger brother, Dagoberto.[10]

Andrés Pascal Allende and Mary Ann Beausire

After escaping the DINA's encirclement and reaching Santiago, Andrés Pascal Allende contacted Gerardo Whelan, someone he knew to be a strong believer in nonviolence. Whelan told Pascal Allende to go to the Holy Cross House, where Phil Devlin would shelter him, but said he should not be armed. Allende said, "Sure, yes." But he had no intention of being unarmed. On November 2, when both Allende and Beausire fled, riding on the back of Phil Devlin's motorcycle to the Trappist monastery, he had both a machine gun and a grenade hidden in his bag.[11]

Pascal Allende entered Chile clandestinely from 1978 to 1980, directing insurgent campaigns. He left MIR in 1986 over a split in the organization. During the 1990s, he lived in Mexico, Argentina, and Cuba, finally returning to Chile in 2002 to work at the University of Arts and Sciences (Arcis).[12]

Mary Ann Beausire was part of the production team for the film *Calle Santa Fe, un Amor Revolucionario,* directed by Carmen Castillo and shown at the 2007 Cannes Film Festival. In a 1998 interview, Mary Ann's sister, Juana Francisca Beausire, stated that Mary Ann and Pascal Allende were separated.[13]

Michael Townley

I referred to him as the "eyes of the DINA" and "the American commander." In 1978, Townley pled guilty to the 1976 murder of Orlando Letelier and Ronnie Moffit Karpen. On May 11, 1979, Townley was sentenced to ten years in prison, with credit for time already served. "Townley, under the federal witness protection program, received a new identity and was confined to an undisclosed medium-security prison, with parole eligibility as early as October 1981."[14] His plea deal kept him from extradition to Argentina to stand trial for the 1974 car bombing and deaths of Chilean general Carlos Prats and his wife.

While many scholars have studied Townley's role in Chile, one question remains unanswered: Was Townley both a DINA *and* a CIA agent? In their book *Assassination on Embassy Row*, John Dinges and Saul Landau say, "We have not seen any evidence that shows Townley to be a CIA agent, a mole, or double agent." Yet in the book's Epilogue they devote twenty-one pages to the "paradoxes" of the case, the "withholding, destruction, or concealment of key evidentiary documents," and the refusal to follow investigatory leads or share documents among governmental entities. From my viewpoint, this means that not only was Townley's role not clarified, but more importantly, the role of the U.S. government remains equally obscured.[15]

Pepe (José) Ahumada

In my interviews with David Farrell and Pepe, I learned how Pepe, then a Holy Cross seminarian, escaped from the DINA on November 2, after the arrest of Gerardo Whelan. The DINA said the seminarians could leave, but Pepe believed it might be a trap. When one of the DINA cars drove away, he fled. He knew he had to go into hiding. But first he wanted to see his parents to let them know he was alive. Fifteen minutes after he left his parents' house, the DINA arrived looking for him.

To attain asylum for Pepe, Fr. David Farrell first reached out to Archbishop Marcos McGrath of Panama, a member of the Holy Cross order, to help Pepe enter the Panamanian embassy. McGrath was reluctant to act, because it meant seeking a favor from Manuel Noriega, then chief of military intelligence under Omar Torrijos. McGrath eventually intervened, and Panama offered Pepe asylum.

Farrell and Fr. Juan Baga devised a ruse to evade the security agents posted at the embassy. Pepe dressed as a workman, carrying a bag of tools. As he approached the entry, the ambassador's wife rushed out scolding him, saying, "It's about time! I have company coming and you have to get that furniture fixed." She pulled Pepe to her side, bypassing the *carabineros*. Later, Farrell made arrangements to have a Panamanian agent accompany Pepe out of Chile. After some years in the United States, Pepe returned to Chile to work at Colegio St. George, both as a teacher and its rector. He is currently the superior of the Holy Cross priests in Chile and Peru.[16]

Kathy Osberger

I spent the months of December 1975–January 1976 with Rosita Arroyo's family in La Punta, Callao, in Peru. After Christmas, with Rosita and two of her sisters, we took trains and hitchhiked to Machu Picchu and Lake Titicaca. I traveled to Chimbote and sought out the Holy Cross priests. Several had been expelled or had left Chile right after the coup.

They were anxious to hear what had happened in Chile since the events of Malloco. I also met up with the Notre Dame students, who were days away from relocating to Canto Grande. They introduced me to the director of the primary school where they had been volunteering. In need of a substitute preschool teacher, the director offered me a position beginning in mid-February. That left me enough time to attend the Summer Pastoral Institute in Lima, taught by Fr. Gustavo Gutiérrez.

I relocated to Chimbote in February, at the start of the school year. A few months later I moved into *pueblo joven San Juan de Dios,* to live with the Guzmán Ortiz family. In June, I was asked to be the godmother of their newborn son, Ronald César. It was a profound experience to live among the families of the children I taught. I learned so much from the parents and young teachers at my school. But politically it was a tumultuous year with strikes, a change of government, and the imposition of a curfew. By the end of the year, I realized it was time for me to return home to confront the realities and injustices in my own country.

I arrived home in December 1976. I was very happy to see my family, play with my two-year-old nephew, Eric, and enjoy the Christmas holiday. But it was a disorienting time. I found my footing a few months later when I traveled to New York City to see my college roommate, Mary Beckman, who was working in the social action office of the Brooklyn diocese. One day I traveled by subway to meet with Connie Kelly, who was now working at St. Francis Parish in the South Bronx. When the subway train emerged from the underground onto the elevated tracks in the Bronx, I couldn't believe what I saw below: vast stretches of burned-out buildings, rubble-strewn lots, and children playing on a dump of discarded mattresses. I thought to myself, "And this is the First World?"

Over lunch Connie told me about the dynamic work that was happening in the South Bronx vicariate, led by Fr. Neil Connolly.[17] She urged me to be in touch with him.

I met with Neil, who sat with me for two hours, asking about my experiences in Chile. I told him about the generosity and solidarity among the Chileans, the powerful witness of priests and nuns risking their lives to save those around them. It was the sense of a living church working for justice that Neil and others were trying to build in the South Bronx. Would I be interested in working with them? he asked.

I thought about the moment when I was blindfolded, of my surrender in the back seat of the DINA's car. There where God had joined me, had soothed my trembling body, and where God gave me the courage to live my improbable life.

"Yes," I said.

Kathy Osberger

Notes

Part I. Journey: 1953–1975

Chapter 1: Descent

1. "Chile: Terror under the Junta," *Time* 105, no. 25, June 16, 1975.
2. Ascanio Cavallo, *Memorías Cardenal Raúl Silva Henríquez, Vol. III* (Santiago, Chile: Ediciones Copygraph, 1991), 58–61. Cardinal Silva identifies Zamora's case as "a turning point that determined the energy with which we began to assume the defense of human rights." Note: A discrepancy exists between Zamora's name in the 1975 *Time* article and Cardinal Silva's 1991 memoir, possibly due to the use of a pseudonym.

Chapter 2: Invisible Passports

1. Jim and Jane Gillis, *The Cemetery beneath the Golden Dome: A History of Cedar Grove Cemetery at the University of Notre Dame, 1830–2013* (San Ramon, CA: Falcon Books, 2013), 15.
2. https://www.lorainhistory.org/puerto-rican-origin.
3. Jack Cowell, "Breaking the News: Studebaker Closing," *South Bend Tribune,* December 8, 2013.

Chapter 3: San Miguelito, Panama

1. Ramón Hernández, *San Miguelito, tierra de misión, 50 años de evangelización, 2013,* Instituto Nacional de Formación Profesional y Capacitación para el Desarrollo Humano. See also John Ickis, "San Miguelito, Case Study," *INCAE Business Review* 2, no. 5 (May–August 2010).

Part II. Immersion in Santiago

Chapter 5: Los Desaparecidos—"Where Are They?"

1. "Miristas muertos en Argentina eran buscados en Chile," *El Mercurio,* July 16, 1975, Third Section, 1.
2. John Dinges, *The Condor Years: How Pinochet and His Allies Brought Terrorism to Three Continents* (New York: New Press, 2004), 235–36.
3. "Oficio religioso por Miristas muertos—Monseñor Alvear y Obispo Frenz," *El Mercurio,* August 7, 1975, Third Section, 1.

4. Luke 24:13–35, *The Harper Collins Study Bible*, New Revised Standard Version, 2006, 1812.

5. "Chile: Missing Persons," *Time*, August 18, 1975.

6. "Oficio religioso por Mirisitas," Third Section, 1.

7. "Chile," *Time*, August 18, 1975.

8. "Helmut Frenz no puede regresar a Chile," *Revista Mensaje*, October 17, 1975.

9. Ascanio Cavallo, *Memorías Cardenal Raúl Silva Henríquez, Vol. III* (Santiago, Chile: Ediciones Copygraph, 1991), 74–75; and "Obispo Helmut Frenz no podrá entrar Chile," *El Mercurio*, October 4, 1975, 1.

Chapter 6: In the Población and Los Chicago Boys

1. Elizabeth Earley, SC, *The Sisters of Charity of New York, 1960–1996, Vol. 5* (Bronx, NY: The Sisters of Charity New York Press, 1997), 441–50.

2. Ricardo Lagos, *The Southern Tiger: Chile's Fight for a Democratic and Prosperous Future* (New York: Palgrave Macmillan, 2012), 26–27.

3. Stephen Kinzer, *Overthrow: America's Century of Regime Change from Hawaii to Iraq* (New York: Henry Holt, 2006), 185–86.

4. Naomi Klein, *The Shock Doctrine: The Rise of Disaster Capitalism* (New York: Picador/Henry Holt, 2007), 8.

5. Klein, *Shock Doctrine,* 99–102.

Chapter 7: Weekends

1. In 1975 Fr. David Farrell was the assistant superior of the Holy Cross priests in Chile. In 2021, I asked him what he thought when the LAPEL program was first introduced. He answered, "I thought we'd be babysitters."

Part III. A New Consciousness and a Coup: 1968–1973

Chapter 10: Touching the Soul

1. CELAM II: El Consejo Episcopal Latinoamericana.

2. Sol Serrano and Luz María Díaz de Valdés, "Catholic Mobilization and Chilean Revolutions, 1957–1989," 159–97, in Kathleen Sprows Cummings, Timothy Matovina, and Robert A. Orsi, eds., *Catholics in the Vatican II Era: Local Histories of a Global Event* (New York: Cambridge University Press, 2018). See also Hosffman Ospino and Rafael Luciani, "How Latin America Influenced the Entire Catholic Church," *America Magazine,* August 21, 2018.

3. Joseph Gremillion, *The Gospel of Peace and Justice: Catholic Social Teaching since Pope John* (Maryknoll, NY: Orbis Books, 1976) (Medellín: Poverty of the Church, paragraphs 9, 10, 11), 474.

4. Gremillion, *Gospel of Peace and Justice* (Medellín: Justice, paragraphs 5, 17), 447, 452.

5. Gremillion, *Gospel of Peace and Justice* (Medellín: Peace, paragraph 2, 25), 455, 462.

6. Gremillion, *Gospel of Peace and Justice* (Medellín: Justice, paragraph 3), 446–47.

7. The award-winning film *Machuca* was dedicated to Fr. Gerardo Whelan by Chilean filmmaker Andrés Wood. He depicts Colegio St. George's implementation of "*educación integral*" through the friendship of two boys from vastly different economic backgrounds.

Chapter 11: The Allende Years until the Coup

1. Salvador Allende surpassed Jorje Alessandri, a former president of Chile, who earned 34.9 percent, and Radomiro Tomic, a Christian Democrat, who gained 27.8 percent of the vote.

2. Denise Chadwick was the niece of President Salvador Allende; her mother, Laura Allende, was Allende's sister.

3. Juan de Onis, "Assembly, in Chile Urges Socialism," Special to the *New York Times*, May 4, 1972.

4. Salvador Allende, *Monthly Review online*, posted September 11, 2006, https://mronline.org/2006/09/11/allende110906-html.

5. The United Nations Conference for Trade and Administration building was erected under Allende to host a UN conference. After the coup it was the headquarters for the Ministry of Defense and the offices of Pinochet and the junta members.

6. Marvine Howe, "Chile Takes Over Church School Run by Americans," Special to the *New York Times*, October 30, 1973. Note: The Archdiocese of Santiago negotiated the return of Colegio St. George to the Holy Cross Congregation in 1986.

7. CIME: the Comité Intergubermental de Migraciones Europeas, a UN-affiliated agency led by Robert Kozak, aided foreign nationals to relocate.

Part IV. It Happened So Fast

Chapter 13: Dinner with Isabel

1. Philip Agee, *Inside the Company: A CIA Diary* (New York: Farrar, Straus & Giroux, 1975).

2. Stephen Kinzer, *Overthrow: America's Century of Regime Change from Hawaii to Iraq* (New York: Henry Holt, 2006), 186.

Part V. The Church Bears Witness: October 15–31, 1975

Chapter 15: Malloco

1. The date and time of the confrontation varies. *El Mercurio's* article "Alla-nado refugio en Padre Hurtado: Muerto el subjefe del MIR," October 17, 1975, stated the confrontation began "on October 15 at 8:30 p.m., continuing into October 16, 1975." *The Report of the Chilean National Commission on Truth and Reconciliation* stated: "On October 16, 1975, the DINA succeeded in locating the underground leadership of MIR in Malloco."

Chapter 16: I Was Sick and You Looked After Me

1. Chile Comisión Nacional de Verdad y Reconciliación, *Report of the Chilean National Commission on Truth and Reconciliation, Vol. II.* Translated by Phillip Berryman. Published in cooperation with the Center for Civil and Human Rights, Notre Dame Law School (Notre Dame, IN: University of Notre Dame Press,1993), 470.

2. Chile Comisión Nacional de Verdad y Reconciliación, *Report of the Chilean National Commission,* 551.

3. "Allanado refugio en Padre Hurtado: Muerto el subjefe del MIR," *El Mercurio,* October 17, 1975, 1, 8.

4. "En dos vehículos huyen los extremistas prófugos," *El Mercuri*o, October 19, 1975, 1, 8.

5. "En Santiago: Aparecío Citroneta Robabda en Malloco," *El Mercurio,* October 20, 1975, 1; and "Los cuatro prófugos del MIR," *El Mercurio,* October 21, 1975, 1.

6. Mariana was referred to in *El Mercurio's* news reports with various spell-ings of her first name: Anne Marie, Marie Anne, and Mary Ann Beausire.

Part VI. The Day of the Dead: November 1–2, 1975

Chapter 18: El Día de Todos los Santos

1. In Sheila Cassidy's autobiography, *Audacity to Believe* (Cleveland: William Collins and World Publishing, 1978), her housekeeper is named Mar-garita. In the Declaration to the *Comité Pro Paz* given by Fr. William Halliden on November 4, 1975, he refers to her as Mercedes. I have chosen to use her name as it appeared in the affidavit.

2. The poem is in the public domain.

3. Her actual birthday was November 2.

Chapter 19: El Día de los Muertos

1. The Centro de Investigaciones Sociales (CISOC) is now part of the Universidad Alberto Hurtado in Santiago, Chile.

2. In an email exchange with Sr. Katherine Gilfeather, MM (January 11–12, 2022), she said the Maryknoll Sisters hosted Fr. Brian's guests, but she did not know the reason for their visit. She confirmed that "The Maryknoll Sisters were never involved in adoptions." The issue of adoption was very sensitive in Latin America, as many children were taken by the security forces during raids.

3. American Embassy Santiago, "American Churchpersons Involved with GOC Security Authorities" (Cable, Santiago, November 2, 1975).

Part VII. Solidarity: November 3–8, 1975

Chapter 21: Another Fiat and Solidarity

1. Parma (Italia), 3 (AP): "Leighton perdió la voz," *El Mercurio*, November 4, 1975, 6; and Parma (Italia), 3 (AFP): "Fue operado," *El Mercurio*, November 4, 1975, 6.

2. Maria de los Angeles Marinóm Z. was a member of the Religious of the Sacred Heart (RSC) from Spain.

Chapter 22: Reading between the Lies—November 5

1. "Sacerdotes ocultaron a Miristas prófugos," *El Mercurio*, November 5, 1975, 1, 20.

2. Interview with Sr. Elizabeth Gilmore, SHCJ, by phone and email, January–February 2022.

3. Interview with Fr. David Farrell, CSC, by phone, August 31, 2021, and email, December 3, 2022.

4. "Sacerdotes Ocultaron," 1, 20.

5. Cassidy, *Audacity to Believe*, 68–69.

Chapter 23: Sheila's Night of Torture—November 1–2

1. Cassidy, *Audacity to Believe*, 171–94.

2. Cassidy, *Audacity to Believe*, 186.

3. Cassidy, *Audacity to Believe*, 191. Inside Villa Grimaldi where Sheila Cassidy was being tortured, a live telephone line picked up the interrogations, led by "the American commander," of Sr. Paula Armstrong and this author.

Chapter 24: Bando 89—November 6

1. Bando No. 89: "Tribunales Militares Juzgar A Quienes Ayuden a Extremistas," *El Mercurio*, November 6, 1975, 1, 8.

2. Bando No. 89: "Tribunales Militares" 1, 8. See heading: *"Declaración del Arzobispado."*

3. Bando No. 89: "Tribunales Militares" 1, 8.

4. "Doctora detenida podrá ser visitado por cónsul Ingles," *El Mercurio*, November 6, 1975.

Chapter 25: Inside the Nunciatura—November 7

1. ORBE, UPI, and AP, "Mirista Gutiérrez en la Nunciatura," *El Mercurio*, November 7, 1975, 1.

2. Cassidy, *Audacity to Believe*, 188–91.

Chapter 26: Pudahuel—November 7

1. Police or other investigative authorities issued the pass attesting to one's "good character," i.e., no criminal record.

Chapter 27: Pascal Allende, Devlin, and Diplomats—November 8

1. "Asilado Pascal Allende," *El Mercurio*. November 8, 1975, 1.

2. "Asilado Pascal Allende," 1.

3. "Asilado Pascal Allende," 1.

Chapter 28: No Need to Say Anything—November 2–8

1. "Asilado Pascal Allende," 1, 12.

2. Interview with Sr. Paula Armstrong, November 11, 2005: Sometime in the first three months of 1976, Paula Armstrong, Isabel Donoso, and Phil Devlin attended a hearing in Washington, DC, on human rights in Chile. A government official approached Paula and referred to the number of letters they received, saying, "We couldn't imagine what was happening. We have never had a response like that!"

3. Maryknoll sister Ita Ford ministered in Chile from 1973 to 1980. In 1980, both she and Sr. Carla Piette responded to Archbishop Romero's call to help war refugees in El Salvador. Carla died on August 23, 1980, in a flash flood, while transporting refugees. Carla's last act was to push Ita out the car's window. The next morning Ita was found alive on the river bank. On December 2, 1980, returning from a Maryknoll meeting in Nicaragua, Ita and Maryknoll sister Maura Clark were met at the airport by Ursuline sister Dorothy Kazel and lay missioner Jean Donovan. On their drive home, the four women were murdered by the Salvadoran military. They are considered martyrs. https://maryknollmissionarchives.org/deceased-sisters/sister-ita-ford-mm.

Part VIII. Take Cover: November 9–19, 1975

Chapter 29: Isabel
1. MAPU: "Popular Unity Action Movement."
2. https://www.bcn.cl/historiapolitica/partidos_politicos/wiki/Movimiento_de_Accion_Popular_Unitaria; "Partidos, movimientos y coaliciones, Movimiento de Acción Popular Unitaria, de la Biblioteca del Congreso Nacional de Chile, February 3, 2021.

Chapter 30: Conflict in the Pews—November 9–10
1. "Iglesia Ortodoxa se retiró del *Comité Pro Paz*: Por ayuda de sacerdotes al MIR," *El Mercurio,* November 10, 1975, 1, 8.
2. "Obispos reprueban ayuda a los Miristas," *El Mercurio,* November 8, 1975, 1, 8.
3. T. P. Mac Hale, "Holy Cross y St. George: Extremismo en orden religiosa y en un colegio Catolico," *El Mercurio,* November 9, 1975.
4. "Iglesia Ortodoxa," 1, 8.

Chapter 31: Testing the Waters—November 10–16
1. "Nueve asilados en la Nunciatura," *El Mercurio*, November 11, 1975, 1, 8.
2. "Pascal perdió un millón," *El Mercuri*o, November 12, 1975, 10.

Chapter 32: A Photo of Sheila—November 12
1. Cassidy, *Audacity to Believe*, 227–28.
2. Cassidy, *Audacity to Believe*, 234.
3. "Nueve asilados en la Nunciatura," 1, 8.
4. Photo caption: "En la fiscalía," *El Mercurio,* November 12, 1975, 1.

Chapter 33: Quintero—November 14–16
1. Gremillion, *Gospel of Peace and Justice* (Medellín: Poverty of the Church, I, paragraph 2), 258.

Chapter 34: A Bait and Switch—November 15–17
1. Cassidy, *Audacity to Believe*, 246–50.
2. Ascanio Cavallo, *Memorías Cardenal Raúl Silva Henríquez, Vol. III* (Santiago: Ediciones Copygraph, 1991), 81–84.
3. Cassidy, *Audacity to Believe*, 254.
4. "Prohiben informar sobre caso Mirista," *El Mercurio,* November 15, 1975.

Chapter 35: The United Nations Condemns Chile—November 12

1. UN Secretary-General, UN Commission on Human Rights, Ad Hoc Working Group to Inquire into the Situation of Human Rights in Chile, *Protection of Human Rights in Chile: Note by the Secretary General.* 13th Sess., Agenda Item 12, UN Doc. A/10285 (7 October 1975).

2. "Resolución contra Chile aprobada por comisión de ONU," *El Mercurio,* November 13, 1975, 1, 8.

3. Peter Kornbluh, *The Pinochet File: A Declassified Dossier on Atrocity and Accountability. A National Security Archive Book* (New York: New Press, 2013), 236.

4. "Embajadores citados a la cancillería," *El Mercurio*, November 14, 1975; Third Section, 1.

Chapter 36: Cardinal Silva in Rome—November 16–28

1. "Cardenal Raúl Silva Henríquéz con el papa: Declaraciones en Roma," *El Mercurio,* November 28, 1975, 1, 8.

2. Interview with Sr. Lucy Giacchetti, SSND, on June 26, 2012, in Chicago: While in Rome to meet with the pope, Cardinal Silva also met with Sr. Georgina Segner, the superior general of the SSND community. Sr. Lucy, the secretary general of the SSNDs, served as the translator during Silva's meeting with Sr. Segner and recorded his comments.

3. Ascanio Cavallo, *Memorías Cardenal Raúl Silva Henríquéz, Vol. III* (Santiago: Ediciones Copygraph, 1991), 82.

Chapter 37: Rattled—November 17

1. London (Reuter-Latin) 18, "Protesta Britanica en contra de Chile: Por la situación de la doctora Sheila Cassidy," *El Mercurio,* November 18, 1975; third section.

Chapter 38: Elfriede and Edelweiss—November 18

1. Maryknoll sister Elfriede König.

Part IX. Inside the Consulate: November 18–December 5, 1975

Chapter 39: Charles Stout—November 18

1. In 1975, the U.S. embassy was located in downtown Santiago; the U.S. consulate was in a separate building.

Chapter 40: Inside the Consulate—November 19

1. At that moment we had no insight as to the numbers of people who had been hidden in the personal homes of U.S. Foreign Service personnel. No doubt the embassy and consulate staff faced both insecurity and inconvenience by housing fellow citizens targeted by Chile's security forces.

Chapter 41: Daniel Panchot—In the Vortex—November 14–18

1. Interview with Fr. Daniel Panchot, CSC, via Zoom and email on January 14, February 7, 14, 15, 2022.

2. American embassy Santiago, "Detention of Holy Cross Priest Daniel Panchot" (Cable, Santiago, November 19, 1975).

3. American embassy Santiago, "Detention of Daniel Panchot," November 19, 1975.

4. American embassy Santiago, "Detention of Daniel Panchot," November 19, 1975.

Chapter 43: Comité Pro Paz Dissolved—November 20–22

1. "Cardenal aceptó disolver el Comité Pro Paz: Así lo dío a conocer en nota dirigida a S.E.," *El Mercurio,* November 20, 1975, 18.

2. Ascanio Cavallo, *Memorías Cardenal Raúl Silva Henríquez, Vol. III* (Santiago: Ediciones Copygraph, 1991), 80.

Chapter 44: The Memo Tells All—November 21

1. Washington, 20 (EFE): "Cargos contra la CIA en informe senatorial, Documento fue publicado a pesar de protestas de la Casa Blanca," *El Mercurio,* November 21, 1975, 8.

2. Stephen G. Rabe, *The Killing Zone: The United States Wages Cold War in Latin America* (2nd ed.; New York: Oxford University Press, 2016), 131.

3. "Alleged Assassination Plots Involving Foreign Leaders," An Interim Report of the Select Committee to Study Governmental Operations with respect to Intelligence Activities," United States Senate together with Additional, Supplemental, and Separate Views, November 20 (legislative day, November 18), 1975 (Washington, DC: U.S. Government Printing Office, 1975), 227–29.

4. "Alleged Assassination Plots," 227.

5. "Alleged Assassination Plots," Prologue (XIII), Introduction and Summary, 1–2.

Chapter 45: Consulate Woes

1. John Dinges and Saul Landau, *Assassination on Embassy Row* (New York: Pantheon Books, 1980); see asterisked note on page 264.

Chapter 46: Exile—November 24–26

1. Jeanne Derbeck, "Chile Police Release South Bend Woman," *South Bend Tribune,* November 9, 1975, 1. See also Jeanne Derbeck, "Chile Conflict Reaches N.D.: Priests Captured," *South Bend Tribune,* November 9, 1975, 21.

2. Interview with Fr. David Farrell, CSC, by email and telephone, August 31 and September 17, 2021.

3. "Religioso Detenido Viajo a E.E.U.U," *El Mercurio*, November 26, 1975.

Chapter 47: The American Commander—November 28

1. John Dinges, *The Condor Years: How Pinochet and His Allies Brought Terrorism to Three Continents* (New York: New Press, 2004), 122–25.

2. Dinges, *The Condor Years*, 122–25.

3. Fr. William Halliden's affidavit: *Relación homicidio de Doña Enriqueta Valerio y allanamieto del convento de la Congregación de San Columbano, Centro de Documentación Vicaría de Solidaridad 106300*, November 4, 1975. A copy was sent to me by Tom Connelly. Before I interviewed him on October 14, 2021, he emailed saying: "By way of a spoiler, I can mention that Michael Townley . . . was in charge of the squad that attacked the Columban House and took Sheila."

4. Alo Connaughton*, 9/11 to 1984: Notes from a Chilean Diary* (Bangkok, July 2019). This memoir of Fr. Patrick Aloysius Connaughton, SSC, was copyrighted, privately published, and distributed on the fiftieth anniversary of his ordination. See also his article "Mission in Pinochet's Chile: A Memoir," *Irish Migration Studies in Latin America* 7, no. 4 (November 2011).

5. Interview with Sr. Elizabeth Gilmore, SHCJ, by phone and email, January 10 and 27, 2022.

6. Dinges, *The Condor Years*, 71–77.

7. Dinges, *The Condor Years*, 130–33.

8. Jeremiah O'Leary, "U.S. Threatening to Sever Chile Relations," *Washington Star,* March 3, 1978.

9. John Dinges and Saul Landau*, Assassination on Embassy Row* (New York: Pantheon Books, 1980), 321–27.

10. Interview with Tom Connelly by Zoom on October 19, 2021.

11. Interviews with Sr. Elizabeth Gilmore, by phone and email, January-February, 2022.

Chapter 48: Thanksgiving—November 27–30

1. New York, 25 (Reuter-Latin), "Chile en el exterior," *El Mercurio,* November 26, 1975.

2. Washington, 27 (UPI), "Orden del Ford: Agencias de inteligencia no participarán en complots," *El Mercurio,* November 28, 1975.

3. Washington, 27 (UPI), "Ford elogia a secretario H. Kissinger," *El Mercurio,* November 28, 1975.

4. Gabriela Barranechea, the youngest daughter in the family, was a good friend to Bernard and me. Exiled with her young children from Chile to France in the 1980s, she became a well-known singer, guitarist, and actress, performing in Europe, Mexico, and Benin.

Chapter 49: A Letter to the Editor—December 2

1. Tomás Mac Hale, "Extremismo en orden religioso y en un colegio Católico," *El Mercurio,* November 9, 1975, 30–31.

2. Cartas, "Labor de Holy Cross," *El Mercurio,* December 2, 1975.

3. Cartas, "Alusiones a Holy Cross y St. George," *El Mercurio*, December 15, 1975.

Chapter 50: Neither Yes nor No—November 7–December 2

1. Dinges, *The Condor Years,* 113. Dinges writes: "At one point, Pascal—an AK-47 assault rifle in his backpack—his companion Mary Anne Beausire, and an American priest rode a motorcycle to a hiding place in a Trappist monastery in the Santiago foothills."

2. Interviews with Fr. David Farrell, CSC, by phone and email, August 31 and September 17, 2021.

3. "En la embajada de Costa Rica: Asilado Pascal Allende," *El Mercurio,* November 8, 1975, 1, 12.

4. San José (Costa Rica), 2 (EFE), "Caso Pascal Allende: Costa Rica aún no comunica el asilo," *El Mercurio,* December 3, 1975.

Chapter 51: Balcony Doors—November 28–December 5

1. Bonn, 3 (EFE), "Chile en el exterior—Comité Para Paz," *El Mercurio,* December 4, 1975.

Epilogue

1. Chile Comisión Nacional de Verdad y Reconciliación, *Report of the Chilean National Commission on Truth and Reconciliation, Vol. I/II.* Translated by Phillip Berryman. Published in cooperation with the Center for Civil and Human Rights, Notre Dame Law School (Notre Dame, IN: University of Notre Dame Press, 1993), 551.

2. https://memoriaviva.com/nuevaweb/ejecutados-politicos-r/reyes-valerio-enriqueta-del-carmen.

3. https://es.wikipedia.org/wiki/Enriqueta_Reyes_Valerio.

4. "Viajó a Londres Doctora Cassidy," *El Mercurio,* December 30, 1975, 1, 29.

5. Kay O'Connell, SSND, *The Northeastern Province of the School Sisters of Notre Dame, Wilton, Connecticut, 1973–1989: Events in Latin America, Chile, Dominican Republic, Perú,* published by the SSND Wilton, CT, Congregation, October 24, 2006, 248.

6. Susan Cabezas and Carmen Duran, *El arcoiris nace al poniente: Casa Malen, su historia* (Santiago: Congregation of the Maryknoll Sisters of St. Dominic, 2005).

7. Ed Langlois, "Priest-Educator an Inspiration for Film," *Catholic Sentinel*, a journal of the Portland, Oregon, diocese, February 10, 2005.

8. Patricio Hidalgo Gorostegui, *Acto de fe: Testimonios de la vida de Gerardo Whelan en Chile* (Santiago: Colofón, 2009), 80–81.

9. Rodrigo Ruiz, *Nelson Gutiérrez: "El MIR nunca fue miltarista,"* elDESCONCIERTO.cl, 06.10.2014.

10. Hidalgo Gorostegui, *Acto de fe,* 80–81.

11. Hidalgo Gorostegui, *Acto de fe,* 78–80.

12. https://es.wikipedia.org/wiki/index/.php?oldid=142272800&title=Andr%C3%A9s_Pascal_Allende.

13. https://carabcarwww.wsws.org/en/articles/1998/11/int-n18.html.

14. John Dinges and Saul Landau, *Assassination on Embassy Row* (New York: Pantheon, 1980), 379.

15. Dinges and Landau, *Assassination on Embassy Row,* 379–98.

16. Interviews with David Farrell, CSC, on August 31, September 17, and October 17, 2022; and email correspondence with Pepe (José) Ahumada on November 12, 2022.

17. Angel Garcia, *The Kingdom Began in Puerto Rico: Neil Connolly's Priesthood in the South Bronx* (New York: Empire State Editions/Fordham University Press, 2021).

Bibliography

Agee, Philip. *Inside the Company: A CIA Diary.* New York: Farrar, Straus & Giroux, 1975.

Agosin, Marjorie. *Scraps of Life: Chilean Arpilleras.* Translated by Cola Franzen. London: Zed Books, 1987.

Allende, Isabel. *House of Spirits.* Translated by Magda Bogin. New York: Atria, 1985.

———. *A Long Petal of the Sea.* New York: Ballantine Books, 2020.

Berryman, Phillip. *Memento of the Living and the Dead: A First-Person Account of Church, Violence and Resistance in Latin America.* Eugene, OR: Wipf & Stock Publishers, 2019.

Bolaño, Roberto. *By Night in Chile.* Translation by Chris Andrews. New York: New Directions Books, 2003.

Branch, Taylor, and Eugene M. Popper. *Labyrinth.* New York: Viking Press, 1982.

Briggs, Kenneth. *Double Crossed: Uncovering the Catholic Church's Betrayal of American Nuns.* New York: Doubleday, 1988.

Cabezas, Susan, and Carmen Duran. *El arcoiris nace al poniente: Casa Malen, su historia.* Santiago: Congregation of the Maryknoll Sisters of St. Dominic/Colectivo Con-spirando, 2005.

Cassidy, Sheila. *Audacity to Believe: An Autobiography.* Cleveland, OH: William Collins and World Publishing, 1978.

Cavallo, Ascanio. *Memorías Cardenal Raúl Silva Henríquez, Vols. I, II, III.* Santiago: Ediciones Copygraph, 1991.

Cavanaugh, William T. *Torture and Eucharist.* Malden, MA: Blackwell, 1998.

Chittister, Joan. *The Time Is Now: A Call to Uncommon Courage.* New York: Random House, 2019.

Chile Comisión Nacional de Verdad y Reconciliación, *Report of the Chilean National Commission on Truth and Reconciliation, Vol. I/II.*

Translated by Phillip Berryman. Published in cooperation with the Center for Civil and Human Rights, Notre Dame Law School, Notre Dame, IN: University of Notre Dame Press, 1993.

Connaughton, Patrick Aloysius. *9/11 to 1984, Notes from a Chilean Diary.* Bangkok, Thailand, 2019. (Copyrighted, privately published, and distributed; a PDF copy was shared by Tom Connelly.)

Connaughton, Alo. "Mission in Pinochet's Chile: A Memoir." *Irish Migration Studies in Latin America* 7, no. 4 (November 2011), 299–304.

Constable, Pamela, and Arturo Valenzuela. *A Nation of Enemies: Chile under Pinochet.* New York: W. W. Norton, 1991.

Cooper, Mark. *Pinochet and Me: A Chilean Anti-Memoir.* New York: Verso, 2001.

Cummings, Kathleen Sprows, Timothy Matovina, and Robert A. Orsi, eds. *Catholics in the Vatican II Era: Local Histories of a Global Event.* New York: Cambridge University Press, 2018. See "Catholic Mobilization and Chilean Revolutions, 1957–1989," by Sol Serrano and Luz María Díaz de Valdéz, 159.

Dinges, John. *The Condor Years: How Pinochet and His Allies Brought Terrorism to Three Continents.* New York: New Press, 2004.

———, and Saul Landau. *Assassination on Embassy Row.* New York: Pantheon Books, 1980.

Donoso, José. *Curfew.* Translated by Alfred MacAdam. New York: Grove Press, 1986.

Dorfman, Ariel. *Heading South, Looking North: A Bilingual Journey.* New York: Farrar, Straus and Giroux, 1988.

Earley, Mary Elizabeth, SC. *The Sisters of Charity of New York 1960–1996, Vol. 5.* Bronx, NY: Sisters of Charity New York Press, 1997.

Fernández, Nona. *The Twilight Zone.* Translation by Natasha Wimmer. Minneapolis, MN: Greywolf Press, 2016.

Garcia, Angel. *The Kingdom Began in Puerto Rico: Neil Connolly's Priesthood in the South Bronx.* New York: Empire State Editions/Fordham University Press, 2021.

Golden, Renny. *The Hour of the Poor, the Hour of Women: Salvadoran Women Speak.* New York: Crossroad Publishing, 1991.

Gremillion, Joseph. *The Gospel of Peace and Justice: Catholic Social Teaching since Pope John.* Maryknoll, NY: Orbis Books, 1976.

Hernández, Ramón. *San Miguelito, tierra de misión, 50 años de evangelización* (Fiftieth Anniversary Commemorative Book). Panama: Instituto Nacional de Formación Profesional y Capacitación para el Desarrollo Humano, 2013.

Hidalgo Gorostegui, Patricio. *Acto de fe: Testimonios de la vida De Gerardo Whelan en Chile.* Santiago: Colofón, 2009.

Hitchens, Christopher. *The Trial of Henry Kissinger.* New York: Verso, 2002.

Ickis, John. "San Miguelito, Case Study." *INCAE Business Review* 2, no. 5 (May-August 2010), 54–73.

Kinzer, Stephen. *Overthrow: America's Century of Regime Change from Hawaii to Iraq.* New York: Henry Holt, 2006.

Klein, Naomi. *The Shock Doctrine: The Rise of Disaster Capitalism.* New York: Picador/Henry Holt, 2007.

Kornbluh, Peter. *The Pinochet File: A Declassified Dossier on Atrocity and Accountability, Updated for the Fortieth Anniversary of the Coup in Chile.* New York: New Press, 2013.

Lagos, Ricardo, with Blake Hounshell and Elizabeth Dickinson. *The Southern Tiger.* New York: Palgrave Macmillan, 2012.

Markey, Eileen. *A Radical Faith: The Assassination of Sister Maura.* New York: Nation Books, 2016.

McPherson, Alan. *Ghosts of Sheridan Square: How a Washington Assassination Brought Pinochet's Terror State to Justice.* Chapel Hill: University of North Carolina Press, 2019.

McSherry, J. Patrice. "Tracking the Origins of a State Terror Network, Operation Condor." *Latin American Perspectives* [Issue 122] 29, no. 1 (January 2002), 38–60.

Neafsey, John. *A Sacred Voice Is Calling: Personal and Social Conscience.* Maryknoll, NY: Orbis Books, 2006.

O'Connell, Kay, SSND. *The Northeastern Province of the School Sisters of Notre Dame, Wilton Connecticut, 1973–1989: Events in Latin America, Chile, Dominican Republic, Perú* (a booklet published by the SSND Wilton, Connecticut, Congregation, October 24, 2006).

O'Shaughnessy, Hugh. *Pinochet: The Politics of Torture*. New York: New York University Press, 2000.

Ortiz, Dianna, with Patricia Davis. *The Blindfold's Eye: My Journey from Torture to Truth*. Maryknoll, NY: Orbis Books, 2002.

Politzer, Patricia. *Fear in Chile: Lives under Pinochet*. Translation by Diane Wachtell. New York: New Press, 2001.

Rabe, Stephen G. *The Killing Zone: The United States Wages Cold War in Latin America*. Second edition. New York: Oxford University Press, 2016.

Riefensberg, Steve. *Santiago's Children*: *What I Learned about Life at an Orphanage in Chile*. Austin: University of Texas Press, 2008.

Smith, Brian H. *Church and Politics in Chile: Challenges to Modern Catholicism*. Princeton, NJ: Princeton University Press, 1982.

Terrazas Guzman, Mario. *¿Quien se acuerda de Sheila Cassidy? Crónica de un conflicto religioso-político-diplomático*. Santiago: Ediciones EMETE, 1992.

Index